RELIGIONS OF
THE SILK ROAD

BY THE SAME AUTHOR

Mughal India and Central Asia

Conversations with Emperor Jahangir (trans.)

RELIGIONS OF THE SILK ROAD

Overland Trade and
Cultural Exchange from Antiquity
to the Fifteenth Century

RICHARD C. FOLTZ

St. Martin's Griffin
New York

ISBN 0-312-23338-8

Library of Congress Cataloging-in-Publication Data

Foltz, Richard, 1961-
    Religions of the Silk Road : overland trade and cultural exchange
from antiquity to the fifteenth century / by Richard C. Foltz.
        p. cm.
    Includes bibliographical references (p.   ) and index.
    ISBN 0-312-21408-1 (cloth) 0-312-23338-8 (pbk)
    1. Asia, Central—Religion. 2. Silk Road—History. I. Title.
    BL1050.F65 1999
    200'.958—DC21   98-43092
                                                                 CIP

Design by Acme Art, Inc.

First published in hardcover in the United States of America in 1999

10

CONTENTS

Eight pages of illustrations appear between pages 88 and 89.

To my parents, Ruth Bilbe Foltz and Rodger Foltz

PREFACE

This book is an attempt to weave some two thousand years of Asian history around a particular thread—that of the movement and transformation of religious ideas—into a readable and informative account. It is more concerned with presenting a reasonably coherent overall pattern than with resolving disputes over fineries of detail in the design; these I leave to the specialists in the many fields such a broad survey necessarily encompasses.

I do not claim expertise in any of these fields, but rather beg those more knowledgeable than myself to indulge me for my trespasses into their various territories, much as the Silk Road traveler was bound to solicit the goodwill of the many authorities through whose lands he would pass. Although I hope that specialists will find my effort to compose a meaningful "big picture" of some interest and value, this book has been written first and foremost with the student and general reader in mind. For this reason I have tried to keep transliterations as simple as possible, avoiding diacritics. In the case of Chinese, I have chosen the Wade-Giles system in preference to Pinyin, as being somewhat more immediately pronounceable to the non-Chinese speaker.

Without the love and support of my wife, Aphrodite Désirée Navab, I could not have produced this book, or if I had, it would mean little. Our daughter, Shahrzad, who fills our every day with joy, is the major source of motivation for everything we do. My mother, Ruth Foltz, also encouraged me with her enthusiasm from the time I first began to envision this project. For this and for all she has done for me throughout my life, with love and gratitude I dedicate this work to her.

My original interest in the topic of religions in Central Asia came from a lecture by Hans-Joachim Klimkeit at the Harvard Center for World Religions. It is no exaggeration to say that had it not been for his inspiration, this book would not have been written. I will remember him for sparking my interest nearly seven years ago, and more recently for his encouraging comments as I came to complete this book. His untimely passing on February 7, 1999 comes as a great loss.

Jerry Bentley, Richard Bulliet, and Nicola DiCosmo also read the typescript and offered many useful suggestions. Richard Frye's remarks improved an early version of chapter 2, and Jan Nattier helped guide me through a much-needed overhaul of chapter 3. The criticisms of two anonymous reviewers for the *Journal of Early Modern History* helped me to strengthen my discussion of the Islamization of Inner Asia. For any remaining errors of fact or interpretation, I alone remain responsible.

Some of the material in this book has previously appeared in the form of journal articles. These are: "When Was Central Asia Zoroastrian?" in *The Mankind Quarterly* 38/3 (1998), "Judaism and the Silk Route," in *The History Teacher* 32/1 (November 1998), and "Ecumenical Mischief Under the Mongols," in the *Central Asiatic Journal* 43/1 (1999). I thank the editors of those journals for permission to rework and reprint this material here.

I am indebted to Susan Roach of interlibrary loan at Gettysburg College for so patiently and efficiently dealing with my unending requests throughout the academic year 1997-98. Finally, I would like to extend my thanks to Michael Flamini, Alan Bradshaw, and all at St. Martin's Press for helping to bring this work to publication.

New York
April 23, 1999

CHINESE TRANSLITERATIONS
COMMONLY OCCURRING IN THIS BOOK

WADE-GILES	PINYIN
An Shih-kao	An Shigao
Chang Ch'ien	Zhang Qian
Ch'üan-chou	Quanzhou
Fa-hsièn	Faxian
Fu-ch'ien	Fujian
Fu-chou	Fuzhou
Hsiung-nu	Xiongnu
Hsüan-tsang	Xuanzang
Hsüan-tsung	Xuanzong
Lao Tze	Laozi
Lo-yang	Luoyang
Sinkiang	Xinjiang
Sung dynasty	Song dynasty
Taoism	Daoism
T'ien Shan	Tianshan
Ts'ao-an	Cao'an
Tun-huang	Dunhuang
Yüeh-chih	Yuezhi

© Richard Foltz

The Silk R

MONGOLIA

Karakorum

Khanbaliq

Beshbaliq

ghun

Qocho

ucha

K'ai-feng

shgar

Tun-huang

Khotan

Ch'ang-an CHINA

Lo-yang

TIBET

Lhasa

Zaytun

Nalanda

ad

miles 100   500   1000

Central Asia

© Richard Foltz

© Richard Foltz

Religious Minorities
Along the Eastern Silk Road

miles 100   500

I Muslims   C Christians   M Manichaeans   J Jews   Z Zoroastrians

CHAPTER ONE

The Silk Road
and Its Travelers

During the latter decades of the nineteenth century, popular European fascination with the world beyond reached an all-time high. The British and French empires spanned the globe, and their colonial agents sent home exotic goods and stories. Poets and painters put their own visions of the seductive Orient onto paper and canvas.

The last remote corners of the world were completing the list of European discoveries; mountains were measured and the sources of great rivers determined and mapped. Tibet and other far-off lands were penetrated for the first time by Europeans, as British, Russian, and German agents ventured into the most inaccessible reaches of Central Asia, attempting to pave the way for colonial claims.

The Silk Road dates from this romantic period, in name if not in reality. In fact, the trans-Asian trade network linking the Mediterranean with East Asia had been past its prime for over four hundred years,[1] when a late-nineteenth-century player in that web of intrigue known as the Great Game,[2] Ferdinand von Richthofen, invented the term "Silk Road"

(*Seidenstraße,* in his native German), which came to epitomize a sense of exoticism and adventure.

The "Silk Road" was not one road but many; it was actually a network of roads, generally going East and West, but with spurs into southern Iran, the northern Eurasian steppe, and south over the Hindu Kush to the Indian subcontinent. In all of history Richthofen appears to have been the first to conceptualize the land routes across Asia in such a singular way—no one else, at least, had come up with such a catchy label.

Yet in the century since its invention as a concept, the Silk Road has captured and captivated the Western imagination. It has given us images of fabled cities, exotic peoples, awe-inspiring mountains and deserts, and the death-defying feats of hardy long-distance travelers. Explorers' accounts from the turn of the century were best-sellers and continue to be reprinted today. Novels have been written, feature films and documentaries produced, travel packages sold, archeological expeditions funded, and international conferences held, all using the Silk Road as their theme. Like any catch-phrase of vaguely defined beauty, the Silk Road can be whatever we wish it to be; it can be the substance of all of our dreams.

Modern-day Silk Road storytellers usually begin their tale with the mission of Chang-ch'ien, who was sent by the Han emperor of China, Wu-ti, to the "western lands" in 139 BCE to propose an alliance with a nomadic Indo-European people known to the Chinese as the Yüeh-chih against another steppe confederation which they called the Hsiung-nu (possibly predecessors to the Huns), who constantly harassed the Chinese with sporadic raids that even the Great Wall could not prevent. Chang did not succeed in his appointed task but learned quite a bit from his travels, which lasted thirteen years and may have taken him as far as northwestern India. During this time he was captured and imprisoned by the Hsiung-nu, escaped, and was imprisoned by them again on his way home before finally managing to return and offer his report to the emperor.

One writer has suggested that Chang's mission was less an official embassy than "an intelligence mission staffed with expendable personnel."[3] Whatever the case, the traveler's tales of lands and peoples to the west suggested to Wu-ti tempting opportunities for trade. Within a few years Chinese merchants were regularly braving the difficult journey west through the Gansu corridor, around the forbidding Takla Makan desert, and into Central Asia.

For the next twenty years or so this trade seems to have thrived. Wu-ti was particularly keen on obtaining horses from Ta-yüan, probably the Ferghana valley in modern Uzbekistan, which Chang had visited. The Chinese referred to these mounts as "heavenly horses" that "sweat blood" (an appearance caused by skin parasites). The people of Ta-yüan were reluctant to part with large numbers of them, however, and eventually in 104 BCE the Han emperor sent his general Li Kuang-li at the head of a large army with instructions to acquire these horses by force. Supplies were insufficient and much of the army starved en route. Massively reinforced by Wu-ti, they reached their destination only after two years and finally succeeded in gaining the inhabitants of Ta-yüan to capitulate. In the end the Chinese managed to bring home only thirty or so of the "heavenly horses," but the trade route had been definitively opened and its eastern portion put under Han control.

Despite the prominence of these events, which are detailed in the Chinese sources, trans-Asian overland trade probably linked the West with China much earlier than Han times. (Silk has been found in Egypt from around 1000 BCE and in Europe from around three hundred years later.[4]) Few if any individuals ever made the long and dangerous transcontinental journey as a single trip, however. Silk and other high-value goods were transported in contiguous stages, each part of more or less distinct economic systems and under the control of various political ones.

The experience of Niccolo, Maffeo, and Marco Polo, who did cover the whole distance from Venice to China and back during the thirteenth century, was so unusual as to have sounded utterly unbelievable to their fellow Italians. The Polos owed their success to the *pax mongolica*, which brought most of Eurasia under one administration for the first time in history. During the subsequent century others, Asian as well as European, would make this great journey as well. One fourteenth-century Italian merchant even wrote a sort of Asian travel guide for businessmen.[5]

Overall, however, this kind of direct personal contact between East and West was rare.

The historical norm was that most participants in the moving of goods across Asia played relay roles. Central Asian middlemen might travel East or West into foreign lands and even set up trading offices there, but of individuals who personally conveyed silk or anything else from China to the Mediterranean in the pre-Mongol period, history has given us no confirmed examples.[6] Still, the overall connections are apparent in hindsight. Therefore, having admitted that the Silk Road nomenclature is a recent invention, we will retain it as a general term to represent the complex network of land routes across Asia.

SCHOLARS OR SCOUNDRELS?

If it is to the explorer-agents of the turn of the century that we owe the Silk Road as a concept, then it is likewise to them that we owe much of our knowledge of its history. Many of these individuals—Aurel Stein, Albert von le Coq, Paul Pelliot, and Langdon Warner (the Harvard professor who was the model for Steven Spielberg's Indiana Jones)— were scholars and had a real interest in the histories and cultures of the regions they visited. Often armed not only with government funding and diplomatic support but connections with museums and universities as well, they were keen if not always careful archeologists. By diligence and by skill, by means and by ruse, they uncovered long-lost treasure troves of architecture, art, and literature, much of it religious in nature.[7]

One example of the lasting contribution of these men to the history of religions is that prior to their activities, next to nothing was known of the once-great tradition of Manichaeism. During its early life from the third through the ninth centuries, this gnostic religion enjoyed massive appeal throughout the Mediterranean and western Asia, to the extent that defenders of Christianity, Zoroastrianism, and Islam all saw it as the single greatest threat to the very survival of their own traditions. Manichaeism was rooted out and eradicated by force in the West, and all remnants of its existence destroyed by the end of the sixth century. By the tenth century few Manichaeans survived in the Muslim heartlands. Farther east along the Silk Road, however, the religion survived another seven hundred years.

For many centuries Manichaeism was known only through the polemics of its enemies (such as St. Augustine, himself a former Manichaean), and it was not until the beginning of the twentieth century that actual Manichaean written works were found to have survived, locked up in forgotten vaults and buried beneath the deserts of East Turkestan, modern Xinjiang. (Later, further Manichaean texts would turn up in Egypt.) These writings, along with architectural ruins and fragments of wall paintings, were the relics of a Manichaean kingdom of the ninth and tenth centuries, after the religion had been made the official faith of the Uighur Turkish empire.

This is not to say that the intentions of the turn-of-the-century adventurer-scholars were always purely noble ones. Aurel Stein, finding that a large cache of ancient manuscripts had been inadvertently discovered by a Buddhist monk while restoring a grotto shrine, gained access to the site and later pilfered the manuscripts by persuading the monk that although European in outward appearance, he was really a spiritual disciple of the famous Buddhist traveler Hsüan-tsang. Stein insisted that just as that seventh-century pilgrim had "saved" so many Sanskrit works by bringing them from India, he now had a mission to save these works by carting them off to England. "I was performing a pious act," Stein rationalized, "in rescuing for Western scholarship those relics of ancient Buddhist literature and art which local ignorance would allow to lie here neglected or to be lost in the end."[8]

Von le Coq used similar reasoning but with more tragic results. He had his workers attempt to chip off entire walls of medieval Buddhist and Manichaean fresco work, but they did a somewhat careless job, and in the process of removal and transportation to Germany many of the paintings were severely damaged. The final blow came at the end of World War II, when most of them were destroyed in the Allied bombing of Berlin. Today the lost paintings survive only in the color reproductions which von le Coq published in 1913.[9]

The cavalier nature of Stein's claim notwithstanding, it is true that the bulk of subsequent research on Silk Road texts has been done by

Westerners, albeit with notable contributions from Japanese and Chinese scholars. The manuscripts were found to be written in seventeen different languages, many of which were unknown to anyone alive at the beginning of this century. The majority are Buddhist works, but a substantial number are Manichaean and Nestorian Christian. A Jewish business document in Hebrew letters from the eighth century unearthed by Stein has provided the earliest known example of the "Islamic" New Persian language.[10]

European philologists have succeeded in deciphering most of these long-forgotten tongues, and begun the process of translating them into modern ones.[11] In addition, today there are numerous active archeological digs in western China, now under the sponsorship and surveillance of the Chinese government. Much of the material in this book owes itself to these twentieth-century finds preserved by the dry desert air of western China and to the efforts of contemporary scholarship to explain their content and meaning.

The religious texts and paintings found in East Turkestan (or Xinjiang, as it is now called in Chinese), together with archeological and written evidence from elsewhere in Central Asia, attest to a bizarre amalgamation of religious ideas drawn from Christianity and Judaism, Buddhism, and Zoroastrianism. Often this mixture is expressed in the deliberate, peculiar syncretism of Manichaeism.

It would seem, in fact, that eastern Central Asia in the premodern period became a melting pot of religious traditions because it served as a remote refuge for heterodox beliefs, and that well into the Mongol period it was one of the most religiously diverse places on the globe. How this very pluralistic religious environment came to be one of the world's most uniformly Muslim regions is one of the more intriguing questions of Silk Road history.

RELIGION AND TRADE

It is no coincidence that throughout history ideas and technologies have spread along trade routes, and that merchants have been among their prime transmitters. One only has to think about it to realize that traveling businessmen do not simply convey, sell, and acquire goods, and move on. They socialize, interact, and observe while on the road, and they take their impressions home with them.

Nor are businessmen the only utilizers of trade routes; many other kinds of travelers benefit from the networks fostered by commercial activity. In the modern world business travelers are the driving force behind the airline industry, even if the average flier thinks little about that connection. Likewise, the interstate highway system in the United States was devised as a means to encourage trucking—a thought to temper one's curses when struggling to control the steering wheel in the wake of a passing eighteen-wheeler!

Increasing attention has been given in recent years to the role of long-distance trade in the cross-pollination of cultures and ideas.[12] Taking as its theme the specific example of the spread of religious ideas, this book tells the story of how religions accompanied merchants and their goods along the overland Asian trade routes of pre-modern times. It is a story of continuous movement, encounters, mutual reactions and responses, adaptation and change. This is part—though, the reader is cautioned, only a part—of a much broader historical dynamic of cultural interaction, exchange, and cultural conversion. While long-distance trade is not in and of itself an "explanation" of how religions spread across Asia or why Asians converted to them, a case will be made here that it is an important factor, important enough to serve as the theme of a book-length treatment.

Although some of the religious traditions in this story (Christianity, Islam, Judaism, and Buddhism) are familiar to us living today, it would be misleading to project too much of what we know of their modern manifestations into the Silk Road context. Religions are not monolithic, fixed institutions existing each in their own realm of dominance, although we often speak of "Christendom," "the Islamic World," and so on. In reality, religions are like organisms: They are born into this world at a point in time, they grow, develop, undergo diverse influences, and adapt to their environment. They quibble with their neighbors, experience periods of painful soul-searching, have good days and bad. At some point they may split like cells, each taking on a new life. Over time, having proven themselves, they may settle into the self-confident stasis of maturity. Sometimes, eventually, they die. In China, especially, they are more often simply absorbed. Nothing could better illustrate the organic nature of religious traditions than the example of their experiences along the Silk Road.

The Silk Road was more than just a conduit along which religions hitched rides East; it constituted a formative and transformative rite of passage. No religion emerges unchanged at the end of that arduous journey. Key formative influences on the early development of the Mahayana and Pure Land movements, which became so much a part of East Asian civilization, are to be sought in Buddhism's earlier encounters along the Silk Road. Manichaeism, driven underground in the West, appears in the eighth century as a powerful political force in East Turkestan, then gradually blends into the amorphous mass of Chinese popular religion. Nestorian Christianity, expelled as a heresy from the Byzantine realm, moves eastward, touches hundreds of thousands among the Eurasian steppe peoples, and appears centuries later like a bad dream to the first Catholic missionaries in China, who find it comfortably entrenched there as the recognized resident Christianity of the East.

Islam, carried along by the momentum of the Arabs' military success, makes its appearance on the Silk Road in the eighth century but comes to a temporary halt halfway, following the Battle of Talas in 751. Directly and indirectly, Islam would be carried east through trade, just like its predecessors. Nor would the new tradition remain Arab property: It would belong instead to the Persians, the Turks, the Chinese—and it would feed from their cultures. Ideas, after all, like individuals, need to acquire new tastes and new sponsors if they are to thrive in foreign climes.

The existence of trade routes and constant commercial activity linking diverse cultures from ancient times meant that religious ideas (like technology and other aspects of culture) could spread easily along trade networks which spanned Eurasia. Indeed, like running water finding open channels, this spread was probably inevitable. But the religion-trade relationship was mutually reinforcing. For example, the expansion of Buddhism brought an increased demand for silk, which was used in Buddhist ceremonies, thereby further stimulating the long-distance trading activity that had facilitated the spread of Buddhism in the first place.[13]

THE CARAVAN EXPERIENCE

If one needed or wanted to travel from one place to another in premodern Asia, the most prudent way (indeed, virtually the only way) of ensuring one would survive the trip was to join up with a caravan heading in the direction one wished to go. Travel was an exceedingly expensive and dangerous proposition, especially the farther one got from areas of dense population.

Inner Asia contains vast tracts of inhospitable land, often with little water and sparse human settlements frequently separated by great distances. The road from the Mediterranean to China is barred by some of the world's highest and most rugged mountain ranges, some of its driest, most expansive deserts, and an extreme continental climate which makes either winter or summer travel extremely difficult. The most physically challenging regions also tended to be those farthest from the reach of governmental administrations, making them prime grounds for banditry. And where there was local government, it might be hostile to outsiders.

Caravans coped with all of these problems in a variety of ways. There is safety in numbers, and caravans could be made up of anywhere from several dozen to several thousand travelers at a time. They followed established routes, so were unlikely to get lost, and traveled in set daily stages, stopping in places where the locals expected them and were prepared to meet their needs. Usually they were led by professional caravaneers who had made the trip before, and attempts were made to secure the approval and protection of all the authorities through whose lands the caravan was to pass. Occasionally caravans would receive military escorts through particularly dangerous or unruly areas.

The oases of the Silk Road—Marv, Balkh, Bukhara, Samarqand, Kashgar, Turfan, Khotan, and others—owed their prosperity and often their very existence to the regularity of passing caravans. They offered way stations, or *caravansarays*, where large numbers of travelers could stop and rest for a night or more, stock up on food and supplies, buy local goods and sell the locals imported ones. Travelers would also often exchange their beasts of burden, either to obtain fresh, healthy, and rested animals or to trade in one type of animal for another more suitable for the next stage of the journey.

Caravan travelers transported their goods and personal belongings mainly on horses, mules, and donkeys. For desert regions camels were used: dromedaries in southwestern Asia and Bactrians in the colder, higher elevations of Inner Asia. In the most extreme conditions the choice was rather a yak or a *hainag*, which was a cross between a bull yak and a cow. Donkeys and mules carried packs, while horses, oxen, and camels often drew carts. The pace, set by the camels, was tediously slow: four miles an hour unloaded and two and a half to three miles an hour when loaded up. The average load was around three hundred pounds per camel. At this pace, a caravan might cover thirty miles a day.[14]

Even with the protection and regularity provided by a caravan, disasters were not uncommon. Dehydration, starvation, and exhaustion could befall even the best-planned expedition. Snowstorms or sand-storms could make a caravan lose its way, and even large caravans were not immune to attack from highwaymen. All in all, to travel was to assume an immense amount of risk, not to mention the expense. Exotic tales notwithstanding, a reasonable person would hope as much as possible to *avoid* romance and adventure, and pray just to arrive home again safely one day!

Clearly caravan traffic existed primarily by and for long-distance trade. For the most part no one but a merchant would have the means, the motivation, or the mettle to undertake travel when its conditions were so rigorous and its outcome so uncertain. This also explains why it was mainly goods of high value in proportion to their bulk that were carried along the Silk Road: one had to stand to make a considerable profit from his wares for such a daunting endeavor to seem at all worthwhile.

Even so, there were people who joined caravans for other than purely commercial reasons. Diplomatic missions attached themselves to caravans. Sometimes people who had some special talent, or thought they had, would travel to distant courts in hopes of receiving patronage. A few hardy souls traveled merely to satisfy their own curiosity. Others had scholarly interests and traveled for purposes of research.

With the appearance of proselytizing religions came missionaries. First Buddhists, then Christians and Manichaeans, and finally Sufi Muslims latched on to caravans which would take them and their "spiritual goods" into new lands. As new religious traditions carried by the Silk Road disseminated eastward and took root along the way, travelers were increasingly able to find coreligionists in even the most far-flung and out-of-the-way places who could provide them with assistance and fellowship and to whom in return they could bring some contact from the outside world.

The spread of religious traditions across Asia also stimulated religious pilgrimage. For example, once Buddhism had established itself in China, Chinese Buddhists began to feel the need for direct contact with the sources of their tradition in India. Chinese monks, the most famous of whom are Fa-hsien in the fifth century and Hsüan-tsang in the seventh, traveled the Silk Road through Central Asia and down into the Indian subcontinent. Over time Korean and Japanese Buddhist pilgrims also appeared.[15] And by the thirteenth century Christian Turks from Mongolia such as Rabban Sauma and his disciple Markos were undertaking the pilgrimage west to Palestine.

From the tenth century or even earlier, Sufi masters attached themselves to Silk Road caravans in order to spread their interpretations of Islam eastward into Inner Asia and China. They frequently won large local followings, converting people perhaps more by their own personal charisma than through the canonical teachings of the faith. Often such figures were attributed with miraculous powers, and when they died their disciples typically would erect a shrine in their honor which might later become a focus of pilgrimage.

It was not only, or even primarily, through missionary activity that religious ideas spread along the Silk Road, however. The earliest of the "mobile" religious systems to take this eastward path, the Iranian and the Hebraic, were not proselytizing faiths. Even the later so-called missionary religions won converts at least as much through their prestige as foreign, cosmopolitan traditions as they did through active proselytization.

This is a phenomenon that historian Jerry Bentley has aptly characterized as "conversion by voluntary association."[16] According to this interpretation local communities, especially in remote areas, would tend to see foreign traders as being their link to the outside world, a world that wasn't hard to imagine as being far more advanced and civilized than the isolated settlement one lived in. Likewise, any local who adopted the cultural trappings of the foreigners (religion being a particularly visible example) could feel and might be considered by others as being more connected to that greater outside world.

A significant aspect of this tendency for anyone involved in commerce was the practical consideration of maintaining the strongest and broadest connections possible with one's business associates. Numerous cases in world history serve as illustration. For example, the spread of Islam through the Sahara and around the Indian Ocean Basin is generally attributed to the success of Muslims in dominating the trade networks of those regions, with the resulting dominance of shari'a law in the marketplace and favorable concessions and taxation terms being extended to Muslim traders in areas under Muslim control.[17] The same pattern applies to Central Asia beginning in the eighth century, but even before Islam a similar process was at work there. It is surely no coincidence that the periods in which Buddhism, Manichaeism, and Nestorian Christianity experienced their most active spread through Inner Asia were connected with the adoption of those traditions by merchant communities.

THE SOGDIANS

The prime actors in this cross-cultural scenario are the people of Transoxiana, roughly modern Uzbekistan. This is a dry but fertile region of Central Asia lying between two great rivers: the Amu Darya (known to the Greeks as the Oxus and to the Muslims as the Jayhun) and the Syr Darya (the Jaxartes, or the Sayhun). Early inhabitants of this arid land were among the first peoples to develop irrigation. For over three millennia agriculture thrived there, until the Russians imposed their rule late in the nineteenth century and turned the land over to a soil-destroying, water-depleting cotton monoculture, which the post-Soviet governments of Central Asia have so far chosen to maintain.

While irrigation ensured Transoxiana's survival, however, its prosperity depended on trade. Situated halfway between the Mediterranean and East Asian centers of civilization, the peoples of this region were ideally situated to be middlemen, and throughout history they have answered this call. From the earliest times it is the natives of Transoxiana who appear as the central figures in trans-Asian trade, and with their role as traders comes their role as transmitters of culture and ideas.[18]

From ancient times the principal inhabitants of Transoxiana were an Iranian stock known as the Sogdians.[19] A sedentary Indo-European people related to their nomadic neighbors the Sakas, or Scythians, they spoke an Iranian language, Sogdian, which survives today as Yaghnobi in remote areas of Tajikistan.

The Sogdian merchants were for centuries among the most successful in Asia, and their trading activities formed the major link connecting East and West. They were like cultural bees, cross-pollinating ideas and traditions from one civilization to another. In the centuries immediately before the common era Buddhism took hold among the Bactrians, another Iranian people living to the northwest of India in what is now Afghanistan. Sogdians living or trading in Bactria adopted Buddhism and spread its teachings throughout their trading colonies all along the Silk Road as far as China. Later Sogdians became enthusiastic converts to Manichaeism or Nestorian Christianity and became the representatives of these faiths through their string of merchant communities across the Asian interior.

With their international connections Sogdians knew foreign languages, and many were literate. They were often engaged as interpreters and translators. It was Sogdian scribes who translated most of the religious texts of Buddhism, Manichaeism, and Christianity into the various languages of the Silk Road, from Indian Prakrits (vernacular dialects), Aramaic, or Parthian into Bactrian, Tokharian, Khotanese, Turkish, or Chinese, either via Sogdian or directly. For that matter, it was Sogdians who brought the technology of paper production from China to the West, and well into the Islamic period the ancient Sogdian city of Samarqand was known throughout the world for the quality of its paper.

In 1907 the British agent-explorer Sir Aurel Stein found the earliest known example of rag paper, dating from the fourth century, in the Tarim Basin of modern China; it consisted of business letters written in the Sogdian language in Aramaic script.[20] In his account of his expeditions, Stein remarks in connection with his discovery of Sogdian Buddhist texts, "What a large share this Iranian element must have had in the propagation of Buddhism along the old 'Northern Route' to carry its particular language and writing to these marches of China proper!"[21] The Sogdians' role in spreading other religious traditions was equally important.

During the eighth century Muslim armies based in Khurasan, composed of Arab settlers and native Iranian converts, gradually conquered and absorbed the Sogdian lands in Central Asia and brought them into the fold of the Muslim empire under the Caliph of Baghdad. First the ruling elite and aristocracy, then over time the general population, converted to Islam in increasing numbers, to such an extent that since the fifteenth century the native sedentary population of Central Asia has been almost completely Muslim.

It would seem that even before Muslim power was fully consolidated in Central Asia, Sogdian merchants were among the earliest and most enthusiastic converts to the new religion. The practical element lurking beneath this trend is not hard to see. Muslims had taken over control of the trade networks which connected Central Asia with the Mediterranean world; if Sogdian traders wished to maintain business in that direction, the advantages of being part of the dominant tradition were obvious. Once their own Central Asian homeland had come under Muslim rule (and their markets under shari'a law), merchants would have had particular incentives not to cling to the old ways.

As Sogdians in western and Central Asia turned to Islam, this led, following the established pattern, to the conversion of their fellow Sogdian trading partners farther East. This in turn facilitated the participation of non-Sogdian Muslims in the Sogdians' trading activities beyond the lands

under Muslim rule, so that when Islam came to China it was not only
Sogdian but also Persian and Arab Muslims who were its bearers.

Thus from the eighth century Sogdians and others in Central Asia
adopted Islam and became active participants in the formation of
Muslim culture. But Islam came to Central Asia through the filter of
Persian civilization, which it had already absorbed and which was its most
prominent non-Arab influence. The Arab Muslims' most dramatic
accomplishment was the defeat and absorption of the entire Persian
Sasanian Empire during the 640s. In 750 the so-called "Abbasid
revolution" displaced the center of Muslim power and administration
eastward into the Persian world. The new Abbasid Empire then in many
respects merely maintained the preexisting Persian cultural and political
realities under a new Islamic identity. Islam became increasingly Persian
in character: To a large extent, Islamic law, philosophy, literature, art,
and mysticism all developed in the Persian cultural sphere.[22]

It was therefore a very Persianized form of Islam that penetrated and
transformed Central Asia over the next several centuries. Islamic religion
and Muslim culture were communicated to Central Asians mainly in the
Persian language. Just as in Egypt and in Syria, where the local Semitic
languages gradually gave way to Arabic, in Central Asia Sogdian and
other Iranian languages ceded to Persian. Although Central Asia had
been incorporated at times into previous Iranian empires, from the
Achaemenids to the Parthians to the Sasanians, it was under the Islamic
Caliphate that local identity essentially disappeared and Central Asia
became an integral part of the Persian world. Indeed by the tenth century
a new Bukhara-based Persian dynasty, the Samanids, had made Central
Asia the center of that world,[23] and it would remain so for several
centuries to come.

LANGUAGE AND PROSELYTIZATION

Attitudes and choices about language are central to questions about the
spread of religions. The Iranian and Hebraic traditions apparently did not
proselytize along the Silk Road but remained the faiths of expatriate Iranian
or Jewish communities. Coincidentally, the sacred texts of Zoroastrianism

and Judaism remained bound to languages which were no longer spoken or understood by the majority of their adherents, whereas actively prose-lytizing movements such as Buddhism, Manichaeism, and Christianity consciously attempted to reach potential converts through both preaching in and translating texts into vernacular languages.

Yet in the wake of the first translation of Hebrew texts into a popular language, the Greek Septuagint, throughout the Roman period the Hebraic tradition which would evolve into Judaism did win many converts; it would seem, in fact, that at no time in its history did the tradition experience such growth. By contrast, the story of Judaism along the Silk Road at a later stage in its life is one of far-flung and, over time, increasingly isolated communities struggling to maintain their religious identity. The tragedy of this trend underlies contemporary treatments by Jewish scholars of the demise of the ancient Chinese Jewish commu-nity in the middle of the twentieth century.[24]

When and why conversion to Judaism began to decline is beyond the scope of the present work, but the issue may be pursued briefly. It may be that the Talmudic approach represents Judaism on the defensive, following the destruction of the Second Temple by the Romans in 70 CE. This case highlights the importance of noting, in any discussion pertaining to a religious tradition, where that tradition stands within its own historical lifecycle of development.

The spread of Islam across Central Asia presents a special case in regard to language, but one which perhaps ultimately fits the pattern. It has been argued that no religious tradition is more scripture-bound than Islam, and since Muslims do not believe a translation of the Qur'an remains the Qur'an, Islam has tended to be seen as strongly tied to the Arabic language.

While in theory such a tie certainly exists, in reality Arabic played less of a role in the transmission of Islam to the peoples of the Silk Road than Persian did. An early twelfth-century Bukharan translator into Persian of an Arabic work on local history explains in his preface that "Since most people do not show a desire to read an Arabic book, friends of mine requested me to translate the book into Persian."[25] Similarly, among the steppe nomads Islam was learned not so much from Arabic texts as through the often highly personalized teachings of charismatic individuals who preached in local languages such as Turkish.

In general, there would appear to be a connection between the success of a religion in winning converts and the readiness with which the substance of that religion was translated into local vernaculars. It should be noted that successful translation is not merely linguistic; meaningful analogs must be found for symbols and concepts. In many cases such analogs between one cultural vocabulary and another simply do not exist and must be invented. It is thus easy to see how the substance of religious traditions often was transformed along the Silk Road, sometimes radically, as a result of the translation process.

MIXED MARRIAGES AND WOMEN'S ROLES IN RELIGIOUS EDUCATION

For the most part long-distance travelers were men. In the case of traveling businessmen, liaisons or marriages with local women frequently ensued. Formally speaking, in most cultures the offspring of such mixed unions tended to be considered members of the father's community, but in reality it was often the mothers who exercised the greater influence on their children's religious education.

This informal level of passing on religious tradition is far less documented than that reflected in standard male history and often must be reconstructed from secondary evidence. It is therefore difficult to make assertions about women's roles and influence that can be clearly substantiated; nevertheless, a growing number of historians are attempting to round out the picture drawing on whatever sources they can.

The anthropological fieldwork of Sergei Poliakov conducted in Tajikistan during the last four decades of the Soviet period has shed much light on the roles of women in passing on religious tradition to their children.[26] At a time when even men were cut off from the influence of the mosque, Poliakov demonstrates how Islam—or, more accurately, a popular local expression of it—survived seventy years of enforced official atheism by being preserved through a culture of shrine visitation, a culture which was largely the province of women.

Although the shrine custodians who acted as teachers and transmitters were men, it was mainly the women who went to the shrines, often to pray for offspring. An American friend of mine recently visited such a shrine in Uzbekistan in the company of his wife; the attendant assumed they were there to pray for children and recited the *fatiha* (the opening chapter of the Qur'an) for them. My friends joked about it afterward—they had no plans for children. But four months later the wife was pregnant!

Normally wives visit such shrines alone, and in the course of such visits the custodian usually serves as a religious instructor. The knowledge passed on through this type of system belongs more to oral culture than it does to canonical texts, and it was this oral culture, transmitted principally by women to their children, that formed the backbone of Central Asian religious life throughout the Soviet period.

Historian Richard Eaton has described a similar system for the transmission and dissemination of Islamic vocabulary and symbolism in southern India dating back at least to the sixteenth century and probably earlier.[27] The folk literature of this region suggests that the spread of Islam—or, perhaps more accurately, of Islamic ideas and symbols— among the Indian masses was facilitated to a large extent by Sufi shrine attendants who composed "Islamic" songs in the local language and taught women to sing them while spinning, cooking, as lullabies, or at weddings. Since merely singing such songs did not require any kind of formal conversion or profession of faith, they spread widely and became a significant element of popular culture. As Islamic concepts and symbols worked their way into Indian society in this way, it would not always be easy to tell Muslims from Hindus on the basis of their religious vocabulary. At the village level such communal distinctions became most marked during the British period, as the colonial government sought to conduct censuses and place people into categories.

Still, even to this day in India one finds ostensible Hindus, Christians, Jains, and Sikhs visiting the shrines of Muslim saints, and vice versa. While men too participate in shrine culture, especially festivals, on a daily basis the normative influence of the mosque is more open to them, whereas women's access to "Islamic" teaching is more through the shrines.

While women's history is only recently beginning to emerge as a corrective to the established male-oriented view ("*his*-story"), it is likely that female-centered patterns of religious education within the family existed in many different historical contexts. That is a matter for future research, but women's roles may be borne in mind as one seeks to understand the various expressions of religious syncretism which continuously emerge from within the multicultural and cosmopolitan societies of the Silk Road.

OTHER HISTORICAL PROBLEMS

The largely unwritten history of women is not the only obstacle to a clear understanding of religious history. Another fundamental problem is that of defining the religious traditions themselves and of determining which religious ideas can be attributed specifically to each of them. Especially as we go farther back into prehistory and perceive borrowings between traditions, in many cases it is far from clear which culture borrowed from which. Such is the case with the many shared ideas found among the ancient Semitic Israelites and the Indo-European Iranians.

A related problem is determining the very nature of any given tradition. Religious belief and behavior varies inevitably even over brief stretches of space or time, often even within the boundaries of what we consider to be a single tradition; thus, any attempt to circumscribe belief and practice within a particular definition is bound to be to some degree arbitrary. We are stretching things, and possibly seriously anachronizing, if we refer to ancient Yahweh-worshippers as Jews or Ahura Mazda devotees as Zoroastrians. By the same token, the beliefs of second-century Parthian Buddhists or thirteenth-century Turkish Nestorians may be hard to reconcile with standard modern definitions of Buddhism or Christianity.

A third dimension to this problem of categorization is that in any given place and time, people more likely than not exhibit beliefs and practices that are to some degree heterogeneous. Where we perceive evidence of the presence of a recognizable tradition, we nevertheless often lack evidence that the people in question thought of themselves as adherents to that tradition in any way that matches what we project back onto them.

When we find, for example, material from fifth-century Central Asia that we associate with Buddhism and other evidence we deem to be Zoroastrian, we may draw a variety of conclusions: (1) that both Buddhist and Zoroastrian native communities existed there; (2) that both communities existed but one was foreign and the other native; (3) that *local* religion was a mixture of Buddhism and Zoroastrianism; or (4) that the original local religion, although surviving, had incorporated Buddhist and Zoroastrian elements. In actual fact it is very difficult, if not impossible, to settle on any of these interpretations definitively.

This brings us to yet another unresolved question, which concerns the extent of conversion to a given tradition in any particular place and time or its proportional representation within the society. Even when we can obtain strong evidence for the presence of an identifiable tradition— say, a monastery containing canonical works in its library and bearing standard iconography on its walls—we often cannot extrapolate with any real accuracy how pervasive that tradition was.

We know that under the Uighur kings in the eighth and ninth centuries Manichaeism attained official status for the only time in its career. But despite its being the state religion, the mass of the population cannot have converted to it, for we see simultaneous evidence for the presence of Buddhists, of Christians, and for the persistence of the traditional Turkic shamanistic religion in Uighur society.

Likewise the decline of Zoroastrianism, Buddhism, Manichaeism, and Christianity along the Silk Road, although a historical fact, is very difficult to trace with any sort of precision. Once the absence of evidence is complete, we can say with relative certainty that by that point a tradition has been extinguished. But if, for example, we find no Nestorian relics in Central Asia that date later than the mid-fourteenth century, neither does that tell us how numerous the Christians were who produced those last relics, nor does it tell us when the last practicing Nestorian died or converted to Islam.

Manichaeism in China ceases to be identifiable as a distinct tradition by the sixteenth century, yet in recent years a Manichaean temple has

been found in Fu-ch'ien Province.[28] Clearly, any observations regarding
the existence and the survival of religious ideas, along the Silk Road or
anywhere else in world history, ought to be advanced with humility.

CHAPTER TWO

Religion and
Trade in Ancient Eurasia

Archeological evidence suggests that urban-based political structures in the Oxus region began to develop from the early part of the first millennium BCE. To the north, within the vast swath of steppelands reaching across the Asian continent from above the Black Sea all the way to the frontiers of China, the culture was mainly nomadic or semi-nomadic. As urbanization developed, the pastoral peoples of the Eurasian steppe entered into a long, rocky partnership with settled civilization which lasted for well over 2,500 years, until the twentieth century, when "modernizing" governments began forcibly resettling nomadic groups and bringing their age-old way of life to an end.

The great Russian Orientalist V. V. Bartold expressed this symbiotic relationship as "the steppe and the sown," a conceptualization which remains popular among many who study the social history of Central Asia. According to this model, Central Asian history is defined largely by the dynamics of nomadic-sedentary relations, often hostile, even violent, but always mutually interdependent.

Specifically, the relationship meant that pastoral peoples would provide raw materials, such as wool and leather from their herds, to be processed by the oasis-dwellers, who would offer back manufactured goods in exchange. On a different level, the nomads would often attack and plunder the settled folk, like wolves raiding chicken coops.[1] Having taken their fill, they might then recede again to the steppes. Or, seduced by the fleshpots of civilization, they might stay on and assimilate, often taking their place as the new ruling class, thereby injecting new blood and new energy into a decadent society. Inevitably conquerors from the steppe who chose to settle in the cities would adopt the culture of those they had conquered and become in their turn the champions and defenders of that culture. This pattern repeats itself again and again over the course of three millennia.

In most cases the dominant peoples of the Eurasian steppe have belonged to either the Iranian or the Turkic language families. Although the Iranian tongues, being Indo-European, are distinct from the Altaic Turkic dialects, the speakers themselves often have been less easy to distinguish, since their shared history has provided them with many shared traits, ideas, and ways of life. This common legacy includes the Iranian and Turkic languages themselves, as can be seen in the bilingualism which remains in some parts of Central Asia to this day.

The same is true for religious beliefs, practices, and myths. Many of the religious concepts of the ancient Iranian peoples appear to fit neatly into the scheme of Indo-European religion and social structure, as reconstructed by the French Indo-Europeanist Georges Dumézil and others.[2] But in many cases the same phenomena are observable among the Ural-Altaic peoples as well. It has been suggested that such widespread phenomena as horse nomadism, fire worship, exposure of the dead, and the concept of universal dominion granted by a sky god were all borrowed from the Indo-European Aryans by other steppe peoples farther east—but this is largely a matter of speculation.[3]

In ancient Eurasian as in other primal societies, religion manifested itself mainly through rituals of daily life, such as in preparation for hunting, funeral rites, and so on. Archeological remains are the primary source for reconstructing these ancient religious rites and beliefs. The tripartite structure of Indo-European society posited by Dumézil, consisting of priests, warriors, and pastoralists, seems to be reflected in the earliest building foundations uncovered at Dashly (in northern Afghanistan) and elsewhere. These appear to be in the form of sacred triads: three gates, nine towers.[4] Burial sites also show evidence of animal sacrifice, especially horses, but also dogs and oxen. The graves often have wooden covers held up by posts, just as described in the *Rig Veda* scriptures of the ancient Indo-European migrants to India, peoples often referred to as the Indo-Aryans.[5]

In another parallel with the Indian culture depicted in the *Rig Veda,* Iranians of the steppes relied heavily on horse-drawn chariots, especially in warfare. This technology may have been vital in enabling the Indo-Aryans to subdue the northern Indian subcontinent. Indeed it is upon the steppes of western Central Asia that the horse was first domesticated and hitched up to a chariot—probably in the area of modern Ukraine—although riding horseback appears to have been a later innovation.[6] Significantly, a horse-drawn chariot is the means by which the ancient Iranians believed the soul departs this world.

Other beliefs characteristic of the ancient Iranians are described in classical Greek accounts of various tribes known to them, especially the Sakas, or Scythians.[7] The Sakas believed that the implements they considered most important—the yoke, the plow, the spear, and the chalice—were divine gifts. They had a cult of the horse, believing the horse to be an intermediary between this world and the next. The steppe Iranians' reverence for horses is seen in the frequency of horse motifs in Saka art, a theme found in the funerary art of the steppes at least as late as the sixth century CE. Horse sacrifice among the Sakas is mentioned by Herodotus, as is a water taboo and the making of drinking vessels from the skulls of slain enemies; all these customs are found later among various Turkic peoples.[8]

The Sakas also had a fire cult and a related cult of the Sun. Herodotus quotes Tomyris, queen of the Massagatae tribe, as swearing "by the Sun our master," and says of them that "The only god they worship is the sun, to which they sacrifice horses: the idea behind this is to offer the swiftest animal to the swiftest of gods."[9]

Herodotus elsewhere states that the supreme Saka goddess was named Tabiti, whom he equates with the Greek Hestia.[10] The Greeks observed religious images, altars, and temples to be in use among the Sakas. They noted the existence of a figure known as an *enaree*, a sort of effeminate divination expert. Greek writers commented on the Sakas' elaborate funeral and burial rites and on their efforts to protect ancestral tombs.[11] Herodotus mentions one Saka tribe, the Argippaei, as having a special sacred status that protected them from attack by neighboring tribes and enabled them to serve as arbitrators in disputes.[12]

As in ancient Greece, local religious activity in the Iranian world often centered on worship of a mythical hero. In Bukhara the major cult focused on the heroic figure of Siyavash. He appears later as a character in the Persian national epic, the *Shah-nama,* or "Book of Kings," which the tenth century poet Abu'l Qasim Firdawsi, like his Greek counterpart Homer, redacted from a variety of ancient oral traditions.

Generally speaking, the Iranian tribes tended to dominate the western part of the Eurasian steppe and the Altaic peoples the east, although there were Altaic groups in the region of the Ural Mountains and elsewhere and Indo-Europeans at least as far east as the Tarim Basin of modern Xinjiang.[13] Thus, we must turn to Chinese sources for references to the Altaic peoples. The earliest mentions of the Hsiung-nu (third century BCE to second century CE), state that, like the Chinese, they offered sacrifices to their ancestors and to the gods of heaven and earth, according to a seasonal ritual calendar. Furthermore, they consulted the stars and the moon before embarking on military maneuvres.[14]

A much-later Western source from a sixth-century Greek envoy to Central Asia describes a Turkish funeral ceremony where mourners lacerated their faces and, like the ancient Iranians, sacrificed horses and also servants.[15] More elaborate information is given in the earliest-known inscriptions in a Turkic language, found on stone pillars by the banks of the Orkhon River in modern Mongolia, which date from the seventh century. These inscriptions specifically refer to a sky god, Tangri, and to a sacred mountain called Ötükän. Tangri comes to be identified as the supreme god of the Altaic peoples and survives as a synonym for Allah in modern Muslim Turkey.

ZOROASTER

At some point in pre-history—exactly when is not known—a prophet appeared among the Iranian pastoralists of Central Asia. Zarathrushtra, or Zoroaster as he is more commonly known, is believed by some to have lived as early as the thirteenth century and by others as late as the sixth century BCE. His home has been placed as far west as Azerbaijan and as far east as Mongolia.[16] Zoroastrianism, the religious tradition which traces its foundations back to his teachings, is represented today by small communities of believers in India (especially Bombay), Iran, and North America. Some compositions, actually hymns, attributed to Zoroaster himself are preserved in the sacred book of the Zoroastrians, the *Avesta*, where they are known as the *Gathas*. These hymns are in a very old Iranian dialect, close to Vedic Sanskrit, and were passed down orally for centuries before being included in the Avesta sometime in the early centuries of our era.

Zoroaster was a preacher, perhaps of priestly family background, who sought to reform the religious practices of his community. He opposed certain tendencies common to various Indo-European peoples, such as bull sacrifice and the ritual drinking of *haoma* (Skt. *soma*), an intoxicating beverage, which often led to drunken orgies.[17] (In the *Rig Veda*, Soma is the second most important god after Indra.) The prophet also singled out one god, or *ahura* (Skt. *asura*), from among the Iranian pantheon for exclusive worship and referred to this god as Ahura Mazda, or "Lord Wisdom." The other Iranian gods, the *ahuras* and the *daevas* (Skt. *deva*), he demoted to demons: The English word "devil" is, like the concept itself, of Iranian origin.[18]

Thus, Zoroaster, like Moses, who may have been his contemporary, seems to have been among the earliest of the world's prophets to sow the seeds of monotheism. His vision differed from that of the ancient Israelites, however, in that it accounted for evil by positing an evil divinity, Angra Mainyu (Ahriman). For this reason Zoroastrianism is often characterized as a dualistic rather than a monotheistic religion.

It is often assumed that the various Iranian peoples of "greater Iran"—a cultural area that stretched from Mesopotamia and the Caucasus into Khwarazm, Transoxiana, Bactria, and the Pamirs and included

Persians, Medes, Parthians, and Sogdians, among others—were all "Zoroastrian" in pre-Islamic times. As one writer recently put it, "After the conversion of King Vishtasp [by Zoroaster], all of Iran is thought to have become Zoroastrian, and it continued to be so up to the end of the Sasanian empire."[19] Other scholars continue to characterize virtually the entire ancient Iranian world as Zoroastrian, a sweeping generalization supported by little or no evidence.[20]

These blanket assertions must, therefore, be taken with caution. Like Judaism, the Zoroastrian religion has ancient roots, but is essentially a product of the Christian era. Zoroastrianism was first codified only from the third century CE as the official state religion of the Iranian Sasanian Empire, anywhere from a thousand to fifteen hundred years after the life of Zoroaster. We know relatively little about the religious beliefs and practices of the Central Asian Iranian peoples of early times, compared to the documentation available for Sasanian Zoroastrianism.

What is known of Sasanian Zoroastrianism, furthermore, does not necessarily apply to the religious beliefs and practices of ancient Iran. No known Achaemenid sources even mention the prophet Zoroaster. Clearly, we should be wary of projecting back onto Achaemenid- and Parthian-era Iranians the "Zoroastrian" tradition in its Sasanian form.[21] The same is all the more true for Central Asia.

We can, however, speak of Iranian religion in a broad sense, by identifying certain elements which clearly belong to an Iranian religious "pool" of myths, deities, symbols, and rituals. Iranian religion can then be understood in its various local contexts to be made up largely of elements drawn from this pool. The mix varies depending on the time and locale, with different elements having greater or lesser relative weight, or none at all, and with diverse non-Iranian regional elements filtering in.

It appears that before as well as after Zoroaster many Iranian communities considered the sun to be the visible form of Ahura Mazda. Assyrian inscriptions give the form *Asara Mazas* (proto-Iranian **Asura mazdas*), and in the Saka language *urmaysde* is the word for sun.[22] The sun, and its earthly analog, fire, both served to purify. It is worth noting that the Indo-Aryans worshipped Agni, the god of fire, and that the Indian practice of purifying the bodies of the dead on funeral pyres has at its root the same purpose as the Iranian practice of exposing their remains to the sun. As one writer has remarked, ". . . fire and light are purifying agents, destroying dead matter and releasing the nonmaterial soul to paradise. Paradise itself is conceived of, in both cases, as a place of light."[23]

A moon cult also figured in the Iranian religious world. The moon was equated with the figure of a heavenly bull, which was widespread in ancient times, especially in Mesopotamia. In the Avestan language the moon is called *gao chithra*, "having bull semen." According to Iranian myth all earthly animals were born of this semen, while plants were created from its dripping onto the ground. Evidence of bull worship from the early second millennium BCE has been found at Altin Tepe in present-day Turkmenistan. It has been suggested that the Makh temple at Bukhara mentioned in early Islamic sources was originally a temple of the moon (cf. Pers. *mah*, "moon").[24]

Perhaps the most visible element of Iranian religion is the festival of the new year, called *Naw ruz* ("new day") held at the vernal equinox. This pan-Iranian festival seems to have originally been connected with Jamshid (Av. *Yima*), the "Primordial Man" figure in Iranian mythology.

By Achaemenid times quite a few of the Iranian deities which Zoroaster had attempted to demote to demons were creeping back into the Iranian religious pantheon, even in the central Persian lands. Still, the Achaemenid ruler Darius could say critically of the Sakas and Elamites, "they do not worship Ahura Mazda,"[25] indicating the official primacy the Achaemenids accorded to that god.

It seems that the Achaemenids attempted to impose their calendar on their Central Asian subjects, but it does not appear to have been a great success. The Sogdians substituted names of their own for most of the months and invented new names for the intercalary days (the *epagomenae*), which, in the words of one Iranologist, "shows little regard for the *Amesha Spenta* ['Bounteous Immortals', a class of divinities] and lack of familiarity with the *Gathas*."[26]

Among the divinities popular in Central Asia was Baga (cf. Skt. Bagha, Rus. Bog), a god associated with wine and marriage.[27] The Sogdian "Ancient Letters," documents from near Lou-lan in Xinjiang which probably date to around 313 CE, before Buddhism, Christianity, or Manichaeism took hold among the Sogdians, mention only "the lord of the temple" *(Vgnpt)* and not the chief of the Magi *(Mogrt)*, leading us to understand that the former was more important in the Sogdian world even in the early Sasanian period.[28] The goddess Nanai (equated with Anahita, or Venus) is frequently mentioned. The figure of the devil carries a distinctly Sogdian name, Shimnu, which is derived independently of the Avestan Angra Mainyu.[29]

THE ENCOUNTER OF
IRANIAN AND JUDEAN RELIGION

The Israelite monarchy established in Palestine by King David in the tenth century BCE was obliterated by powers from the East in two major stages, beginning in the eighth century BCE and concluding in the sixth. The Assyrians crushed the northern kingdom of Israel in 722 and forcibly relocated its inhabitants to other parts of their empire. The book of II Kings states that Ten Tribes of Israel were exiled to "Halah and Habor by the River Gozan and in the cities of the Medes" (18:11). Since the former locations have been situated in Khurasan, it has been suggested that Israelite presence in Central Asia should be considered as originating at that time.[30] Accordingly it has been proposed that these earliest exiles may have engaged in long-distance overland trade.[31] Such hypotheses are not implausible, but solid evidence is lacking.

The southern kingdom of Judah managed to survive for another century and a half through diplomacy, but in 587 a new power, the Babylonians, put an end to Judean independence, destroying Jerusalem and its Temple, which had been the center of the priest-dominated sacrificial religion of the Israelites since the time of King Solomon (tenth c. BCE). Like the Assyrians, the Babylonians deported the Judean survivors to Mesopotamia to work as slaves.

Less than thirty years later, in 559 a Persian army under Cyrus the Great conquered Babylon and freed the various enslaved peoples there, including the Judeans. Allowed to return home to Judah, most Judeans chose instead to stay in Babylon as free citizens of the new Persian Empire or elected to try their luck elsewhere in the Persian-controlled lands. Many relocated eastward to Iran proper and laid the foundations for Jewish communities that have survived there to the present day, especially in the cities of Hamadan (ancient Ecbatana) and Esfahan.

As Cyrus had also made conquests to the east, as far as Bactria and Sogdiana, it is likely that some of the Babylonian Jews relocated to those provinces as well. The Book of Esther states in several places (3:6, 8; 8:5, 12; and 9:20) that the Jews lived "in all the provinces" of the Persian Empire. The modern-day Jewish communities of Bukhara and Samarqand, in particular, like to trace their history back to Assyrian times and consider themselves to be descended from the Ten Tribes.[32] Although this origin is attested by Saadia Gaon of Fayyum in the tenth century,[33] there is no direct evidence for Jewish presence in Central Asia earlier than the Achaemenid period as described in the Book of Esther.

Recently an attempt has been made to argue that Samarqand was originally founded as a Jewish refugee colony, on the basis of some popular etymologies (Samar + qand = "Samarian city") and other evidence. While some of the examples given are intriguing, the clear fallaciousness of others undermines the argument's credibility. For example, the author, being ignorant of Persian, suggests that the Persian new year, *Naw ruz* ("new day"), is derived from the Hebrew *navra* ("fire").[34] In any event it is certain that Samarqand was already an important city by the time of Alexander's conquest in 329–327 BCE; his chronicler Arrian mentions it as Maracanda. Therefore the Muslim legend, according to which the city was founded by two of Alexander's slaves, Samar and Qamar, must be discounted as well as the recent Jewish explanation.

It does seem likely that many of the postexilic Judean settlers in Persian lands took up commerce. It would have been consistent with later patterns for them to set up trade networks with relatives or other Judeans in other parts of the Persian Empire or elsewhere. Roman sources show that by the Parthian period, both Palestinian and Babylonian Jews were involved in the silk trade from China. Hebrew names appearing on pottery fragments from Marv dating from the first to the third centuries CE attest to the presence of Jews living along the Silk Road at that time.[35] Because Jews were spread across a wide geographical area spanning both the Parthian and the Roman lands, they were ideally situated to participate in trade between the two empires.[36]

Iranian Influences on Judaism

Influences that Jewish communities picked up in one cultural environment could easily travel to connected communities in another. Beginning in the Persian period and continuing through Hellenistic and Parthian times, a number of Iranian beliefs and concepts began to work their way into the religious outlook of the Judeans, a tradition that would later evolve into Judaism.[37]

Eschatological ideas such as warnings of the "last days" and belief in a messianic savior, a bodily resurrection, and a last judgment are just some of the notions that Judaism (and subsequently Christianity and Islam) seems to have borrowed from the Persians. The concepts of a heavenly paradise (Old Pers. *paira daeza*) and a hell of punishment for the wicked are also seen in ancient Iranian religion, but not in Israelite sources prior to the Babylonian period. The Iranian evil spirit Angra Mainyu, or Ahriman, evolves into the Christian and Muslim devil, who first appears in the book of Job as *ha-satan*, "the accuser." The concept of angels and demons, likewise, seems to derive from Iranian beliefs. Ancient Iranian cosmology, with its numerology based on the number seven, may be the precedent for later evolutions in Greek philosophy and in Jewish, Christian, and Muslim mysticism.[38]

The biblical Book of Esther, composed apparently in Iran sometime in the fourth century BCE, provides one of the most explicit examples of interaction between the Iranian and Israelite religious traditions. It also provides the earliest record of numerous Iranian cultural traditions, such as court protocol, which continue to be attested through the Islamic period. The drinking custom mentioned in Esther 1:8 and echoed by the tenth-century Arab writer al-Jahiz is one example. Others are the function of the chamberlain in Esther 6:4-5, and the role of eunuchs in 1:10.[39]

The Book of Esther has been shown to contain numerous elements derived from Iranian religion. The plotter Teresh and the disloyal minister's evil wife Zeresh appear to be reflections of the demons Taurvi and Zairik in the Avesta. Together they can be seen to represent the Iranian paradigm of "the lie" *(druj)* opposed to the king's law *(data)*, and by extension lewdness versus chastity and violence versus the pacifism of the righteous.[40]

The Jewish festival of Purim, which comes out of the Esther story, was likely derived from the ancient Iranian springtime festival of Fravardigan, which, like Purim, began on the fourteenth day of the month of Azar and included an exchange of gifts.[41]

Like some other Indo-European peoples, Iranians believed time would end in a great apocalyptic event. This final catastrophe (which is known as Ragnarök in later Scandinavian mythology) was called Frasho-kereti or Fraoshkart by the ancient Iranians. It is surely no coincidence that the apocalyptic writings of Jewish tradition, such as those found in the books of Ezekiel and Daniel, appear in the context of the Babylonian captivity and after.

Iranian origins have even been seen in aspects of the Christian apocalypse of St. John the Divine. The passage in Revelation 11:1-2 prophesying that Jerusalem, but not its Temple, would be destroyed, is derived from an earlier Jewish apocalyptic text written in Greek, the *Oracles of Hystaspes.* The latter work, composed most likely in Parthia, was in turn based on an old Iranian story about King Vishtasp, the royal convert won over by Zoroaster; the anonymous Jewish author presumably sought thereby to imbue his tale with the authority of an ancient Iranian prophecy.[42] Eventually the "Great King" of the original Magian story evolved into the figure of Christ in the Revelation of John. Thus, over a period of centuries, what had originally been a uniquely Iranian eschatology was developed into a Hellenic and eventually Christian concept.[43]

It has been observed that concepts apparently Iranian in origin become most evident in Jewish sources not from the Persian period (the sixth to the fourth centuries BCE) but later during the Hellenistic period, when they become evident in Greek-ruled Palestine.[44] This supports the theory that Iranian ideas found their way into Jewish culture through the agency of Jews who had settled in the Iranian world and were thus immersed in Iranian culture. Iranian Jews would then have transmitted these ideas westward to the Jewish communities of the Mediterranean world with which they remained in contact. We have already suggested that the basis of this preserved contact was, to a significant extent at least, Jewish involvement in long-distance trade.

JUDAISM IN EAST ASIA

A single stone inscription from a synagogue in K'ai-feng along the lower reaches of the Yellow River offers a tantalizing suggestion regarding the earliest Jewish presence in East Asia. The inscription, which dates from 1663, reads: "The religion started in *T'ien-chu* [lit. 'India,' but probably just meaning the West], and was first transmitted to China during the Chou [the Chou dynasty, ca.1100–221 BCE]. A *tz'u* (ancestral hall) was built in Ta-liang (K'ai-feng). Through the Han, T'ang, Sung, Ming, and up till now, it has undergone many vicissitudes."[45]

If we are to believe this inscription, the Jewish community discovered at the turn of the twentieth century in eastern China would appear to have been founded by traders who came to East Asia, presumably via the Silk Road, prior to the end of the third century BCE. It has even been suggested that this process was already occurring in the time of King David! Supporters of the latter theory point to terms in the Hebrew Bible which they take to mean "silk," although detractors point out that these meanings are far from established.[46] For a long time enthusiasts identified "the land of Sinim" in Deutero-Isaiah with China, a connection since disproven.[47] In 1993 archeologists in Egypt found a sample of silk dating to the tenth century BCE,[48] and Israelite traders are certainly as likely as anyone to have played a role in bringing it there. It may be said that to argue Jews *may* have participated in trans-Asian trade from the earliest times is fine, but so far the more extreme dates are purely speculative.

Unfortunately, the K'ai-feng inscription is uncorroborated by any other piece of evidence and may just reflect the Chinese Jewish community's boldest claim to antiquity in its own origin myth. An earlier inscription from 1512 and a slightly later one from 1679 both date the Jews' first arrival in China to the Han period (202 BCE–221 CE). Consistent with this dating, some Chinese Jews told a Jesuit missionary in the early eighteenth century that according to their own oral tradition, their ancestors had first come from Persia during the reign of Ming-ti (58–75 CE).[49] The founders of the K'ai-feng community, meanwhile, appear to have arrived by sea no earlier than the ninth century CE, separately and distinctly from the Jews who had come overland into Chinese territory much earlier.[50]

IRANIAN AND JEWISH
RELIGION ON THE ANCIENT SILK ROAD

Although firm evidence is lacking, it is not unlikely that both Iranian and Jewish merchants were active along the Silk Road from a very early time, perhaps 3,000 years ago or even more. Naturally their religious ideas would have accompanied them on their travels and therefore would have become familiar to peoples these merchants encountered along the way. There is evidence that Iranian soothsayers were employed by the Western Chou dynasty of China prior to the eighth century BCE.[51]

So we can say that in ancient times certain religious ideas may have spread geographically eastward, in the sense that the *possessors* of those ideas physically went there; this is not to say, however, that Iranian or Jewish religious systems "grew" or won converts. The great missionary religions had not yet entered the stage of world history.

In traditional societies religions, like people, are generally considered as being attached to a particular locality or region and, by extension, to their own local culture. From an Inner Asian or Chinese point of view, whatever religion a foreign merchant of Iranian or Israelite origin practiced was simply the home religion of the Iranians or of the Israelites; one would no more think of embracing such religion oneself than of pretending to be from Iran or Palestine.

Still, as Turks, Chinese, and other East Asian peoples came into contact with these merchants from the West and became familiar with their ways of thinking, subtle influences must have penetrated in both directions through everyday encounters and conversation. For example, it has been suggested that Taoists of the late Han period (i.e., sometime before 221 CE) borrowed their term for "the highest heaven," *ta-lo,* from the Iranian *garo-dmana,* the "house of praise," the highest of the four heavens, associated with Ahura Mazda who is referred to in parts of the Avesta as Dadhvah.[52]

It has been argued by a Japanese scholar that the so-called "ghost festival," an annual ritual for "feeding" untended souls, which became extremely popular during the T'ang period, actually had Iranian origins. The Chinese name for the festival, *yu-lan-p'en,* may be derived from the Sogdian *rw'n* ("soul"), and a popular tale associated with the festival, in which a monk, Mu-lien, descends into hell to retrieve his mother, seems to be based on the Greek myth of Dionysos and Semele.[53] There is evidence for other such influences from the early centuries of our era,[54] but similar exchanges of ideas may have been going on much earlier, and if Iranian soothsayers did serve the Chou, they probably were.

CHAPTER THREE

Buddhism
and the Silk Road

At some time during the seventh to the fourth century BCE in northern India lived a man named Siddhartha Gautama, who came to be known as the Buddha, or "Enlightened One."[1] A spiritual reformer who sought a "Middle Path" between worldliness and asceticism, the Buddha preached a message based on Four Noble Truths: that life is suffering; that there is a cause of that suffering, namely desire; that there is a way to end suffering; and that the way is by following an Eightfold Path of right opinion, right thought, right speech, right activity, right livelihood, right effort, right attention, and right concentration.

During his lifetime the Buddha founded a quadrapartite community of followers, called the *sangha,* divided between male and female monks and laity. Soon many of them began to travel throughout India and beyond in order to spread the Buddha's message, which they believed to be universal. This was the first large-scale missionary effort in the history of the world's religions.

This activity was intensified under the Emperor Ashoka of the Maurya dynasty (r. ca. 268–239 BCE), a convert to Buddhism who, repenting of the death and suffering caused by his military conquests, raised Buddhism to official status (although not state religion) within his vast northern Indian empire. Since the time of the Buddha the leading Buddhist monks had held two councils in an attempt to resolve disagreements over correct doctrine and practice.[2] A surviving legend states that Ashoka, troubled by these disputes, called a third council in 244 BCE in order to formulate a Buddhist orthodoxy.[3] If this third council actually happened, it only intensified the divisions.

Traditional views have it that the dispute within the *sangha* centered on a controversy regarding the nature of the monks who had attained Enlightenment, referred to as *arhat*s. Five theses were proposed, purportedly by a monk named Mahadeva, which challenged the status of the *arhat*s by suggesting that they were still subject to worldly distractions such as erotic dreams, residue ignorance, lingering doubts, and so forth.

Another argument was that the *arhat*s' approach restricted the possibility of Enlightenment to a very small group of people. Yet another layer of disagreement had to do with the infiltration of popular religious practices into the tradition, especially the veneration of relics of the Buddha. The more "conservative" monks felt that this type of innovation was a threat to the purity of the Buddha's message and to the rigor of commitment to a Buddhist lifestyle.

The conservatives, according to the traditional view, defended the *arhat*s' exalted status as leaders within the community, while the majority supported the five theses that aimed at bringing the *arhat*s down from their pedestal of privilege. The conservative party came to be known as the Sthaviras and their opponents, the Mahasanghikas, or "the majority community."[4]

Recently some scholars of early Buddhism have sought to revise this version of history, suggesting that much of the disagreement may actually have come later and gotten projected backward as a "historical" explanation for existing schisms. It may be that the central point of tension within the early *sangha* was over additions to the body of rules governing the monastic lifestyle, called the *vinaya*. A "majority" of monks rejected the adding of new rules, accepting as binding only those laid down by the Buddha himself. According to this more recent interpretation, the Sthaviras were those seeking to "reform" the *vinaya* by adding to it; the Mahasangikas, who claimed to possess the older, shorter version, were therefore the "conservative" party.[5]

To complicate matters further, there evolved diverse schools of commentary on the Buddha's teaching. Each of these schools, which were collectively known as *nikaya*, compiled its own canon of texts purporting to be the Buddha's teaching, along with the particular interpretations of it which they considered to be authentic and authoritative. Legend states there were eighteen such schools. Many have left texts, but the only school surviving to the present day is the Theravada (Skt. Sthaviravada, lit., "the way of the elders"), which is the dominant form of Buddhism in Sri Lanka and Southeast Asia.

Buddhism has produced a body of texts more vast than any other movement in human history, making the study of even one school a potentially lifelong task. In China today philosophy professors warn their students, "The serious study of Buddhism is a Black Hole—if you enter, you will never re-emerge!"[6]

BUDDHIST SCHOOLS OF THE SILK ROAD

Since most of the early Buddhist schools no longer exist, their thought must be reconstructed on the basis of surviving texts. The available texts even of defunct schools date to hundreds of years after these schools arose, so it is difficult to know the positions of the various early schools and their relationship to each other with any certitude.

The major *nikaya* schools connected with the regions traversed by the Silk Road were the Dharmaguptakas and the Sarvastivadins. The Mahasanghikas were also active early on. The alternative approach, a more inclusive movement which came to be known as the Mahayana, or "Great Vehicle," first gained influence in Central Asian regions such as Khotan, before eventually displacing the *nikaya* schools from the Silk Road altogether.

The Mahasanghikas

The Mahasanghika attempt to reduce the singular importance of the *arhat* ideal, or perhaps simply their resistance to innovations in the *vinaya*, created the first great schism within the Buddhist community. Many of the Mahasangikas also believed that intuition *(prajña)* happened instantaneously, not gradually as the Sarvastivadins and others taught; this idea later became central in the Mahayana as well, especially in its Zen form.

The famous colossal Buddha statues at Bamiyan in Afghanistan, which stand 150 and 100 feet high carved into a rock cliff face, may have been the work of Mahasanghikas in the northwest.

The Dharmaguptakas

The Dharmaguptaka school was probably the most influential along the Silk Road up to the time of the Kushan Empire in the first centuries of the common era. The Dharmaguptakas wrote their texts mainly in Gandhari Prakrit, the dominant vernacular language of the Kushan heartland in northwestern India. Many Dharmaguptaka texts were transmitted to China by early Central Asian missionaries. By the time of Hsüan-tsang's travels in the seventh century, however, the school had disappeared from India completely and had very few representatives left in Central Asia.

The Dharmaguptakas appear to have been distinguished primarily by their doctrine that the Buddha was separate from, and superior to, the Buddhist community, and not a part of it as other schools believed. A practical ramification of this attitude was the belief that only gifts given to the Buddha could bring merit, not gifts to the community. Since the monastic community depended for its survival on gifts from lay followers, this doctrine may have played a role in the school's ultimate decline.

The Sarvastivadins

The name of this school derives from the phrase *sarvam asti*, "everything exists," which characterized its theory of time. According to this view, the past, present, and future all exist simultaneously. According to Theravada tradition, one of the main accomplishments of the third Buddhist council called by Ashoka was the rejection of the Sarvastivadins.

If true, this may have been a factor in pushing the Sarvastivadin school into Central Asia. By the second century the Dharmaguptakas were losing ground to the Sarvastivadins there. Unlike other schools which used Pali or other regional languages, the Sarvastivadins wrote their texts for the most part in Sanskrit, the ancient priestly language, in an archaizing attempt to give their works a higher authoritative character.

The Mahayana

The Mahayana was not a school per se but rather a "pan-Buddhist movement" defined mainly by the acceptance of new scriptures.[7] The origins of the self-styled "Greater Vehicle" to enlightenment are not fully clear and may never be. The interpretation of earlier scholarship which saw the tradition as growing out of the Mahasanghika school is no longer generally accepted, but the question of whether the Mahayana arose primarily within the lay or the monastic community continues to be debated.[8]

This movement, which appears to have been rather small at first, probably began in northwestern India or Central Asia during the first century BCE. Although a few Mahayana scriptures were recently discovered in northern Pakistan, many of what would later become the main Mahayana texts were probably composed in Central Asia along the Silk Road, where the constant mixing of cultures and ideas must have contributed diverse influences. As one contemporary scholar has cautiously put it, "it is just possible that the popularization of the Mahayana was a phenomenon which took place outside the Indian subcontinent, for reasons connected perhaps with the transmission of Buddhism to other cultures."[9]

Among the distinctive themes of the new scriptures was an elevation of the Buddha to the "supramundane" (*lokattara*), reflected in the belief that his death was a mere appearance (an idea adopted from the Mahasanghikas). There was also an emphasis on compassion for the less fortunate and, most important, the idea that all beings contain "the buddha-nature" (*tathagatha*) and should aspire to no less than full buddhahood. One who embarked upon this quest toward becoming a buddha was known as a *bodhisattva*, a state considered superior to that of an *arhat*.

A *bodhisattva* can be defined as one who vows to be reborn as many times as it takes to work toward becoming a full buddha, for the sake of helping all sentient beings to salvation. This is contrasted in Mahayana "Perfection of Wisdom" literature *(Prajñaparamita)* with the narrower goal of purely personal salvation that characterized the traditional approach.[10] An additional element of early Mahayana works is a strong hostility toward those who wouldn't accept the new texts as authentic.[11] Eventually Mahayanists began to refer derisively to the traditional schools as *Hinayana,* the "Lesser Vehicle."

Furthermore, while schools such as the Theravada can be considered atheistic, the Mahayana expression eventually allowed for treating buddhas and *bodhisattva*s as divinities. According to some Mahayana interpretations, *bodhisattva*s who acquired more merit than they needed could pass it on to others. Devotees would therefore often pray to the Buddha or other *bodhisattva*s to help save them from the cycle of rebirth into the world *(samsara).*

The Mahayana did not develop its own *vinaya,* however. Instead, monks followed the rules laid down by the *nikaya* school of their preference. Thus, while the Mahayana tradition largely displaced *nikaya* schools from China, Chinese monks continued to follow either the *vinaya* of the Sarvastivada or the Dharmaguptaka schools, precisely those that were the first to dominate the Silk Road.[12]

THE GANDHARA
SYNTHESIS AND THE KUSHANS

According to a legend preserved in Pali, the language of the Theravada canon, Buddhism's first contact with the Silk Road took place during the life of the Buddha himself.[13] This legend relates that two merchant brothers from Bactria (medieval Balkh, in the north of Afghanistan), named Tapassu and Bhallika, visited the Buddha in the eighth week after his enlightenment and immediately became his disciples. According to the story, the brothers then returned to Balkh and built temples dedicated to the Buddha.

While there is no evidence to confirm the legend of Tapassu and Bhallika, edicts inscribed on rock pillars set up by Emperor Ashoka state that he sent missionaries into his northwestern territories.[14] Over the following centuries Bactria did become a major Buddhist region, and it remained so up to the Muslim conquests. In the seventh century, on the eve of the Arab invasions, the Chinese Buddhist pilgrim Hsüan-tsang found that Balkh had some one hundred Buddhist monasteries and three thousand priests.

The northwestern region was home to a diverse mix of cultures. It was the meeting ground between the Indian and Iranian worlds, and from the latter part of the fourth century BCE there was added a Greek presence as well. Alexander of Macedon conquered much of this territory between 332 and 327 BCE, and left in his wake a Hellenic administration which would survive in parts of Asia for another two centuries as the Seleucid Dynasty.

Greek settlers in Bactria and Gandhara (what is now north-central Pakistan) brought with them the gods of the classical Greek pantheon and have left coins and other archaeological evidence in testimony. Some Greeks adopted local religions—for example, Heliodoros, ambassador of the Seleucid ruler Antialcidas, erected a pillar to Vishnu at Besnagar.[15] Although evidence of widespread conversion in either direction is lacking, religious ideas must have been exchanged on some level with the native Iranian and Indian populations of those areas. Greeks in Asia, as elsewhere, attempted to identify local deities as corresponding to their own.[16]

A tale of the blinding of King Ashoka's son Kunala relayed by Hsüan-tsang appears to a Buddhist recasting of the Greek tragedy of Hippolytus and Phaedra. Hsüan-tsang reports that in the seventh century, blind pilgrims would pray at the *stupa* of Kunala, near Taxila in what is now Pakistan, for the restoration of their sight.[17] In a remarkable example of cultural continuity, a modern-day hospital there is known for the excellence of its eye facilities.[18]

As one would expect, cross-cultural influences in Gandhara went in both directions. In some cases there is evidence that local cults adopted Greek forms of worship, as at a Greek-style sanctuary to the god Vaxshu (Oxus) at Takht-i Sangin in northern Afghanistan. Or, alternatively, both Greek and Bactrian rites may have been practiced at that same temple, since it appears to be dedicated to both fire and water gods.[19] Likewise, certain Indian notions may have made their way westward into the budding Christianity of the Mediterranean world through the channels of the Greek diaspora.

Religious tolerance appears to have been the norm. The Greco-Bactrian general Menandros, who conquered part of northern India and ruled there as king from around 150 to 135 BCE, treated Buddhist communities under his control with benevolence. His memory is preserved in a Buddhist treatise called the *Milindapañha,* or "The Questions of Menander," a dialogue in the Platonic style between the king and an Indo-Greek monk named Nagasena.[20]

Herakles with a lion-skin served as an artistic model for the Buddhist Vajrapani, a protector of the Buddha. The image of Ganymede's abduction by Zeus in the form of an eagle was taken up by Gandharan artists and recast onto a Buddhist tale, the *Sussandi-jataka* story of a *bodhisattva* who falls in love with a married woman and takes the form of the bird Garuda in order to carry her off. This image appears in Buddhist paintings and sculptures throughout the Indian subcontinent and all across the Silk Road into China; it also finds its way into Sasanian art, where it acquires a Zoroastrian interpretation.[21]

By around 130 BCE Greek rule in Bactria had succumbed to nomadic incursions from Sakas and other steppe peoples. The Sakas too absorbed some Buddhist influence and left a number of Buddhist inscriptions. After a century or so of Saka rule a new power, the Kushans, arose in what is now northwestern Pakistan.

The Kushans' origins are not entirely clear, although it appears they were an ethnically mixed group consisting partly of Indo-European immigrants from farther east along the Silk Road, a people known to the Chinese as Yüeh-chih. They ruled over a population which included native Indians, Iranian-speakers, and Greek settlers, and came to control the trade routes connecting the Indian subcontinent with the Silk Road to the northwest.

Kushan coins bear images of a variety of deities, Iranian, Indic, and Buddhist, suggesting that the new ruling elite had a tolerant attitude toward diverse religions. They held the Iranian goddess Ardoxsho and the Indic god Shiva both in particularly high regard.[22] Votive figures of Hariti, the Indian goddess of smallpox, are an ominous presence of this time; the smallpox epidemic which hit the Mediterranean world during the second century BCE probably started in the Kushan lands and spread west via the trade routes.[23]

From the beginning of their rule, the Kushans adopted the symbol of the Greek Nike, goddess of victory, a clear attempt to appropriate the royal ideology of their Greco-Bactrian predecessors. Yet the second Kushan ruler, Vima, was a devotee of Shiva. It has been suggested that Vima's sympathy for Indic religion was a reflection of his desire to gain control over the Silk Road, since by that time Indians were active in trade throughout the Oxus region and even as far as China.[24]

Vima's successor, Kanishka I, while presumably maintaining the desire to become master of the Silk Road, turned his attention toward mustering the support of his Iranian subjects to the west. During his rule the Iranian forms of divine names reemerge from beneath the Greek ones, although Shiva retained a high official status. His grandson, Kanishka II, helped the spread of Buddhism through the building of *viharas* (monasteries) and *stupas* (temples to house relics). He is also said to have called a Buddhist council in Kashmir, in which it was decided to rewrite the original Gandhari vernacular, or "Prakrit" texts in the high literary language of Sanskrit, a turning point in the evolution of the Buddhist literary canon. Although Kanishka II was not himself a convert to Buddhism, Buddhist sources refer to him as a "second Ashoka."

It is in the Kushan period that the Buddha is first depicted in human form, a development which some scholars have attributed to Greek influence. Statues and busts of the so-called Gandhara school, which developed under the Kushans, show a marked blending of Indian and Greek elements and formed the basis for the later development of Buddhist art in China and elsewhere. A late-first-century statue of the

Buddha flanked by two *bodhisattvas*, with an inscription mentioning the transferal of merit, may be the earliest explicit evidence yet discovered of Mahayana ideas.[25]

Greek as well as Iranian influences appear to have shaped the evolution of Mahayana images (and perhaps thought as well) during the Kushan period. The most popular representation of the Buddha in Kushan art is Maitreya, the "future Buddha," some of whose soteriological and eschatological qualities seem to echo those of the Zoroastrian Saoshyant and the Jewish and Christian Messiah. In a particularly striking parallel, in Buddhist mythology Maitreya will be welcomed by a disciple named Kasyapa; the name of a similar figure in Zoroastrianism, awaiting the Saoshyant, is Karashaspa.[26]

Later, in Manichaeism, Maitreya becomes connected with the Iranian god Mithra and with Jesus. The buddha Amitabha and *bodhisattva* Avalokitesvara, who figure prominently in later Chinese and Japanese expressions of Buddhism, bear features that have been associated with the Iranian gods Zurvan and Mithra. In some cases Amitabha (which means "infinite radiance") seems to be simply understood as the Iranian god of light, equated with the sun.[27]

Stories about the life of the Buddha appear that contain Jewish and Christian elements.[28] Even the Trojan horse turns up in an Indian Buddhist story—now it is a wooden elephant, however, and the beseiged *bodhisattva*, unlike the Trojans, is not fooled.[29] All of these commonalities may reflect the attempts of Indian Buddhist missionaries to present their message through figures, terms, and symbols familiar to a western, Greco-Iranian audience.

A third-century Chinese Buddhist source states that the Kushan lands were one of the main centers of Buddhism.[30] The Kushans may have had Buddhist texts translated into their own language and later into Sogdian for the benefit of Central Asian converts. No such translations have survived, however. Extant Sogdian translations are later and from Chinese, not Indian, versions.

Sometime in the Kushan period, a monk by the name of Sutralanka, who was a native of the Kushan capital Puskaravati (modern Charsadda, near Peshawar), traveled to Shash (modern Tashkent) in Central Asia in order to decorate a Buddhist *vihara* there.[31] This implies the existence of a Buddhist host audience in that part of Central Asia at the time.

Sogdiana does not appear ever to have experienced widespread conversion to Buddhism, however. Hsüan-tsang was disappointed to see how poorly the faith was represented when he visited Samarqand in the seventh century, and a Korean Buddhist passing through several decades later found only one Buddhist monk living alone in a monastery.[32] Buddhism seems to have been carried farther east along the Silk Road by small groups of Sogdian converts associated with diaspora merchant communities. We are faced with the apparent irony that while Sogdians were among the principal agents in the eastward spread of Buddhism, the faith never took root in their homeland.

The Kushans were dislodged from northwestern India and western Central Asia by the Iranian Parthians beginning in the late first century. By the fifth century most of the former Kushan lands were being raided and plundered by nomadic armies, known as Hephthalites or White Huns, from the steppes to the north. The Hephthalites looted Buddhist monasteries and dealt a severe blow to the Buddhist culture of western Central Asia. They cannot have destroyed the religion itself, since people must have continued to practice it, but by looting the monasteries and ravaging the land they took away the financial base which had enabled it to thrive.

PARTHIAN BUDDHISM

The Greek Seleucids were displaced in Iran and Central Asia by an Iranian dynasty, the Parthians, at the beginning of the second century BCE. The Parthians became the new middlemen on the Silk Road, controlling the overland trade from China at a time when Romans were becoming passionate customers for silk.

The Silk Road city of Marv (Grk. Margiana), situated in the eastern part of the Parthian Empire, became a major Buddhist center by the middle of the second century of the common era.[33] Several scholars have been reluctant to concede the importance of Iranian Buddhism at this early date,[34] apparently due to their lack of familiarity with the wealth of archeological evidence that Soviet scholars turned up in Turkmenistan beginning in the early 1960s.[35]

Inscriptions using the Kharosthi Indian script found in the Oxus region farther east date from 58 BCE to 129 CE, attesting to the presence of Mahasangikas there.[36] Later inscriptions found in the Oxus valley from the fourth and fifth centuries are in Brahmi, another Indian script. This together with the discovery of fifth-century Sarvastivadin texts in Marv, suggest that the latter school, although coexisting with the Dharmaguptakas, eventually predominated in western Central Asia.[37]

The picture painted of Gandharan and Parthian Buddhism by archeological finds from the region is dominated by various *nikaya* schools. This poses a historical problem, in that a number of Parthian Buddhists who went to China are mentioned as having translated Mahayana texts there. If there was an early Mahayana presence in western Central Asia, evidence by which it can be reconstructed remains to be discovered.[38]

THE TARIM BASIN

Buddhist missionaries probably reached Khotan on the southern loop of the Silk Road skirting the Takla Makan desert sometime in the first century, although legend has it that a monk from Kashmir arrived there during Ashoka's reign. Khotan was inhabited by Iranian-speaking peoples. The people of Kucha north of the desert, who were also Indo-Europeans, spoke a language closer in some respects to Celtic. Buddhist paintings found in Kucha early in this century are derived from the Gandharan style, indicating close contact between the regions at that time. The light-complexioned figures are distinctly Europoid, often blue-eyed. Farther East, in Miran, has been found the work of a Buddhist painter named Tita (Titus?), perhaps a Roman artist who traveled east along the Silk Road in search of employment.

The major source of Buddhist influence on Khotan in the early centuries of the common era seems to have been from Kashmir, a predominantly Sarvastivadin region at that time. The kings of Khotan played an important role in sponsoring Buddhist schools, first the

Sarvastivadins and Mahasanghikas and later, by the fourth century, the Mahayana, which became dominant there. Still later, in the seventh century, the presence of Tantric schools can be detected.[39] In Kucha, meanwhile, the Sarvastivadins remained the favored school, and when Hsüan-tsang visited in the seventh century he found the local monks scornful of Mahayana texts.

It may be asked why the kings of these oasis city-states in the Tarim Basin welcomed and even solicited Buddhist monks from India. While spiritual factors need not be discounted, it is certainly likely that these rulers also saw this as a way of encouraging contact with a larger, more prosperous civilization. As we have seen, cultural exchange tends to be good for business, and vice versa.

THE ARRIVAL OF BUDDHISM INTO CHINA

During the first half of the first century BCE, the Han dynasty of China succeeded in extending its power westward well into Central Asia. The pretext for this westward expansion is said to have been the Han emperor's desire for Central Asian horses, "horses of heaven," as they were known. Once the Chinese controlled the eastern half of the Silk Road, Western merchants and other travelers would have had increased access to China. Thus it is probable that foreign Buddhists entered China sometime before the common era.

The first clear mention of Buddhism in a Chinese source is a reference in the *Hou Han shu* (*Late Han History*) to a Buddhist community at the court of the governor of Ch'u Province that included some Chinese lay followers. The governor is described as observing both Buddhist and Taoist rituals; this indicates that, from its earliest penetration into Chinese culture, Buddhism had begun to blend with and adapt itself to local religion.[40] When the governor sent a gift of silk to Ming, the Han emperor, as a token of submission, the Emperor sent the following reply: "The king of Ch'u recites the subtle words of Huang-lao [a Taoist cult], and respectfully performs the gentle sacrifices to the Buddha. . . . Let [the silk which he sent for] redemption be sent back, in order thereby to contribute to the lavish entertainment of the *upasaka*s and the *sramana*s."[41] The fact that the emperor uses the Indian terms for lay followers and monks indicates that he was already familiar with Buddhism, which must therefore have been established in China by that time.

Buddhist legend has it that in that same year Emperor Ming dreamed of a "golden man." Told that he had dreamed of the Buddha, the emperor is said to have sent a request to India for Buddhist missionaries.

The first Buddhist missionary who is named in Chinese sources is a Parthian monk who arrived in the capital Lo-yang in 148. An Shih-kao, as he is called in Chinese, may have been the first to organize the systematic translation of Buddhist (in his case, *nikaya*) texts into Chinese. He may also have been one of the first teachers in China of the system of mental exercises known in Sanskrit as *dhyana* (Ch. *ch'an,* Jap. *zen*). And, consistent with the ancient pattern of royal interest in fortune-tellers, his knowledge of Western astronomy is mentioned.

Another Parthian Buddhist, a traveling merchant referred to as An Hsüan, went to China in the year 181 and joined An Shih-kao's translation team. He is best known for participating in the translation of a Mahayana text, the *Ugrapariprccha* (Ch. *Fa-ching ching*). From this early date, therefore, Mahayana and *nikaya* schools appear to have coexisted at Lo-yang.

The early Mahayana in China is most commonly associated with the efforts of a translator of Kushan origin, Lokaksema, who was active at Lo-yang in the last decades of the second century. The eleven earliest known Mahayana texts are Chinese translations, most of which were probably done by Lokaksema or his students.[42] Two of his three principal Chinese assistants were members of a local Taoist sect, a fact that gives further evidence of the process of syncretism at work.[43]

Other translators associated with Lokaksema included several Indians and Sogdians. Later figures bearing the Parthian surname An, such as An Fa-hsien and An Fa-ch'in in the third century, must also have come from Transoxiana, where a remnant Parthian administration survived through the fifth century. (The western part of the empire had been conquered by the Sasanians from 226).[44]

The oasis town of Kucha on the northern branch of the Silk Road was another Buddhist center from which missionaries traveled to China proper. One Kuchean monk of mixed Indian ancestry, Kumarajiva (born in 344), became the first major translator of Mahayana texts into Chinese. Although Kucha itself was predominantly Sarvastivadin, Kumarajiva had studied Mahayana works in Kashmir as a youth and became a proponent of the Mahayana approach on his return to Kucha. He was taken forcibly to the Chinese capital Lo-yang in 402, where he stayed until his death in 412 or 415. Some 300 translations of Buddhist texts into Chinese are attributed to him.[45]

Some scholars have doubted the Iranian role in early Buddhist penetration to East Asia, emphasizing the more direct transmission from India to China northward over the Karakorum Mountains to Kashgar and the Tarim Basin, and thence back again to the Iranian-inhabited regions of western Central Asia.[46] This view, however, is probably overstated. The abundance of Buddhist remains from the area of Marv dating to as early as the first century CE as well as linguistic evidence showing the evolution of Buddhist terminology via Parthian demonstrate that Buddhism traveled first northwest out of the subcontinent into the Iranian world and then eastward along the Silk Road into China.[47]

This does not preclude a more or less contemporary *additional* channel via the Karakorum route to the Tarim Basin and thence to China. (As we have seen, Khotan in particular had direct links with Kashmir.) And once Buddhist presence was established in China, the Silk Road offered a natural conduit by which Chinese Buddhist influences could later travel westward again through Central Asia.

The existence of Chinese Mahayana texts translated into Sogdian, by Sogdian merchants in China who had learned Chinese, suggests that such westward re-transmission was sometimes the case.[48] Indeed, the very idea of translating Buddhist texts into local vernaculars appears to have come to Central Asians from the Chinese; prior to the sixth century, when Buddhist texts were first translated into their own vernaculars, Central Asians were apparently content to read them in Indian languages.[49] Hsüan-tsang, in the seventh century, personally introduced at least one Chinese apocryphal text into India. Finding that the monks of Nalanda, one of the great Buddhist universities, were unfamiliar with *The Awakening of Faith in the Mahayana,* he "retranslated" this "lost" text into Sanskrit.[50]

If in fact the Sogdians and other West Asians began to translate sacred texts as a result of Chinese influence, we may have an example of how "language policy" can play a major role in the success of a religion. Our first evidence for mass conversion to Buddhism along the Silk Road does not come until we reach China, and if indeed early Sogdian Buddhists did not translate sacred texts into their native language, that may be a reason why large-scale conversions to Buddhism in the Sogdian homeland did not occur.

Political factors also affected the spread of Buddhism in China. During the rule of the T'ang dynasty from 618 to 917, several emperors exhibited a marked taste for the exotic. At such times Westerners as well as Western customs and ideas were unusually welcome in China. Military successes by the T'ang likewise extended the influence of Chinese culture and civilization in the direction of the West. At the greatest point of T'ang expansion in the eighth century, the Silk Road was under Chinese control as far as modern-day Kyrgyzstan. They built garrison towns there as elsewhere, and the ruins of an eighth-century temple at Aq Beshim attest to the westward extension of Chinese Buddhism.[51]

LATER BUDDHIST MOVEMENTS

Pure Land

The early Buddhist idea of a "Buddha land," a paradise where the teachings of the Buddha prevail, was broadened in the Mahayana interpretation to mean that the various *boddhisattvas* would purify the lands where they resided. One such purified realm, called Sukhavati, the "land of bliss" (which, significantly perhaps, is located in the West), is described in two late-first-century texts from northwestern India and a third compiled in Central Asia.

This land of splendor is presided over by the Buddha of Light, Amitabha, who leads his followers to salvation through his own excess of acquired merit. The devotee of Amitabha must focus on him, especially at the moment of death, in order to be transported into the Pure Land. Some have argued that this soteriology has more in common with Western notions of the time than with Indian ones and that Iranian ideas in particular were formative in the Pure Land tradition.

The Pure Land movement spread along the Silk Road to China and Japan, where it became widely popular, especially among the lower classes to whom its very simple message of salvation appealed. To those who would criticize such an "easy" method to salvation, Pure Land teachers replied that while in the past many could follow a more rigorous path, the darkness of the present age required an easier means.

Tantra

Tantrism began sometime around the fifth or sixth century CE as a movement in eastern India. It combined rituals such as the chanting of incantations, called *mantras*, and the burning of sacrificial offerings, with yoga. All of these practices had precedents in Brahmanism but were employed now in a Buddhist context. An esoteric tradition, Tantrism was transmitted secretly from teacher to disciple, at first orally.

During the early eighth century Indian monks such as Subharkara Simha, Vajrabodhi, and Amoghavajra introduced Tantra to China. The teaching briefly interested the court, but among the general populace it could not compete with sects such as the Pure Land, and Tantrism did not survive in the T'ang Empire once the Indian missionaries were no longer present.[52] By contrast, Tibet proved particularly receptive to Tantrism, which became the dominant form of Buddhism there beginning in the eighth century.

Ch'an

A legend states that in the sixth century a Buddhist monk named Bodhidharma, who was from southern India (or possibly Iran), traveled to China in order to bring a new teaching: that the usual rituals, texts, and practices of Buddhists were ultimately useless. Instead he offered the example of spontaneous enlightenment, which could be attained through meditation on paradoxes, called *kung-ans* (Japanese *koan*). Ch'an (from Skt. *dhyana,* meditation), as this approach was known, shows considerable influence from Taoism and is thus an exemplary case of Chinese culture transforming Indian ideas into Chinese ones. The tradition became known in Japan as Zen and provided a philosophical basis for arts as diverse as samurai swordplay, haiku poetry, and the painting of watercolor landscapes.

BUDDHIST PILGRIMS

As Buddhism won increasing numbers of native converts in China, many Chinese Buddhists came to feel dissatisfied with learning their religion through foreign intermediaries and thirdhand translations of texts by Central Asians. It does indeed appear that in attempting to make Buddhist concepts palatable to the Chinese, missionaries and translators often took liberties in their translations of key terms and the pairing of Indian with Chinese concepts.

For example, the Indian terms *dharma* (the Buddha's teaching), *bodhi* ("enlightenment"), and *yoga* were all at times rendered in Chinese as *tao* ("the way"), a word which Taoists and Confucians had each already endowed with very strong connotations of their own. The term *arhat*, similarly, was translated as *chen-ren*, or "True Man," which in Taoism represented one who had mastered the arts of immortality. The ineffable *nirvana* was translated as *wu-wei* ("not-force"), a Taoist term for the ethic of passivity.[53] Ordinary phrases acquired new shades of meaning as well, as in one case where "husband supports wife" became in Chinese "husband controls wife."

Beginning no later than 260 CE, Chinese Buddhist monks began to travel to India in order to discover for themselves the sources of the faith. Fifty-four of these pilgrims are mentioned in Chinese sources, although there were probably many more who remain anonymous. The desire of these monks to experience India firsthand went beyond the desire to acquire original texts, however. They also wished to visit personally the sites associated with the life of the historical Buddha. Additionally, they hoped to find authoritative teachers of the Buddhist tradition, doubting the orthodoxy in some cases of Buddhist proponents in China. Many pilgrims brought home relics as well, such as teeth or bones believed to be the Buddha's.

One of the most celebrated of these travelers was Fa-hsien, who lived at the turn of the fifth century. From his home in Ch'ang-an (modern Xian), Fa-hsien traveled westward to Tun-huang, then via Turfan, Qara Shahr, and Khotan southward over the Karakorum to the Swat Valley in what is now northern Pakistan, and from there to India proper. After spending six years in India, from 405 to 411, he returned to China by sea.[54]

Another well-known Chinese Buddhist who traveled to India was Sung-yün, a native of Tun-huang who set out in 518. Like Fa-hsien, Sung-yün took the relatively direct but exceedingly difficult Karakorum route south from Khotan to Kashmir. According to his account, the dangers of this mountain journey were compounded by the presence of a dragon near some mountain lakes below the Tsung-ling Mountains. This dragon was known to cause travelers "all sorts of inconveniences," such as blinding snowstorms, but, according to Sung-yün, "if they pay some religious service to the dragon, they find less difficulty afterwards."[55]

Fa-hsien's travels inspired a young man who would become the most famous Chinese Buddhist of all time, Hsüan-tsang. Born near Lo-yang in 602, Hsüan-tsang was raised in a traditional Confucian family but came under the influence of an elder brother, a Buddhist monk who inclined toward Pure Land beliefs. At twelve he was admitted to his brother's monastery, and he spent the next fifteen years studying the teachings of various Buddhist schools in Cheng-tu and Ch'ang-an. During this time he grew increasingly frustrated by the apparent errors and inconsistencies he detected in the available Chinese translations of key Buddhist texts. He resolved to go to India and to bring back a copy of the original Sanskrit version of a text to which he was particularly attracted. This was Asanga's *Treatise on the Stages of Yoga Practice,* the main text of an intellectualistic Mahayana sect known as the Yogacara.

Hsüan-tsang quite naturally followed the Silk Road westward and perhaps in doing so retraced in reverse the original path of the religion from the northwestern Indian subcontinent to China. His route took him first through Tun-huang at the edge of the Takla Makan desert and then through the oasis towns of Agni, Kucha, Aqsu, and Nujkand. From there he traveled to Transoxiana, through Talas to Tashkent and

Ferghana, Samarqand, Bukhara, and Khwarazm. He then turned south and passed through Kish, Qunduz, and Termez before crossing the Pamirs through Garm, Kulab, and Wakhsh to Balkh in Bactria. The last leg of his long journey to India took him to Bamiyan and over the Hindu Kush into India. Hsüan-tsang spent the following years traveling throughout the subcontinent, visiting Buddhist sites, debating with scholars, and collecting manuscripts. He returned to China via Khotan after an absence of thirteen years.

Hsüan-tsang personally brought back to China 657 Sanskrit manuscripts, many of which he then translated into Chinese.[56] During his travels he played the role of teacher to Central Asian Buddhists he encountered, in many cases expressing dismay and even outrage at their deviation from what he saw as the orthodox tradition.

Beginning in the eighth century Muslim armies began to win control of the Central Asian Silk Road as far as Talas in modern Kazakhstan. Although Islamic law offered protection to "peoples of the Book," namely Christians, Jews, and by some interpretations Zoroastrians, the early Muslims were generally hostile toward Buddhists. They referred to Buddhists as "idol-worshippers," which had unfortunate associations with the portrayal of the Prophet's Meccan enemies in the Qur'an. This probably at least in part accounts for the unabatingly harsh treatment Muslims reserved for the Buddhists they encountered in the course of their conquests.

As a result of the increasing Muslim dominance of the Silk Road, it became more and more difficult for Buddhist monks and pilgrims to travel between India and China.[57] By the second half of the eleventh century this contact ceases, and Buddhism in East Asia, cut off from its Indian sources, is left to go its own way.

BUDDHISM AND
ZOROASTRIANISM IN CENTRAL ASIA

Certain passages in the account of Hsüan-tsang's travels have led scholars to perceive a Central Asian Buddhism in decline vis-à-vis Sasanian-sponsored Zoroastrianism. For example, Hsüan-tsang's biographer,

Hui-li, who was one of his disciples, comments sadly that in Samarqand, "The king and people did not believe in Buddhism but worshipped fire. There were two monastery buildings but no monks lived in them. If a guest monk attempted to stay in them, the native people would drive him out with fire."[58]

It seems the Sogdian king was impressed by Hsüan-tsang's piety, however. When two of Hsüan-tsang's accompanying disciples were chased from the temple by fire-worshipping priests, the king ordered the priests to be punished. Hsüan-tsang then "turned the other cheek" by intervening on the priests' behalf. According to Hui-li, Hsüan-tsang thereby won the respect of the local people, and "the king and people believed in Buddhism and a great meeting was held to ordain some people, who afterwards lived in the monasteries."[59]

Since Hui-li's work is as much hagiography as biography, his assertions about the success of Hsüan-tsang's efforts should be taken with a grain of salt. The Chinese traveler was certainly a charismatic individual, and often such figures are able to generate personal followings wherever they go. This account does not in itself enable us to understand, however, that the Sogdian population had converted from Buddhism to Zoroastrianism and that Hsüan-tsang had managed to set them once again on the straight path.

Furthermore, even if Hui-li's assertions about his master's successes in Sogdiana are true, the "converts" may have been at least partly made up of individuals who were already Buddhists (or at least to some degree "Buddhistic"), and who merely saw in him an authority whose "corrective" entreaties they were willing to listen to. There were numerous schools of Buddhism as well as variants in local belief and practice spread out across Asia at that time, and if Buddhists existed in Sogdiana, as it is not impossible that they did, it may simply have been their local version of Buddhism that Hsüan-tsang saw as heretical.[60] Hui-li's phrasing about "correcting evil customs" would seem to be consistent with this interpretation.

Even more likely, perhaps, is that with the rise in Sasanian influence from Iran, any existing local form of Buddhism, which probably would have been colored by local Iranian religiosity to begin with, had increasingly taken on aspects of the newly institutionalized Sasanian Zoroastrianism. The eastern Iranian world has provided documented examples of Zoroastrian influence on the evolution of Buddhism there. One such case can be seen in the layout of the circumabulatory corridor around Buddhist *stupas*, which is modeled on that of fire temples.[61]

Again, we cannot assume that the population of Sogdiana was ever in any uniform sense Zoroastrian or Buddhist as we understand the terms. For one thing, they lived at some remove from the centers of both Zoroastrian and Buddhist institutionalizing forces. Furthermore, we have evidence of the persistence of strictly local elements, such as the cult of the hero Siyavash at Bukhara, which included the sacrifice of a rooster every New Year.[62] Most probably, the local religiosity of Sogdiana was made up of many elements drawn from the Iranian/Indo-Aryan pool from which both major religions had evolved, and any attempt to categorize them at any period as Zoroastrian or Buddhist is bound to be misleading.

TIBET AND THE SILK ROAD

The Silk Road skirted the forbidding highlands of the Tibetan plateau, but spur routes connected Tibet to the busier overland tracks. Paintings and rock inscriptions along the upper Indus River in Ladakh at the southwestern corner of the Tibetan world indicate the passing of Christian and Manichaean Sogdian merchants there. Sogdians of various faiths probably carried their business into the Tibetan interior.[63] Buddhism reached Tibet both from India via Nepal to the south and from China via the eastern Silk Road.

From around 655 until 692 a short-lived Tibetan empire gained control over the oasis towns of the Tarim Basin, bringing the passing Silk Road trade under its jurisdiction. A century later, from just before 794 until 851, they controlled predominantly Buddhist Khotan.[64] This meant temporary increases in traffic channeled off into Tibet proper, which allowed for a greater penetration of Buddhist ideas from China. The first Buddhist temple in Tibet was constructed in around 779 at Samye. There, as in the Tarim region and elsewhere, monks prospered from the contributions of lay devotees engaged in trade.

Tibet's relations with China, which from the late seventh century made them rival competitors for control of the eastern Silk Road, tempered the influence of Chinese Buddhism. Although it is not entirely clear why or how Tibetan Buddhists came to look more to Indian sources, especially Kashmiri Tantrism, Tibet's political need to limit Chinese cultural hegemony was likely a factor. Khotan, with its long-standing Buddhist connections to Kashmir, was probably a major transmission point, especially during the periods when it was under Tibetan control.

CHAPTER FOUR

A Refuge of Heretics: Nestorians and Manichaeans on the Silk Road

It was during the first four centuries of the common era that the major religions of West Asia defined themselves and began to take the shape in which we recognize them today. To a large extent this was a process resulting from mutual antagonisms: in the Eastern Roman world between Christians and Jews and among proponents of diverse interpretations of Christianity, and in the Iranian sphere between the caretakers of traditional Ahura Mazda–based worship and the emergent threat of Manichaeism.

Human groups tend to hasten toward self-definition mainly when challenged by something they could conceivably be, but, for fear of losing their identity, must demonstrate they are not. (That is why belief systems in traditional societies often appear so frustratingly flexible and inclusive to modern, description-minded observers.) In religion, preoccupation with "us/them" distinctions is characteristic of the priestly class. We see evidence for this in the legalistic sources of the Hebrew Bible and in the Talmud of the rabbis who succeeded the priests as guardians of Hebraic tradition; we see it in the polemics of the church fathers; and we see it in the merciless efforts of the Zoroastrian magi in suppressing the Manichaean alternative.

The doctrinal disputes of the early common era are inseparable from the political sponsors with which they aligned themselves. When one party proved stronger, rivals were branded heretics. This left the way open to persecution, banishment, or even execution. In the case of two movements which proved highly significant for world history, the losers chose exile. What is striking is that they each followed a similar pattern and headed eastward out of harm's way. In both cases exile ensured their survival for another thousand years, and even some periods of success. The logical channel for this eastward migration, as we have seen, was to join up with the caravans of the Silk Road.

Both Christian and Manichaean sources attest to the close relationship between mercantile and missionary activity. Syriac, the lingua franca of West Asian trade, became the liturgical language of the Eastern church. Among the early Christians the Syriac word for merchant, *tgr'*, was often used as a metaphor for those who spread the gospel. A fourth century Syriac hymn includes the following stanza:

> Travel well-girt like merchants,
> That we may gain the world.
> Convert men to me,
> Fill creation with teaching.[1]

THE CHURCH OF THE EAST

What we call Christianity first emerged as a movement within the Jewish society of Roman Palestine. The interpretations which Jesus' followers gave to Jewish history, as expressed in text and legend, were sufficiently radical to cause a significant proportion of Jews to reject them. In the process of doing so, Jewish scholars developed a method for determining and stating what their heritage correctly was and did mean; this was eventually institutionalized as the rabbinical tradition, which became normative for Jews and is the basis of Judaism today.

Similarly, among the Christians there were disagreements over interpreting what they should believe and how they should practice their faith. One of the touchiest problems facing the early Christian theologians was to resolve the issue of Christ's true nature, whether divine or human.

Doctrinal disputes within the early Christian church were a reflection of the struggle for supremacy between the highly placed advocates of various interpretations and thus tended to be identified with particular regional power bases. The "diophysite" position of the so-called school of Antioch was that Christ consisted of two distinct persons, one human and one divine, which were brought into coexistence in the person of Jesus, much as the Spirit of God had descended onto the Hebrew prophets. The rival "monophysite" position, associated with the theologians of Alexandria, was that Christ was the eternal Divine Logos, incarnate as a human being—that He was God living under human conditions.

During the early fifth century this controversy expressed itself in terms of a dispute over how Mary should be described, whether as the "Bearer of Christ" *(christotokos)*, or as the "Mother of God" *(theotokos)*. When a Syrian bishop named Nestorius was appointed Patriarch of Constantinople in 428, he taught the Antiochan view, which he summarized with the remark that he "could not imagine God as a little boy." Nestorius' privileged position at Constantinople as spokesman for the Antiochans resulted in a hostile response led by Cyril, Patriarch of Alexandria.

The Byzantine Emperor Theodosius II personally liked Nestorius, but his sister Pulcheria despised him. She had enormous influence over the emperor, and knowing this, Cyril made her a focus of his propaganda campaign against Nestorius. In 431 the emperor called a Council at Ephesus to settle on an appropriate terminology for Mary. Cyril was appointed to preside over this council, so it is no surprise that the Antiochan position was denounced as heretical. (In fact, the Antiochan party refused to attend.) The emperor, under pressure from Pulcheria, supported Cyril, and Nestorius was deposed and banished to Egypt.

The Antiochan teaching being dominant in Syria and lands to the east, however, a large part of the diocese chose not to recognize Cyril's authority and seceded to form the Church of the East, with its seat at Ctesiphon (near modern Baghdad), capital of the Persian Sasanian Empire. This implied a rejection of the Byzantine emperor's authority as well, and from that point onward, the Nestorian church came to be identified with the Persian world in opposition to the Byzantine.

In 451 the Council of Chalcedon proposed a compromise between the monophysite and diophysite positions, namely that Christ combined two natures but not two persons. The Nestorians tended to see this as something like an acknowledgment of their position, but it didn't go far enough. At a synod in 486 the bishops of the East declared their church explicitly Nestorian, repudiating both monophysitism and the Chalcedonian "compromise" and expressing their belief in "one divine nature only, in three perfect persons. . . . " They went on to state that "[Christ had] two natures, divine and human . . . without confusion in their diversity . . . [yet with] perfect and indissoluble cohesion of the divine with the human. . . ." A major problem for the Nestorians seems to have been what living under human form would imply for God, since their statement continued, "if anyone thinks or teaches that suffering and change inheres in the divinity, and if, when speaking of the unity of the person of our Saviour, he does not confess that He is perfect God and perfect man, let him be anathema."[2]

The synod and a subsequent one in 497 put Persian monophysites on the defensive, and henceforth Nestorianism became the official (although not the only) doctrine of Christian Asia.

Christianity in Iran

In the Acts of the Apostles (2:9) it is stated that Iranian Jews from Parthia, Media, Elam, and Mesopotamia were witness to the miracle of the Pentecost. Since Christianity arose within the Jewish world, it is only natural that its eastward spread from Palestine would have been facilitated first and foremost through existing contacts across the Jewish diaspora.[3] Since these contacts were to a large degree commercial in nature, it can safely be said that Christianity's first link with the Silk Road was via the Babylonian Jews.

The Parthian Arsacid dynasty, which ruled Mesopotamia and Iran during the first two centuries of the common era, did not consider religion a particularly important political issue. As a result there is little mention of religious sects in Parthian sources, and we can only guess at the spread of Christian ideas in the East based on analysis of later materials. It would seem that in the western part of the Parthian realm Christian communities grew among various Jewish and other sects, local cults and varieties of Iranian religion.

The earliest reference to Central Asian communities in a Christian source is the comment of Bardaisan around 196 CE: "Nor do our sisters among the Gilanians and Bactrians have any intercourse with strangers." The apocryphal Acts of Thomas, written around the same time, mentions the "land of the Kushans" *(baith kaishan)*.[4]

In 224 a new dynasty, the Sasanians, defeated the Parthians. By then Christians were fairly numerous in the Iranian world: an early church history states that in 225 there were twenty bishoprics throughout the Persian-controlled lands.[5] Following the Sasanian Emperor Shapur I's victories over the Byzantines in 256 and 260, Greek-speaking as well as Syriac-speaking Christian captives were deported to Iran and thus added to the numbers of Christians there.

The first three Sasanian emperors largely maintained the Parthian tolerance of non-Iranian religions. Shapur issued an edict stating that "Magi, Zandiks (Manichaeans), Jews, Christians and all men of whatever religion should be left undisturbed and at peace in their belief." Under Bahram II (r. 276-293), however, the Sasanian house tightened its ties to the Zoroastrian priesthood, whose chief priest, Kartir, had been waging a campaign to make Zoroastrianism the official religion of the new empire. To do this, Kartir felt obliged to eliminate any potentially rival religious organizations. In an inscription from the year 280, he names Christians among those groups he believes should be persecuted. Though Kartir also names Jews among those groups he opposes, there is no evidence that Jewish communities were actually targeted.[6] Presumably they were not numerous enough to constitute a threat.

In the face of this lurking animosity the various Christian communities of Iran gradually built up a common church organization through which their position could be strengthened. By 410 the Iranian church was made up of six provinces, and at a synod in 424 the Eastern bishops declared their church administratively independent of the West. The addition of two new provinces in the East, Marv and Herat, is indicative of Christianity's continuing spread along the Silk Road.

Christians under Sasanian rule lived a precarious existence. More often than not, the impulse of the individual emperors was to tolerate them; Christians served in the Sasanian army (notwithstanding the following accusation), and one Christian general even led the Sasanians into battle against the Byzantines. But the magi, who sought to bind up their religious authority with the political authority of the emperor, were always lobbying against Iran's non-Zoroastrian religious communities. The periods when they most succeeded in their political aims (such as under Shapur II from 309 to 379, Bahram V from 421 to 439, and Yazdigard II from 439 to 457) were those in which Christians, Jews, and Manichaeans suffered most harshly. A royal decree issued by Shapur II lists a variety of points on which Christians seemed at odds with the state and with Zoroastrian values:

> The Christians destroy our holy teachings, and teach men to serve one God, and not to honor the sun or fire. They teach them, too, to defile water by their ablutions, to refrain from marriage and the procreation of children, and to refuse to go out to war with the Shahenshah. They have no scruple about the slaughter and eating of animals, they bury the corpses of men in the earth, and attribute the origin of snakes and creeping things to a good God. They despise many servants of the King, and teach witchcraft.[7]

Conversely, when the state and the magi drifted apart (as under Narseh from 293 to 303, Yazdigard I from 399 to 421, Balash from 484 to 488, Kavad from 488 to 531, and Hormizd IV from 579 to 590), Christians and Jews were able to live in peace and often prospered. Indeed, it has appeared to some observers that Christianity may have been on the verge of displacing Zoroastrianism, on the popular level at least, when Islam appeared on the scene in the seventh century. The Central Asian Muslim scholar Biruni, writing in the eleventh century, claims that in his day "the majority of the inhabitants of Syria, Iraq, and Khurasan are Nestorians."[8]

The adoption of Christianity as the official religion of the Roman Empire had two major effects on Iranian Christianity. The first was that, despite their ideological differences with the Roman church, Christians in Iran were now frequently suspected of foreign loyalties, which many times was used as justification for their persecution. Indeed, most of the major persecutions of Christians in Iran were directly connected to the political situation between the two empires.

The other effect was that with Christianity now enjoying state sponsorship in the West, doctrinal disputes tended to be won by the parties with government support, which they could then use to suppress those holding rival interpretations. Roman citizens who chose not to convert to Christianity, likewise, were out of favor and often in jeopardy. As a result of the church's state-supported persecutions, a large number of intellectuals and others fled the Mediterranean world for sanctuary in the Sasanian Empire. Many Athenian philosophers, Syrian physicians, and Sabean astrologers took this route, to the benefit and enrichment of Sasanian culture.

The now-ruined city of Gundeshapur in southwestern Iran became the new seat of classical Greek medicine, philosophy, and astronomy, and the school founded there was staffed by pagans and Eastern Christians alike. For the next five centuries Gundeshapur was one of the greatest scientific centers of the world. When the Muslim Arabs conquered the region in the mid-seventh century they kept the school intact, and for two centuries more many of the leading minds of the new Islamic faith got their education there from Christian teachers.

Nestorianism among the Sogdians

Sogdiana was—until the Samanid dynasty made it the most dynamic center of the Muslim world in the tenth century—never a region of religious orthodoxy. Settled in prehistory by Iranian tribes, it was at the fringes of both east and west, equally removed from the centers of all the great religious traditions. It had always been middle ground, a transit point, a place where anything could and did pass through sooner or later.

Alexander left Greek influences in Sogdiana in the fourth century BCE. Iranian nomads such as the Sakas, and Turkic nomads as well, were always a nearby presence. The Parthians left the cultural mix there unmolested, and for the Sasanians, the province was too remote for the standardizing efforts of the Zoroastrian magi to be effective.

Sogdian merchants were the real masters of the Silk Road, whoever the ephemeral powers of the time might be. Under the rule of their fellow Iranian peoples the Parthian and the Sasanians, Sogdian merchants moved easily in the Iranian lands to the west, where some of them were won over to the Christian message, just as others active in the former Kushan lands had embraced Buddhism.

There do not appear to have been any obstacles preventing Sogdian converts to either tradition from importing their new faith either to Sogdiana proper or conveying it farther east in the course of their business ventures. By the year 650 there was a Nestorian archbishopric at Samarqand in the heart of Sogdiana and another beyond that at Kashgar; in all over twenty Nestorian bishops had dioceses east of the Oxus River.[9]

For centuries Sogdian was the lingua franca of the Silk Road. But, as has been said earlier, through their widespread dealings Sogdian traders knew foreign languages as well, which made them especially well equipped to serve as translators. Among the Nestorian texts which have been discovered in the Tarim Basin since the beginning of the twentieth century, a preponderance are in Sogdian or show evidence of having been translated from Sogdian versions. Although Syriac was the liturgical language of the Nestorian church, the language in which Nestorian Christianity was disseminated across Asia was principally Sogdian, as it was for Buddhism and Manichaeism as well.[10]

Most of the Christian texts found in the Tarim region were discovered by four German expeditions to the Turfan oasis from 1902 to 1914. The bulk of these manuscripts date to the ninth and tenth centuries from a Nestorian monastery at Buyaliq, north of the oasis. They include hymns, psalms, prayers, lectionaries from the New Testament, and commentaries.[11] Although for the most part they are translations from Syriac, some of the Sogdian versions are older than their known Syriac counterparts, and a few do not have known Syriac versions.[12] The Christian texts in Sogdian, unknown before the twentieth century, have substantially rounded out scholars' understanding of Nestorianism.

Nestorianism among the Turks

Nomadic Turks in Central Asia were first taught the art of writing by Persian Nestorian priests in the entourage of the dethroned Sasanian Emperor Kavad sometime around 550. A group of these priests stayed among the Turks for seven years and baptized many of them. The priests learned Turkish and rendered it in writing for the first time, using the Syriac alphabet.[13]

The Sogdians of Central Asia, who traded directly with the Turkic nomads, were a more regular cultural influence on them. A Chinese writer of the Sui period (581–618 CE) noted that "The Turks themselves are simple-minded and short-sighted and dissension can easily be roused among them. Unfortunately, many Sogdians live among them who are cunning and insidious; they teach and instruct the Turks."[14]

The native religion of the Turkic and Mongol peoples of Inner Asia is generally described as shamanistic. They held the sky god, Tangri, as supreme, the male principle which was balanced by the female earth. Religious behavior was practical; rituals were connected with basic survival needs like hunting, healing, and fertility. The spirit world was accessed through a shaman, a medium who communicated with the spirits after working himself into an ecstatic trance.[15] Shamans still exist in Inner Asia today, even among nominally Buddhist or Muslim populations.

Apparently some of the first Christian priests to win followers among the Turks were perceived by them as shamans. Syriac records of the Nestorian church recount that in the year 644 the metropolitan of Marv, Elias, impressed a Turkish king by using the sign of the cross to stop a severe thunderstorm.[16] The king was thereby enticed to accept Christianity, and his subjects along with him. Scholars of archaic Turkish religion have noted that the stopping of thunderstorms, through use of a stone called a *yat,* was a traditional function of the shamans.[17]

The same sources state that in 781–782 a second major conversion occurred among the Turks, again with the conversion of the king leading to that of his subjects. As a result of this second mass conversion, the Nestorian Patriarch Timothy in Baghdad established a Central Asian metropolitan specifically to instruct Christian Turks.[18] A contemporary writer states that information concerning the successes of missionaries among the Turks comes from a "letter which some merchants and secretaries of the kings, who had penetrated as far as there for the sake of commerce and of affairs of State, wrote to Mar Timothy."[19]

A third mass conversion took place in 1007, when according to the sources 200,000 Turks and Mongols became Christians. The standard identification of this latter group with the Kerait tribe has recently been questioned,[20] but the scale of the conversion was certainly quite large. The medieval Jacobite writer Bar Hebraeus explicitly credits Christian merchants, presumably Sogdians, with bringing the conversion about.

According to Bar Hebraeus' account, the ruler of this nomadic group had been saved from a snowstorm by following a vision of a Christian saint. "When he reached his tents in safety," Bar Hebraeus relates, "he summoned the Christian merchants who were there, and discussed with them the question of faith, and they answered him that this could not be accomplished except through baptism." On hearing this news, the metropolitan sent a priest and deacon to perform the necessary baptisms and offer instruction.[21]

Under the patronage and protection of the Mongol Qara-khitai in the twelfth century, Nestorian Christianity experienced a new surge in popularity. Sometime around 1180 the Nestorian Patriarch Elias III established a new metropoly in Kashgar, with authority extending up into the so-called Seven Rivers region (Turk. Yeti su; Rus. Semirechye) in the southern part of modern Kazakhstan.

By the dawn of the Mongol period Christianity was certainly the most visible of the major religions amongst the steppe peoples. What Christianity meant to them, however, is another question. The sources indicate that the essential test of a Christian was baptism; apart from that initiatory ritual, there is little information available regarding how Christianity among the nomads was practiced. Some tribes apparently had portable tent chapels, but numerous accounts show that many of their rituals were simply Christianized forms of traditional practice, such as the drinking of fermented mare's milk, called *kumiz*.

One may also contemplate what the nomads' interest in Christianity was. Was it merely allegiance transferred to the "shamanistic" power which had demonstrated the greatest capabilities? Or was there some thought of cultivating connections with Christian traders along the Silk Road? Both are likely possibilities.

Nestorianism in China

The Chinese, who have inherited one of the world's oldest and greatest civilizations, have a long history of considering other cultures beneath their interest. Uncharacteristically, some of the early emperors of the T'ang dynasty (especially Hsüan-tsung, who reigned from 712 to 756) had a fascination with things foreign that sometimes verged on a mania.[22] In such an atmosphere the alien traditions of traders from the West were unusually welcome and encouraged.

Sogdian and Iranian merchants and missionaries brought Christianity to China during the seventh century. In fact, the Chinese originally thought the cradle of Christianity was Iran, and referred to it as "the Iranian religion" for over one hundred years before correcting their records in the mid-eighth century. An imperial T'ang edict of 638 relates that an Iranian priest named A-lo-pen (Abraham?) had arrived at court three years earlier.[23] A-lo-pen had brought with him scriptures, which were translated into Chinese so that the emperor could understand them. The emperor approved, and gave the Nestorians authority to propagate their faith throughout the empire. This event is generally considered to mark the introduction of Christianity into China.

A monument erected in the T'ang capital of Ch'ang-an (Xian) in 781 contains a wealth of information about the local Nestorian community's first 150 years. Iranian and Central Asian names occur throughout, indicating a continuous influx of Westerners along the Silk Road. One of the monument's most interesting pieces of information concerns a monk by the name of Adam, who assisted in the Chinese translation: He is said to have collaborated on the translation of a Buddhist treatise as well. Adam knew no Indian languages, so the Buddhist text in question must have been in Sogdian, presumably his native language.[24]

A seventh-century *Eloge of the Holy Trinity* in Chinese found at Tun-huang by the French Sinologist Paul Pelliot states that no less than thirty Nestorian works had been translated into Chinese by the late eighth century. It does not appear that the Nestorians won many Chinese converts, however. Like the Buddhists, they found themselves in the position of having to communicate concepts and values entirely alien and even offensive to the Chinese. Unlike the Buddhists, the Nestorians in China do not appear to have succeeded in adapting their message to Chinese tastes.

This does not appear to have been for lack of trying, since they referred to their treatises as "sutras" and to Christian saints as "buddhas." By the time the Xian monument was erected, Nestorianism was known in Chinese as "the Brilliant Religion" *(ching chiao)*. On the other hand, the name of the Christian savior himself, which is Yishu in Syriac, sounded in the pronunciation of the period like the Chinese term for "a rat on the move."

It would seem therefore that for the most part the Nestorian community in China consisted of foreigners, as was the case with Judaism and Zoroastrianism. All three traditions were brought into China as the faiths of traveling merchants, and their fates were tied to those of the expatriate merchant communities themselves.

The T'ang court's enthusiastic taste for foreign people, ideas, and things also allowed for the proliferation of religious quackery. Many religious figures were engaged not for their spiritual teachings but for their more worldly skills. Christians and Manichaeans especially were valued for their knowledge of astrology and medicine, inherited from the traditions of Mesopotamia.

One Chinese source mentions a priest who had the power to "chant people to death and then revive them"—evidently a hypnotist. A

Buddhist monk from India named Narayanasvamin claimed to be two hundred years old and to possess elixirs of immortality. Taoist alchemists had fantasized about such potions since ancient times, but in this case the Indian's concoctions were found to be ineffective and he was dismissed from court.[25]

Religious buildings often served as "cultural centers" where foreign adherents as well as interested locals could gather. Mazdaean temples in Lan-chow and Lo-yang, for example, regularly hosted magic shows which drew large crowds. Although Hsüan-tsung actually encouraged such activities during his reign, more xenophobic Chinese rulers could perceive this kind of foreign influence as threatening.[26]

In the year 845 the T'ang Emperor Wu-tsung, who was a supporter of Taoism, outlawed all foreign religions (even Buddhism, which was hardly foreign any more), forcing them underground. In 980 a Nestorian monk told a Muslim writer in Baghdad that he had been sent by the church to China seven years earlier in order to "set the affairs of the Christian religion in order" there, but had found no Christians surviving anywhere in the country.[27] Christianity appears to have disappeared from China, to be reintroduced under the Mongols three centuries later.

MANI

Mesopotamia in the third century of the common era was home to a proliferation of religious sects. Long the buffer zone fought over by successive Greek and Iranian empires, it was a meeting ground of cultures where all were represented. Israelites had lived there for a thousand years alongside Iranian Mazda-worshippers and native Mesopotamians, whose original religious beliefs survived among the Sabeans, who were renowned for their knowledge of astrology. By this time there were also various Christian denominations as well as hybrid Jewish-Christian gnostic baptist sects.

It was into one of the latter, possibly Elkesaite or Mandaean, communities that the prophet Mani was born in the year 216 to parents of royal Parthian ancestry.[28] Mani was raised in an ascetic religious environment, where Christian and Jewish ideas were set against a dualistic gnostic backdrop. He received his first revelation at the age of twelve and another when he was twenty-four. From the time of this second revelation, Mani took up the role of prophet and set out to preach his message.

Mani's first missionary journey was to the Kushan lands of northwestern India. This was one of the thriving centers of Buddhism at that time, and Buddhist influences were significant in the formation of Mani's religious thought. The transmigration of souls became a Manichaean belief, and the quadrapartite structure of the Manichaean community, divided between male and female monks (the "elect") and lay followers (the "hearers") who supported them, appears to be based on that of the Buddhist *sangha*.

On his return to Iran, Mani managed to convert at least two princes of the new Sasanian ruling house and spent several years in the entourage of the Emperor Shapur himself. Mani must have aspired to make his new faith the official religion of the new empire; unfortunately his rival at court, the magian priest Kartir, had the same idea.

During Shapur's reign Mani enjoyed official patronage and protection. As a result he was able to send followers to all corners of the Sasanian realm in order to spread his teaching. The new religion rapidly won converts throughout the land. For nearly fifty years the popularity of Mani's vision posed the greatest threat to the authority of the traditional magi led by Kartir.

After Bahram I acceded to the Sasanian throne in 273, Mani's fortunes changed. At the instigation of Kartir, the emperor had Mani arrested in 276, just as the latter was attempting to flee to Parthia. It is interesting that in his final interview with Mani, the emperor reproaches him not on the basis of his religious views but rather on the accusation that he has neglected his duties as a physician: "What are you good for, since you go neither fighting nor hunting? But perhaps you are needed for this doctoring and this physicking? And you don't even do that!" Mani defends himself on the same grounds: "Many are those whom I have made rise from their illnesses. Many are those from whom I have averted the numerous kinds of ague. Many were those who were at the point of death, and I have revived them."[29]

This exchange suggests that religious leaders were valued more for their skills as doctors than as healers of souls, an interpretation which finds ample corroboration elsewhere throughout premodern history.[30]

Following this conversation, the emperor sentenced the prophet to prison. After several months, Mani died in detention at the age of sixty.

Something from Everyone: A New Universal Tradition

What made Mani's message so attractive to so many people was that he made every effort to "speak their language." He did so literally but also figuratively, borrowing ideas, symbols, and religious terminology from every tradition in existence. Religious systems spread most effectively when they succeed in appropriating the mind-set and worldview of their target audience, making the "new" message seem merely a "perfection" of old truth, compatible with people's traditional understanding. Mani and his disciples were unparalleled masters of this technique.

Having been born and raised in the lands where Asian and Mediterranean civilizations had met through the centuries, Mani was conditioned from childhood by heterodox religious notions drawn from a variety of sources. His system blends Semitic and Iranian traditions so completely that scholars today continue to argue over which is its real underlying source.[31]

Manichaeism is generally treated as a gnostic system.[32] The origins of gnosticism are obscure but probably date to sometime before the common era. Gnosticism posits a radically dualistic view of the universe, in which "good" is equated with spirit and "evil" with matter.

Gnostics favored esoteric interpretations leading to salvation through knowledge, a possibility which held special appeal for intellectual elites. It was an *approach* to truth rather than a religious tradition per se; Gnostics were found among Christians, Jews, and other groups. Representatives of the mainstream invariably saw the "hidden" interpretations of the Gnostics as a threat to orthodoxy and continually declared them heretics.

Mani presents himself as the culminating prophet in human history, following Zoroaster, Buddha, and Jesus. His cosmology takes many Iranian figures, including Zurvan, Ormazd (Ahura Mazda), Ahriman (Angra Mainyu), and various good and evil spirits, and imbues them with gnostic interpretations; he equates spirit with light (expressed as the supreme god Zurvan) and matter with darkness. The universe is seen as a realm of struggle between good and evil, with the good, represented as particles of light, striving to be liberated from the evil matter in which it is trapped.

The most visible figure in Manichaean mythology is Jesus. Mani refers to himself throughout his life as "the Apostle of Jesus Christ." Mani's Jesus takes three forms, however: Jesus the Man, Jesus the Living Soul, and Jesus the Splendor. The first is the historical Jesus of the Christians, but whose death on the cross Mani considers to have been an illusion. The second is the "suffering Jesus" *(Jesus patibilis)*, the force of goodness in the form of light particles which are trapped in all living things. Jesus the Splendor, a conceptualization borrowed from the Mandaeans, is the embodiment of Light who visited the First Man and will return as Savior at the end of time.

Mani taught that reproduction is an evil, since with each succeeding generation the light particles trapped in every individual are further divided among one's descendents. The Manichaean "elect," therefore, were to practice abstinence. The following Manichaean parable about a nobleman whose wife has just died (versions of which are found both in early Christianity and later in Islam) illustrates this abhorrence of carnality as well as worldly delusion symbolized by drunkenness:

> He saw [the corpse] and thought, "This is my wife." He went in [to the tomb] and lay down beside the corpse. And because he was drunk and foolish, he put his arms around the corpse, behaved shamelessly and united with it. Because of his exertions the corpse burst open. Blood, pus and foul and evil things in its nauseating body oozed and flowed out. And the noble man lay in blood and pus with his whole body and all his clothes, and he was covered from head to foot. And because of his drunken state, he thought to himself, "I am very satisfied."
>
> When morning came and the sun rose, the noble man's drunkenness passed. He awoke from his sleep. Raising his head, he saw that

he was lying in a tomb, a corpse being at his bosom. Pus and blood were oozing out and spreading a terrible odor. He looked at himself and saw that he was all covered with blood and lying in excrement. He was struck by panic and seized by fear; he screamed loudly, quickly left in his mourning-dress and ran away. The more he ran the more he vomited. Then he quickly tore to bits and to shreds the gown that had been so pure, threw it away and then ran on. He reached a pond, jumped into it, and washed and cleansed himself. . . . [33]

But Mani's highly organized propaganda strategy involved more than simply adopting existing religious stories and symbols and giving them new meanings and interpretations. In most religions, scriptures are handed down orally over long periods before being written down, leaving them open to accusations of human corruption and falsification. Mindful of this danger, Mani made a point of writing down his revelations himself, producing at least seven canonical works which formed the scriptural foundation for his religion.

Mani also believed strongly in the power of images to convey religious truth. (This may have been partly a concession to the fact that literacy was not widespread.) A talented painter, he illustrated his own scriptures. His skill as an artist won him a reputation which, somewhat ironically, is his most enduring legacy, outlasting the very religion he founded. To this day, his heretical beliefs forgotten, he is remembered in the Muslim world as the greatest painter who ever lived.[34]

It was the Manichaean elect who bore the responsibility of spreading the message of the faith as itinerant preachers, following the model of Christian and Buddhist monks. The elect were distinguished by the wearing of white robes and adherence to a vegetarian diet. They had to exercise the utmost care not to engage in any activities which contravened the principles of their religion, even activities necessary for their own survival. Even more than Buddhist monks, the Manichaean elect were utterly dependent on their lay followers, the "hearers," who supported them. They could not even prepare their own food, since that would damage the light particles that were believed to reside in all living things, including vegetables, and before eating they were to recite: "Neither have

I cast it into the oven; another hath brought me this and I have eaten it without guilt."[35]

Manichaeism on the Silk Road

Mani's religion began to enjoy popularity in the Mediterranean world within his own lifetime, although even before the Roman Empire became officially Christian it persecuted Manichaeans as adherents of a "foreign," Persian faith. Once Christianity became the state religion, Manichaeism was considered even a greater threat, since it claimed to be an esoteric, and therefore "truer," form of Christianity itself. Although subject to the most ruthless suppression, dualist and anti-worldly ideas which echoed Manichaeism survived in Europe into the Middle Ages, through the Cathar movement in Provence and the Bogomils in the Balkans.

To the east Manichaeism fared better, at least initially. It enjoyed several decades of protection during Mani's lifetime, during which it had spread into Central Asia along the Silk Road beyond the Oxus River. Once again it was Sogdians who played a major role in the transmission of the faith, with their capital, Samarqand, becoming the center of an early and active Manichaean community.

Using their linguistic skills, Sogdians translated Manichaean texts from Syriac, Middle Persian, and Parthian into Sogdian and thence into Turkish and eventually Chinese. By the end of the sixth century the Sogdian Manichaeans were strong enough to declare their independence from the *archegos,* the head of the church in Baghdad, giving rise to a schism which was to persist for over a century.[36]

An Iranian Manichaean missionary named Mihr-Ormazd traveled to China sometime in the late seventh century.[37] He was granted an audience with the Chou Empress Wu and presented her with a text entitled *The Sutra of the Two Principles,* which would become the most popular Manichaean work in China.[38]

The missionary's success brought on the jealousy of the Buddhists at court, who quickly became opposed to the new teaching. Sometime after 820, Chinese Buddhists began circulating the following story:

Wu K'o-chiu, a man of Yüeh, resided in Ch'ang-an. . . . He began to practice Manichaeism and his wife Wang also followed his example. She died suddenly after more than a year. Three years later she appeared to her husband in a dream, saying, "For my perverse belief I have been condemned to become a snake and I am below the *stupa* at Huang-tzu p'o. I shall die tomorrow at dawn and I wish you would ask the monks to go there and recite for me the Diamond Sutra so that I could avoid other forms of suffering."[39]

The husband does as he is asked and afterward becomes a good Buddhist again.

The T'ang rulers looked on Manichaeism with suspicion after their restoration in 705. In 732 the emperor issued an edict to the effect that the religion could be propagated only among non-Chinese. The reasoning given for this restriction shows that Buddhists were behind it: "The doctrine of Mar Mani is basically a perverse belief and fraudulently assumes to be [a school of] Buddhism and will therefore mislead the masses. It deserves to be strictly prohibited. However, since it is the indigenous religion of the Western Barbarians and other [foreigners], its followers will not be punished if they practice it among themselves."[40] It is clear that just as the Manichaeans in the West attempted to present their religion as an esoteric form of Christianity, in the East they tried to portray it as a type of Buddhism.

As the Sasanian government became increasingly bound up with the Zoroastrian clergy, Manichaeans in Iran gradually moved eastward beyond the reach of the state and the magi. After the Arab Muslims conquered the Sasanian Empire in the 640s, many Manichaeans returned from Central Asia to Iran and Mesopotamia. The Umayyad Arabs, based in Damascus, were generally content to leave the religious matters of their subject populations alone. But in 751 the Abbasid revolution brought a wave of religious reform to the Muslim-controlled lands.

During the second half of the eighth century many Persian bureaucrats in the Abbasid administration began to exert a form of cultural revival vis-à-vis the Arab ruling class. In literature this took the shape of the so-called *shu'ubiyya* movement, through which many Persian literary classics were translated into Arabic. Within the same class of Persian intellectuals, crypto-Manichaeism became a popular form of self-assertion. Soon Mani's faith acquired the dubious status it had possessed in the Sasanian and Roman worlds, as the official religion's archenemy number one. Even those merely suspected of being Manichaeans were ruthlessly persecuted, and many believers chose to flee eastward once again.

The Uighurs

For a relatively brief period of about seventy-seven years, from 763 to 840, the much-maligned Manichaean faith enjoyed the status of an official, state-sponsored religion. This was thanks to the Uighur Turks, who subdued the former Turkish confederation and founded a state on the southern Siberian steppe in 744.

Chinese relations with the steppe had always been characterized by appeasement through bribes, often in the form of silk, as a result of which some of the steppe peoples were able to become quite rich. By the time the Uighurs came to power, the T'ang were beset by frequent internal problems and came increasingly to rely on the Uighurs for support.[41]

Beginning in 755 the T'ang emperor was faced with a rebellion led by a general of mixed Sogdian and Turkish origin, Roshan ("the bright one"), sinicized to An Lu-shan. The emperor called upon the Uighurs to assist him in putting down the rebellion. It was after retaking the T'ang city of Lo-yang in 762 that the Uighur *kaghan,* or king, known in Chinese sources as Mou-yü, made the acquaintance of some Sogdian Manichaeans living there. These Sogdians made a great impression on the *kaghan,* and when he returned home to his capital of Qara-Balasaghun north of the Tien-Shan Mountains he took four of them along. Within a few months they had persuaded him to adopt Manichaeism. In 763 the *kaghan* made it the official religion of the Uighur state, banning the Turkish shamanistic tradition.

Why the *kaghan* did this is something of a mystery. The chief Manichaean monk, known by his Chinese name Jui-hsi, is reported to have had great eloquence and persuasive skill. The *kaghan,* as a military man, may have liked the rigid discipline of the Manichaean lifestyle.

Another aspect of the religion's appeal was that the Chinese didn't like it, and the Uighurs were seeking to demonstrate their independence from the T'ang. A third reason may have been in order to facilitate commercial contacts with the West through the Sogdians.[42]

Characteristically, the Manichaean missionaries among the Uighurs used the strategy of associating their religious concepts with those of the Turks. For example, the Manichaean gods of the two palaces of light are equated with the sun and the moon, which the Turks revered. The term for the palaces themselves was rendered into Turkish as *ordu*, literally the place where a nomadic king's tent is erected. The Manichaeans attached the Turkish word *bilig* ("knowledge"), a term the nomads had associated with leadership from ancient times, to all five of the cardinal virtues (love-knowledge, faith-knowledge, passion-knowledge, patience-knowledge, and wisdom-knowledge). For "soul" they used the Turkish *qut*, or "heaven-granted blessing."[43] Again we see the importance of language and translation in spreading religious concepts to diverse cultures.

With the Uighur state to back them up, Iranian and Turkish Manichaeans living in China were able to obtain increased privileges from the T'ang government, including the building of new temples. Between the years 768 and 771, the T'ang emperor ordered Manichaean temples to be built in Ch'ang-an, Lo-yang, Kinchow, Nanchang, Shao-hsing, and Yangchow.

In the Uighur lands, the Manichaean priests became one of the most powerful social classes. A large number of the Manichaean texts extant today date from the period of Uighur rule in the Tarim region. One text speaks of the efforts to eliminate the practices of the Turks' traditional religion: "Let all sculpted or painted images of the demons be entirely destroyed by fire; let those who pray to genies or prostrate themselves before demons all be [?] and let the people accept the Religion of Light. Let [the country] with barbarous customs and smoking blood change into one where the people eat vegetables; and let the state where men kill be transformed into a kingdom where good works are encouraged."[44]

Manichaeans seem to have enjoyed Uighur protection even after Manichaeism ceased to be a state religion. The Muslim writer Ibn Nadim relates that in the ninth century, the governor of Khurasan heard there was a community of five hundred Manichaeans practicing in Samarqand and wished to kill them. The Uighur *kaghan* sent word to the Khurasan governor that if the Samarqand Manichaeans were harmed, he would kill all the Muslims living under his authority.[45]

The Uighurs used their leverage as supporters of the T'ang following An Lu-shan's rebellion to protect Manichaean communities in China as well, but after the Uighur kingdom was overrun by another Turkic group in 840 there was a backlash. Three years later the T'ang government closed all but three Manichaean temples in China, informing the Uighur *kaghan* that they would be reopened once the Uighurs reestablished their kingdom.

Within a few months, however, the T'ang government went ahead and closed the remaining temples, seizing their property and executing the Manichaean priests. The Japanese pilgrim Ennin describes the event: "An imperial edict was issued, ordering the Manichaean priests of the Empire to be killed. Their heads are to be shaved and they are to be dressed in Buddhist robes and are to be killed looking like Buddhist *sramana*s (monks)."[46]

It has been suggested that this persecution was at least in part economically motivated, since the Manichaean temples were probably functioning as money-lending institutions run by Uighur merchants.[47] Two years later a similar pattern would play itself out against the most successful of the foreign religions in China, Buddhism. Christianity and Zoroastrianism likewise lost their protection within the empire at that time and disappear from the Chinese historical record.

After their defeat in 840 the Uighurs moved eastward into the Tarim Basin and established a new capital at Qocho. Although the majority of the new Uighur kingdom's population was Buddhist or Christian, Manichaeans retained official favor and their monasteries, like those of the Buddhists, prospered from the administration of farmlands.

Panegyrics addressed to the Uighur kings of Qocho indicate that Manichaeans and Buddhists alike saw him as a protector.[48] Texts and art from this period, mostly discovered hidden in monasteries, show markedly syncretistic trends.[49] Over the following centuries Manichaeism seems slowly to have lost its adherents to Buddhism and Christianity, and by the time of the Mongol conquest it may have become extinct among the Uighurs.

In China, however, the religion continued to succeed in winning native converts. Buddhist writers in the thirteenth century were still producing polemics against Manichaeism, disparaging it along with two Buddhist sects, those of the "White Lotus" and the "White Cloud," as deviant interpretations of Buddhism. The Ming Code of the following century outlawed the three altogether.[50] This continued animosity from Buddhists in China drove Manichaeans underground, but the community survived.

BLURRING DISTINCTIONS:
SHARED IDEAS, SYMBOLS, VOCABULARIES

From the earliest times, Manichaeism attempted to portray itself as an all-inclusive, universal religion. Its missionaries consciously drew on the symbols and vocabulary of their target audience, attempting to render the new teaching more familiar and acceptable.

Mani's disciple Mar Ammo, a Parthian, had great success propagating the new teaching in the eastern lands where Buddhism was prevalent. A Sogdian text states that Mar Ammo "fully exposed the Buddhahood of the Prophet of Light."[51] Another hymn, in Parthian, uses Islamic terminology, such as *dhu'l-fiqar*, the sword of Muhammad, perhaps to disguise its content from persecution by Muslims.[52] Another important early missionary, Mar Zaku, was eulogized by Manichaeans living along the Silk Road as "the Great Caravan-Leader," an epithet which Central Asian Buddhists applied to Avalokitesvara.[53] An apocryphal letter from Central Asia has Mani write to Mar Ammo that the faithful should practice meditation and strive to acquire merit.[54]

Although the Uighur court in eastern Turkestan championed Manichaeism for nearly five centuries, probably only a minority of their subject population became Manichaeans. Some remained Nestorian, and many more eventually embraced Mahayana Buddhism. The texts and paintings from the Turfan oasis, especially, show a mixing of the three traditions to an extent that often verges on the bizarre. The "Great

Hymn to Mani" which has been preserved in Turkish is a good
example:

> We have prepared ourselves with hearts full of praise to praise you,
> My praiseworthy, honorable father, my Mani Buddha . . .
> You have taken nescience from the living beings in the five forms of
>   existence,
> You have brought them wisdom.
> You have let them partake of *parinirvana*.
> Hate and many other passions had perturbed their senses and their
>   minds
> When you, our holy father, came down from the Firmament . . .
> You have erected the ladder of wisdom,
> And overcoming the five forms of existence you have saved us . . .
> We, the miserable sentient beings . . . came to see the Buddha-like
>   Sun-God [Jesus], equal to thee.
> Bound in fetters, enduring pain, we remain in this *samsara*.
> [But] you have preached the true, incomparable doctrine to those
>   bound to transient joys and you have led them to good *Nirvana*
>   . . .
> You have shown them the way leading to the Buddha-realms.
> You have heaped up a Sumeru mountain of good deeds . . .
> When you found the unredeemed sentient beings, you saved them all
>   without exception.
> Awakened beings like us you have thoroughly taught the gem of the
>   gospel-teaching.[55]

A Sogdian hymn mentions "the five assemblies of the five Buddhas
of Mahayana,"[56] clearly another conscious attempt on the part of the
Manichaeans to speak the language of the eastern Silk Road. A Parthian
text from Turfan includes the exhortation, "Awake, brethren, chosen
ones, on this day of spiritual salvation the fourteenth of the month of
Mihr, when Jesus, the Son of God, entered into *parinirvana*."[57] The
Christian term "crucifixion" and the Buddhist term "*parinirvana*" were
interchangeable to the eastern Manichaeans; both referred to the

liberation of Jesus' soul from the body of matter and its return to the Realm of Light.[58]

The increasing influence of Buddhism on the Uighur Manichaeans is markedly visible in a Buddhist-style *pothi* (palm-leaf) book from Bezeklik in the Turfan oasis probably dating to the eleventh century, which includes a colophon on the transfer of merit. Also included is the story of a merchant named Arazan, reflecting the identification of Manichaeism with Silk Road businessmen.[59]

In at least one significant case this mixing up of religious ideas was carried back west along the Silk Road to Europe. One of the most popular medieval European tales was the story of Barlaam and Ioasaph, a much-recolored account of the life of the Buddha. Through a series of translations, the name of the hero was transformed from the Sanskrit *bodhisattva,* to the Sogdian Budasaf, to the Uighur Bodhisaf and back again through Iudasaf to Ioasaf.[60]

In China, too, evidence of conceptual sycretism is abundant. The famous ten-foot-high eighth-century Nestorian monument in Xian is topped by a Maltese cross resting on a Taoist cloud with a Buddhist lotus flower beneath it.[61] The text inscribed below summarizes the essence of Christianity in heavily Buddhist-flavored terms and images (e.g., "the eight cardinal virtues," echoing the Noble Eightfold Path, "hanging up the bright sun," and "an oar of the vessel of mercy," a reference to Amitabha ferrying souls to paradise), along with a sprinkling of Confucianism ("how to rule both families and kingdoms") and Taoism (the "New Teaching of Non-assertion"):

> Fulfilling the old Law as it was declared by the twenty-four Sages, He (the Messiah) taught how to rule both families and kingdoms according to His own great Plan. Establishing His New Teaching of Non-assertion which operates silently through the Holy Spirit, another person of the Trinity, He formed in man the capacity for well-doing through the Right Faith. Setting up the standard of the eight cardinal virtues, He purged away the dust from human nature and perfected a true character. Widely opening the Three Constant Gates, He brought Life to light and abolished Death. Hanging up the bright Sun, He

swept away the abodes of darkness. All the evil devices of the devil were thereupon defeated and destroyed. He then took an oar in the Vessel of Mercy and ascended to the Palace of Light. Thereby all rational beings were conveyed across the Gulf. His mighty work being thus completed, He returned at noon to His original position (in Heaven). The twenty-seven standard works of His Sutras were preserved. The Great means of Conversion (or leavening, i.e., transformation) were widely extended, and the sealed Gate of the Blessed Life was unlocked. His Law is to bathe with water and with the Spirit, and thus to cleanse from all vain delusions and to purify men until they regain the whiteness of their nature.

A few lines further down the imagery becomes more pronouncedly Taoist:

But, at any rate, The Way would not have spread so widely if it had not been for the Sage, and the Sage would not have been so great if it were not for The Way. Ever since the Sage and The Way were united together as the two halves of an indentured deed would agree, then the world became refined and enlightened.[62]

An earlier (641?) Christian text in Chinese bears the very Indian-sounding title *The Shastra on One Deva* (or "Discourse on the Oneness of God").[63] In another early text (from 638—written by A-lo-pen?), known as the *Jesus-Messiah Sutra,* is found the following passage, very much expressed in Chinese imagery: "Jehovah, who is Lord of Heaven . . . is like the wind in His countenance. And, who could possibly see the wind? . . . The Lord of Heaven is incessantly going all over the world, is constantly present everywhere. . . . On account of this, every man existing in this world only obtains life and continues his existence by the strength of the Lord of Heaven. . . ."[64] The *Jesus-Messiah Sutra* also mentions "Buddhas, Kinnaras, and Superintending Devas," perhaps an attempt to translate the concept of "angels, archangels, and hosts of heaven."[65]

A well-known early-ninth-century Manichaean text in Chinese begins and ends like a Buddhist sutra. In fact, its conclusion is virtually identical with that of the Diamond Sutra. The Manichaean version reads: "Then, all the members of the great assembly, having heard the *sutra* accepted it with faith and rejoicing, and proceeded to put it into practice." The Diamond Sutra likewise concludes: "all the monks and nuns, lay-brothers and lay-sisters . . . having heard the Buddha's words rejoiced with one accord, and accepting them with faith, proceeded to put them into practice."[66]

To ordinary people, unequipped to sift through doctrinal subtleties, this religious mish-mash often must have been quite confusing. One Chinese text offers the following advice: "Talking about accepting Buddha, one should think of converting to *which* Buddha; not Mani Buddha, not to Nestorian Buddha, nor Zoroastrian Buddha, but Sakyamuni Buddha. . . ."[67]

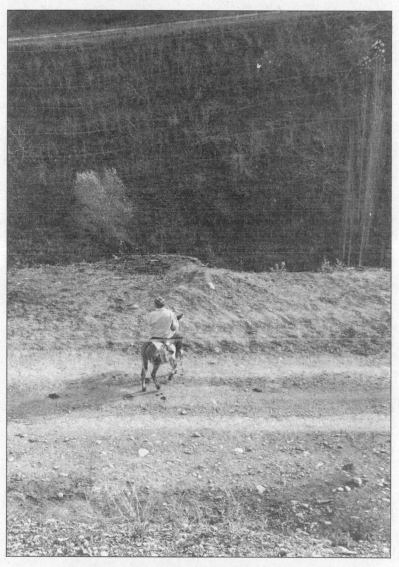

1. A contemporary Central Asian scene, Uzbekistan.
Photo by Aphrodite Désirée Navab.

2. Sogdian (?) caravan leader, Turfan, ninth century. Photo courtesy of the National Museum, New Delhi.

3. Greco-Buddhist Vajrapani modeled on Herakles in a lionskin, Hadda, Afghanistan, third century. Photo by F. Tissot.

4. Previous page: Iranian (Sogdian?) lay-merchants making offerings to Buddha. Detail of a wall painting, Bezeklik, tenth century. Photo courtesy of the Museum für Indische Kunst, Berlin.

5. The Prophet Mani (?) and Electi. Wall painting, Qocho, tenth century. Photo courtesy of the Museum für Indische Kunst, Berlin.

6. Manichean Electi, from an illustrated manuscript, Qocho, ninth-tenth century. Photo courtesy of the Museum für Indische Kunst, Berlin.

7. Cross and lotus atop Nestorian monument, Xian.
From a rubbing obtained by Camilla Foltz.

8. Fourteenth-century Nestorian gravestone with Syriac inscription,
angels, cross, and lotus atop Mazdaean-type altar.
Photo courtesy of the Hermitage Museum, St. Petersburg.

9. Kazakh Muslim shaman (right) and family, northwestern Mongolia.
Photo by Thomas Oller.

10. Kazakh village mosque, northwestern Mongolia. Photo by Thomas Oller.

11. Pagoda-style minaret with dragons, Xian mosque. Photo by Camilla Foltz.

CHAPTER FIVE

The Islamization
of the Silk Road

No religious tradition in world history favored trade as much as did Islam. The Prophet Muhammad himself was a businessman by profession. While in his twenties he became employed by a wealthy merchant woman of Mecca, Khadija, and made his reputation by successfully carrying out a trade mission to Syria; Khadija married him soon after.

Sometime around 610 of the common era, Muhammad, who liked to spend time alone meditating in the mountains outside Mecca, began hearing voices during the course of these retreats. At first he began to doubt his own sanity, but Khadija persuaded him that these voices might be divine in nature and should be listened to. Gradually Muhammad came to believe he was receiving revelations from God, calling upon him to "rise and warn" his fellow Meccans that the time had come to mend their ways.

Mecca was a desert town with little to subsist on apart from its trade. Successful merchants must have been its wealthiest inhabitants. Many of the revelations Muhammad received dealt with social injustice, which was clearly a problem in Mecca at that time. His message found a growing audience of sympathetic ears, while it increasingly alienated the social classes who were the target of his criticism. Before long certain powerful residents of Mecca were making life difficult for Muhammad and his followers.

In 622 the citizens of Yathrib, a town some two hundred twenty miles to the north of Mecca, were involved in factional disputes they could not resolve. Hearing of Muhammad's reputation for fairness and piety, they invited him to come and arbitrate. He accepted. Sending most of his followers ahead of him, the Prophet of Islam put his affairs in order and finally left his hometown, an event known to Muslims as the *hijra,* or migration, which marks the beginning of the Islamic calendar.

Once in Yathrib, the Muslims were not only no longer persecuted, they enjoyed special status. From their new power base they launched raids (Ar. *razzia*) on Meccan-bound caravans, at the same time enriching their own treasury while inflicting damage on their former persecutors. After several battles with the Meccans, the Muslims were able to negotiate the right to return to Mecca for the traditional Arabian pilgrimage to the sacred *ka`ba* stone; by 628 Mecca was under Muslim control.

Raiding caravans was an established part of the economic life of Arabia. The only rule was that one couldn't raid clan members or groups with whom one had made a non-aggression pact. With the successes of the Muslims growing from year to year, eventually all the tribes of the Arabian peninsula sent emissaries to Muhammad in order to seek such pacts. Their professions of loyalty were described by later Muslim writers as "submission," which in Arabic is *islam.* Small wonder that these sources, and the non-Muslim histories based on them, interpret this as meaning all the Arabian tribes had accepted the new religion.

Understanding this term "submission" in its more restricted literal sense, however, more easily explains what happened upon the Prophet's death in 632: Most of the Arabian tribes rebelled. Later Muslim sources refer to these as rebellions of "apostasy." A simpler interpretation would be that the rebel parties simply saw their nonaggression pacts as having been rendered null and void by the Prophet's passing.

The Muslims immediately chose a successor, or caliph (from Middle Pers. *khalifa*), Abu Bakr, under whose leadership the various

Arab tribes were forced to resubmit. Since the Arabian economy required the component of raiding, and since according to the nonaggression pacts no one in Arabia could legitimately be raided, the Muslims were forced to launch forays beyond the Arabian peninsula into Byzantine and Persian territory. Their successes in defeating the armies of both empires probably surprised many of the Muslims as much as it did their imperial enemies.

It is important to recognize the economic aspect of Muslim expansion, driven by the ancient Arabian tradition of raiding. While in hindsight both Muslims and non-Muslims have read into this early expansion a large element of religious zeal, the Arab armies of the time were simply doing what they were naturally acculturated to do, what the economic conditions of their homeland had always constrained them to do. What had changed was that, for the first time, all the Arab groups of the peninsula had excluded for themselves the possibility of raiding other Arab groups. They were forced, therefore, to raid elsewhere. Their new religious self-concept may indeed have inspired them by giving divine meaning to their increasing successes, but other factors were at work as well.

Iranians, in the form of Medes, Achemenians, Parthians, and Sasanians, had been vying with Athenian, Seleucid, and Roman Greeks for hegemony in western Asia for over a millennium. By the seventh century both the Sasanian Persian and Byzantine Greek empires were exhausted and decadent. Neither treated their subject peoples in Mesopotamia, Syria, or Egypt with anything that could be called benevolence. In many locations townspeople threw open the gates to the Arabs and welcomed them as liberators. The Muslims were, in fact, no more foreign in most of the lands they conquered than had been the previous rulers, and at first they were less exploitative.

By the 660s, however, the ruling Arab family, the Umayyads, had set themselves up in Damascus in very much the mold of the Byzantine governors they had dislodged. Throughout the subsequent decades non-Muslims came to chafe under the new regime. Many Arab Muslims, furthermore, resented the imperial manner and "un-Islamic" lifestyles of the Umayyads, many of whom had taken to drinking and debauchery in the best Roman tradition.

But the group which was to bring about the Umayyads' downfall and, in doing so, forever change the very nature of Islam as a cultural tradition was the non-Arabs who chose to adopt the Islamic religion.

Initially and throughout the Umayyad period, the Arabs had seen Islam as a religion belonging to them; their subjects, likewise, referred to Islam as "the Arab religion" *(al-din al-ʿarab)*. The Qur'an enjoined Muslims to spread Muslim *rule* throughout the world but laid down no requirement to spread the faith itself. The original impulse of holy war *(jihad)* was that no Muslim should be constrained to live under the rule of infidels. Once a given locality agreed to submit to Muslim authority and pay the poll tax *(jizya)* levied on protected communities *(dhimmis,* usually "peoples of the Book," i.e., Christians and Jews), there was no further need for coercion on either side.

In fact, Arab Muslims had strong reasons *not* to want non-Arabs to join the faith, since conversion directly affected both their sources of income and the spread of its distribution among Muslims. Conversely, there were numerous reasons why non-Muslims might wish to join the ruling group, which could most obviously be symbolized by adopting their faith. Despite some apparent resistance from the Arab elite, by the early eighth century non-Arab converts were probably beginning to outnumber Arab Muslims.

Islam had attempted to eliminate class and racial distinctions, but even during the Prophet's lifetime this goal was never met. Early converts and their descendants often felt entitled to greater status and privilege than later converts, and members of aristocratic families never forgot who came from humble ones. Tribal and clan loyalties affected government appointments and led to rivalries.

Often these rivalries developed power bases in garrison towns where particular factions were dominant. Local governors, therefore, usually had more or less personal armies at their ready disposal. In areas where the Arabs were quartered among non-Arab majority populations, there was increasing pressure from converts to be treated on equal footing with Arab Muslims.

The problem was that a non-Arab, even after converting to Islam, had no tribal affiliation which could provide him an identity within Arab society. A solution to this was devised whereby an Arab Muslim could take a non-Arab convert under his wing as a "client" *(mawla),* making the convert a sort of honorary tribal member. Of course, such clients were at the mercy of the individual who sponsored them.

Over time this inequality between Arab and non-Arab Muslims became a major pretext for various parties disaffected with Umayyad rule. Not surprisingly it was in eastern Iran, at the fringes of Umayyad power, that a rebel movement capable of overthrowing the central government and completely reshaping Muslim society took place.

In addition to complaints about the un-Islamic character of the Umayyad elite and the inequalities between Arab and non-Arab Muslims, the anti-Umayyad movement could draw on the issue of the very legitimacy of Umayyad rule. The first Umayyad caliph, Mu'awiya, had assumed power by refusing to recognize the selection of the Prophet's nephew and son-in-law, Ali, as fourth caliph. A significant minority of Muslims felt that leadership should be sought in charismatic authority passed down through the Prophet's line. For the "partisans of Ali" *(shi'at Ali),* the Umayyads (and indeed the first three caliphs) had been usurpers from the outset.

All of these antigovernment impulses came together in the so-called Abbasid revolution of 749 to 751, in which a Khurasan-based Muslim army rallied behind an Iranian general, Abu Muslim, in the name of an Arab descendant of the Prophet's uncle Abbas. The rebels succeeded in wresting power from the Umayyads, moved the capital to Mesopotamia, and began setting up a new Islamic administration on the Sasanian imperial model. The new ministers and functionaries were overwhelmingly Iranian, often recent converts from Zoroastrianism or Christianity or, in the case of the influential Barmak family from Balkh, from Buddhism. In 762 the Caliph Mansur built a new capital at Baghdad (Pers. "given by God") and commented that this would put Muslims in touch "with lands as far off as China."[1]

"RELIGIOUS" REBELLIONS
IN IRAN AND CENTRAL ASIA

During the first half of the eighth century, Muslim armies repeatedly attempted to assert and maintain their authority over the easternmost parts of the Iranian world, Sogdiana and Bactria. Following the pattern of the Arab tribes at the time of the Prophet, local rulers would "submit" when overwhelmed and then "apostatize" again as soon as they thought they could get away with it. Some, like the Sogdian king Tughshada, did this several times.

Like the Chinese, Iranians have long considered theirs to be the greatest and most ancient of civilizations. For many Iranians, being conquered by the Arabs, a people they had always considered barbaric, was and remains the greatest single trauma in the history of their nation. The Iranian national epic, the *Shah-nama* ("Book of Kings"), though compiled in the tenth century by a Muslim poet for a Muslim patron, portrays the Arab conquest of Iran as a sort of final and ultimate tragedy.

Because the Zoroastrian priesthood, the magi, were so directly identified with the ruling house throughout most of the Sasanian period, the fall of the dynasty inevitably meant the fall of the priestly class. This did not mean, however, that Iranian religion in other forms could not provide a rallying focus for resistance to Arab rule.

In Sogdiana a resistance movement took shape in 777 around a figure known as Muqanna', or "the Veiled One," a self-declared prophet whose followers, like the Manichaeans, wore white robes. According to Narshakhi, a Sogdian Muslim writing a century later, Muqanna' said of himself: "Do you know who I am? I am your lord and lord of all the world. . . . I am the one who showed myself to people as Adam, then in the form of Noah, also in the form of Abraham, Moses, then in the guise of Jesus, Muhammad the prophet, in the guise of Abu Muslim, and now in this guise which you see. . . . I have the power to be in any guise I wish to show."[2] His missionaries distributed letters which read: "Verily al-Muqanna' has strength, power, glory, and proof. Accept me and realize that I have dominion. Glory and omnipotence are mine. There is no other God but me. He who follows me will go to Paradise, but he who does not accept me will rest in Hell."[3]

Narshakhi writes that in Sogdiana, "most of the villages accepted the faith of Muqanna'" and that the Muslims were "impotent" before them. The movement was so successful in Central Asia, he writes, that the caliph in Baghdad "feared that there was a danger that Islam would be lost and the religion of Muqanna' would spread throughout the entire world."[4]

Like many successful religious figures, Muqanna' may have been a master illusionist. When begged by a crowd to reveal himself, he had assistants direct sunlight into the mob by use of mirrors, in order to dazzle them. Many afterward claimed they had seen God. When after nine years of struggle the Muslim armies finally cornered Muqanna' in his fortress stronghold, he told his followers that he would go up to heaven and bring down angels to help them, then threw himself into a fire. Narshakhi states that in his time Muqanna''s followers still followed their faith in secret. "Their religion is such," he says, "that they neither pray nor fast, nor do they wash after sexual intercourse." He goes on to accuse them of promiscuity: "They say that a woman is like a flower; [no matter] who smells it, nothing is detracted from it."[5]

The single most effective anti-Muslim resistance movement in Iran proper, which lasted from around 816 to 837, was waged in the region south of the Caspian Sea by a sect known as the *Khurram-din,* or "Happy Religion." Led by a prophetic figure named Babak, the Khurram-diniyya were a group descended from a sixth-century social reform movement known as Mazdakism, which enjoyed a period of official favor under the Sasanian Emperor Kavad from 488 to 531 but was brutally crushed under his son and successor, Khusraw I.

The Mazdakites were a sort of proto-communist sect which opposed the possession of private property, including wives. Following the public execution of Babak, which was particularly drawn out and grisly, the movement ceased to be a political force, but continued a secret existence while professing Islam and may still survive today.[6]

ISLAM AND TRADE IN THE EASTERN LANDS

As with any case of mass cultural conversion, the Islamization of Central Asia was a complex process which occurred on more than one level. The first, and most visible level, was the spread of political power. It is worth noting that the spread of a particular religion's rule is not identical with the spread of faith, although historians have often written as if it were.

Muslim rule over the western half of the Silk Road came fairly early and was established, albeit through a period of false starts and occasional reversals, by the mid-eighth century. Muslims thereafter controlled much of trans-Asian trade, which became the second major factor in the Islamization of Central Asian culture. Gradually a third factor, the influence of charismatic Muslim preachers, entered into the process.

The reality of Muslim rule could no longer be reasonably ignored once the numerous eighth-century attempts to rally behind local, non-Islamic religious figures had all failed. Politics was therefore an initial influence encouraging Central Asians to abandon their native cultural traditions and join the growing world culture of Islamic civilization. It appears, however, that only local rulers, especially those who had raised arms against the Muslims, were ever subjected to the convert-or-die alternative that has so long been the stereotype characterizing the spread of Islam. Other people, at least at first, would have embraced the faith of their new rulers for other reasons, in certain cases no doubt spiritual ones.

One of the most commonly cited incentives to religio-cultural conversion is the pursuit of patronage. Anyone directly dependent on the government for his livelihood might sense advantages in joining the cultural group of his patrons and accepting the norms and values of that ruling group. To a large extent, converts to Islam do appear to have held onto their preconquest positions, and being a Muslim increased one's chances of attaining a new or better one.

A second and probably greater influence affecting Islamization was the Muslim domination of commercial activity. A businessman could feel that becoming a Muslim would facilitate contacts and cooperation with other Muslim businessmen both at home and abroad; he would also benefit from favorable conditions extended by Muslim officials and from the Islamic laws governing commerce.

The presence of Muslim rule and the increasing Muslim dominance of trade meant that Islamization came first in the urban areas along the Silk Road and only in later centuries spread to the countryside. The gradual Islamization of the nomadic Turkic peoples of Central and Inner Asia was at first directly tied to their increasing participation in the oasis-based Silk Road trade in the tenth century,[7] accelerated by the political activities of three Turkic Muslim dynasties—the Qara-khanids, the Ghaznavids, and the Seljuks—and supplemented by the proselytizing efforts of Muslim missionaries.[8]

The third major factor accounting for the Islamization of the Silk Road, which follows those of politics and economics, is assimilation. Whatever the reasons for one's converting to Islam, Islamization occurs most profoundly (and irrevocably) among the succeeding generation, since the convert's children in principle will be raised within the father's new community, not his original one.[9] Furthermore, although a Muslim man may marry a non-Muslim woman, Islamic law requires that the children of a mixed marriage be raised as Muslims. However, in light of our remarks in chapter 1 on women's roles in religious education, it may be safe to assume that aspects of pre-Islamic local religion survived through transmission by non-Muslim wives of Muslims.

Central Asians of the countryside, being less directly affected by the factors just described, held onto their Iranian (usually agriculturalist) or Turkic (usually pastoral nomadic) native religious traditions longer than did their urban counterparts. Gradually, though, the same influences were felt throughout the rural areas. An additional and even more significant Islamicizing influence especially on the pastoral peoples came through the activities of Sufi shaykhs, who took it upon themselves to spread Islam to the remotest areas. Their influence stemmed largely from their personal charisma, which often made them the authoritative sources for the religion even above and beyond the Qur'an, *hadith* (stories about the prophet), or Islamic law.

It was the shaykh's own personal interpretations of the Islamic message that formed the basis of the faith as the pastoral folk heard it. Often these personal interpretations were accommodating towards preexisting local beliefs and practices, leading to the development of "popular" expressions of Islam which could deviate significantly from the normative tradition emanating from the cities. In some ways local religion in Central Asia, whether of the Iranian or Turkic variety, never really disappeared. Rather, it acquired Islamic meanings, interpretations, and appearances.

THE FATE OF ZOROASTRIANISM
AND BUDDHISM IN CENTRAL ASIA

By the time of the Arab conquest in the middle to late seventh century
CE, those elements of Sogdian religiosity most noticed and commented on by Muslim writers—such as fire worship and the exposure
of corpses—were elements modern scholars normally associate with
Zoroastrianism. This is in contrast to the Muslim accounts of the
conquest of Sind, located in coastal NW India, where local religiosity
appears to have remained strongly Buddhist-oriented. But even in
the Muslim accounts of Central Asia, we see aspects of local culture
which do not mesh entirely with the canonical Zoroastrianism of
Sasanian Iran.

Narshakhi comments that in his day there were mosque doors in
Bukhara which bore images with the faces scratched out. He explains
that these doors had been taken by lower-class converts to Islam from
the suburban villas of the unconverted rich, each of whose gate bore the
image of a patron idol.

In contrast to this example, Narshakhi elsewhere provides evidence
of more recognizably "Zoroastrian" practice. He relates that upon the
death of Tughshada—the eighth-century Sogdian ruler whose "submission" to Islam was so clearly political—the royal servants "removed his
flesh and brought his bones to Bukhara."[10]

Other cases of the Sogdians' use of iconography incompatible with
both canonical Zoroastrianism and Islam can be seen in their burial
customs. While, like the Sasanians, Central Asian Iranians exposed their
dead to have their bones picked clean by vultures, unlike the Zoroastrians
of the Iranian plateau they then buried the bones in clay ossuaries
decorated with figures.[11]

Accounts of Sogdian merchants and their trading communities
along the Silk Road eastward into China variously identify them as
having Buddhist or Zoroastrian practices. While Sogdians of both faiths
may well have been represented within these expatriate communities, the
lines need not be so clearly drawn, for as we have seen, the Sogdians' pool
of religious beliefs and practices could include elements of both tradi-

tions. In addition, the balance of elements likely differed among various Sogdian communities or even individuals.

As Sogdiana became administratively incorporated into the *dar al-islam,* the Sogdians came to assimilate themselves into the broader Persian cultural sphere, adopting Persian in preference to their original tongue and becoming increasingly identified as Persians. The revival of Zoroastrian letters in the ninth century, which came as a reaction to the mass conversions of Zoroastrians to Islam in Iran, probably improved communication of the institutional form of the religion to those Central Asians who had not yet turned to Islam. Zoroastrians were usually classified as a "protected" *(dhimmi)* community in Central Asia as in Iran, and in Samarqand the Zoroastrian community was entrusted with the maintenance of the water piping system in lieu of paying the *jizya,* the poll tax levied on non-Muslims.[12]

From the seventh century Chinese sources make increasing reference to Zoroastrian communities there. Many Zoroastrians appear to have fled eastward along the Silk Road after the Muslim conquest of Iran, following in the steps of Peroz, son of the last Sasanian emperor Yazdigard III, who was welcomed at the T'ang court at Ch'ang-an as the "King of Persia" and made a general in the imperial guard. Peroz was accompanied by many refugees, who were allowed to build fire temples and practice their faith.

As late as the Mongol period, Zoroastrian exile communities are mentioned as flourishing in China. Zoroastrianism is not a missionary religion, and these communities do not appear to have included local converts, but very likely they included Zoroastrians of Central Asian origin in addition to the refugees and merchants from Iran proper. Numerous T'ang period temples at Ch'ang-an, Lo-yang, K'ai-feng, and elsewhere appear to have been Zoroastrian. Popular Chinese tales from the T'ang period attest to the familiarity of the Chinese population with the figure of the Zoroastrian merchant.[13]

Thus, while we can make certain qualified assumptions about the presence of a recognizably "canonical" Zoroastrianism to the east of Iran in post-Sasanian times, attempts to categorize the Iranian-inhabited Central Asian lands of Sogdiana and adjacent territories as specifically

"Zoroastrian" in any period are unwarranted. On the other hand, religious belief and practice among the Iranians of Central Asia has always had many elements in common with that of Iranians farther west, a truth which holds through the present day.

Despite the Muslims' special aversion to Buddhism as an "idol-worshipping" religion inferior to the religions "of the Book," there is evidence of some Buddhist survivals into the Muslim period. The Barmak family, furthermore, which gave the early Abbasid government many of its most powerful and effective administrators, was originally a family of hereditary Buddhist priests.

The Barmaks controlled a monastery known as Naw Bahar ("new spring" in Persian, a *faux ami* derived from the Sanskrit *nava vihara,* or "new temple") near Balkh, which appears to have been the center of a network of monasteries dispersed throughout Iran.[14] It has been suggested that the Barmaks' conversion to Islam robbed the eastern lands of a major potential anti-Muslim rallying force, thereby facilitating Islamization in those regions.[15] However, after the Abbasids executed Abu Muslim just three years after the Iranian general had led their revolution to success, widespread rumors of his reincarnation arose, pointing to a survival of Buddhist belief among the general population.[16]

The best known of the classical Muslim historians, Tabari, mentions Buddhist idols being brought from Kabul to Baghdad in the late ninth century.[17] Narshakhi gives some interesting information pertaining to Bukhara. He states that at the bazaar adjoining the Makh mosque—which appears to have been a Buddhist temple that the Sasanians had turned into a fire temple before the Muslims came and transformed it once again—a twice-annual fair was held where 50,000 dirhams' worth of Buddhist idols were sold.[18] Another Muslim historian, Ibn Hawkal, writes that in the tenth century, wooden animal figures were for sale in Samarqand.[19]

The Samanids, an Iranian Muslim dynasty which took over many formerly Buddhist lands in Central Asia, seem to have borrowed certain influences into their architecture, such as the four-archway plan of the religious schools, the *madrasas*, which developed during their reign. In fact, the very idea of the *madrasas* themselves may have been absorbed from the Buddhist schools, since these institutions first appear in this part of the Muslim world.

Farther east, where Muslim power took longer to consolidate and Buddhism survived longer as a result, similar patterns can be observed. Aurel Stein in the course of his excavations in the Tarim Basin discovered an early Turkish Muslim shrine purported to be the tomb of four imams, but which he determined had originally been a Buddhist monument.[20] Another such shrine in the Tarim region is mentioned in the sixteenth-century Muslim hagiography *History of the Uwaysis,* which contains a legend about a sufi named Muhibb-i Kuhmar ("Lover of the Mountain Snake") and a holy snake, apparently modeled on a Buddhist snake story connected with the philosopher Nagarjuna.[21]

THE LATER DEVELOPMENT
OF JEWISH TRADE NETWORKS

Jews certainly participated in the Silk Road trade networks which linked the Roman Mediterranean with Han China in classical times. During the Muslim period Jewish traders known as Radanites (Ar. *al-radaniyya,* perhaps from Pers. *rah-dan,* "one who knows the way") held a privileged status, which allowed them to move freely between the Muslim and Christian worlds, but the origins of the Radanite system must go back at least several centuries prior to the coming of Islam, since it is highly developed by the time the Radanites appear in Muslim writings.[22] Latin sources seem to indicate that already in the preceding centuries Mediterranean trade was dominated by Jews from the West and Syrians from the Byzantine East.[23]

The original base of the Radanites was in Roman Gaul, centered in Arles and Marseilles.[24] They trafficked particularly in slaves and controlled a large operation in Verdun for turning them into eunuchs. It was this involvement in the slave trade that brought the Jewish Radanites into contact with the Turkish Khazars of the north Caspian region, a transit point for captured Slavs (from Lat. *sclav,* "slave"; hence Ar. *saqaliba*).

Controlling an important northern offshoot of the Silk Road, the Khazars were ideally situated to serve as middlemen between East and West.

They enjoyed a symbiotic relationship with the settled Iranian peoples to the South and the East along the Silk Road, which was well expressed in the Turkish proverb, "*Tatsiz Türk bolmas; bashsiz börk bolmas,*" or "There is no Turk without an Iranian merchant, just as there is no cap without a head." Perceiving the commercial benefits associated with the Radanites' neutral religious status, the Khazar elite eventually embraced Judaism, although the supreme ruler, the *kaghan,* as well as most of the general population, retained their original shamanistic Turkic religion.[25]

The ninth-century Persian geographer Ibn Khurdadbih describes the Radanites thus: "These merchants speak Arabic, Persian, Roman [i.e., Greek], the language of the Franks, Andalusians, and Slavs. They journey from west to east, partly on land, partly by sea. They transport from the west eunuchs, female and male slaves, silk, castor, marten and other furs, and swords."[26]

Ibn Khurdadbih describes four different trade routes on which the Radanites were active. The first is from Gaul across the Mediterranean and overland to the Red Sea and via the Indian Ocean to the East Asia; the second is via Mesopotamia; and the third across North Africa. The fourth route went northward through the Khazar lands, from whence it joined the Silk Road: "Sometimes they likewise take the route behind Rome, and, passing through the country of the Slavs, arrive at Khamlif [Etil], the capital of the Khazars. They embark upon the Jorjan Sea [the Caspian], arrive at Balkh, betake themselves from there across the Oxus, and continue their journey toward the Yourts of the Toghozghor [the Tüqqüz Oghuz Turks], and from there to China."[27]

Naturally, the raising of Judaism to official status within the Khazar dominions would have facilitated and encouraged the northern alternative. In any event, Ibn Khurdadbih's account makes it clear that Jews were active along all the world's major trade routes at that time, which implies the existence of diaspora communities of Jews living all along the various stages of those routes. The widespread extent of these diaspora communities and the fact that they remained in communication with each other is borne out by the many locations referred to in the Gaonic *responsa* literature (rabbinic instruction on questions of Jewish life) that began in the eighth century.[28]

THE ASSASSINS

Frankish Crusaders in the eleventh and twelfth centuries brought to Europe stories of a secretive extremist sect led by "The Old Man of the Mountain," a group which came to be known as the Assassins. The derivation of this term continues to be debated; popular tales derive it from *hashishiyun,* claiming that members of the sect would drug themselves before carrying out their spectacular and usually public murders of well-known Muslim politicians and other figures. A more sober etymology traces back to *assasiyun,* "the people of the foundation."

The sect in question was an offshoot of the "partisans of Ali," known variously as the Sevener Shi'ites, since their lineage of spiritual leaders *(imams)* diverges from the Shi'ite majority after the sixth imam; as the Isma'ilis, after their seventh imam, Isma'il; or in earlier Muslim sources, as the Batinites (from the Arabic *batin,* "esoteric"), because of their secretive doctrines and practices.

A Sevener dynasty, the Fatimids, ruled from Egypt throughout the eleventh century, drawing much of their prosperity from trade linking the Mediterranean with the Red Sea. The Fatimids provided Sevener Shi'ism with state sponsorship, fostering an active and often quite successful missionary program. The most famous Sevener missionary of this period was the poet-philosopher Nasir-i Khusraw, who traveled the Silk Road westward from his home in eastern Khurasan to Cairo, the Fatimid capital, apparently making a tour of Sevener centers along the way.[29]

The Sunni state based in Baghdad found the Seveners' missionary successes threatening and persecuted Sevener communities wherever they could. It was in response to this persecution that Sevener devotees began their campaign of political killings, designed to strike terror into the hearts of their enemies. The Assassins, as these defenders of their faith have come to be known, were eminently successful in carrying out their missions.[30] Perhaps their most famous victim was Nizam al-Mulk, the Persian prime minister of the staunchly Sunni Seljuk Turks, who was stabbed to death in his litter in 1092.

Two years later the Sevener community split over the issue of succession. The minority faction came to be known as the Nizaris, after a martyred leader. The Nizari cause was taken up by Hasan-i Sabah, a Persian trained in Cairo who had ordered Nizam al-Mulk's killing.[31] Hasan's community operated out of a mountain fortress at Alamut in northern Iran. This region, which had always resisted incorporation into the caliphate and had been home to many heterodox movements, provided safe haven for the Nizaris for over 120 years, until a concerted effort by the Mongols finally dislodged them in 1226.

THE ISLAMIZATION
OF TURKIC DYNASTIES

When the first Muslim merchants and missionaries reached the Tarim Basin, they found one of the most religiously diverse cultures in the world. By that time the majority of inhabitants were probably Buddhists, but there were Manichaean and Nestorian Christian communities as well. Various local cults and traditional religions must also have been represented.

According to local accounts, the Islamization of Kashgar began in the first half of the tenth century when Satoq Bughra, a local Turkish boy from the clan later known as the Qara-khanids, was converted by one Nasr b. Mansur of the Samanid family, which was ruling Transoxiana and eastern Iran.[32] Nasr may have been sent to negotiate trade agreements, since according to the story caravans from Bukhara followed him in large numbers.

Eventually Satoq Bughra became khan of Kashgar and gave Islam official status. Although aspects of this account may belong to legend, it does fit in with the Samanids' well-known policy of sending missions to the various Turkish tribes throughout Inner Asia in hopes of transforming them from raiders into traders.

With the conversion of Satoq Bughra Khan, who died around 955, the Qara-khanids became the first Turkish dynasty officially to espouse Islam.[33] The Muslim historians Ibn Athir and Ibn Miskawayh state that in the year 960 an immense number of Turks—200,000 tents—converted to Islam.[34] The group in question has commonly been identified as the Qara-khanids. Throughout the first half of the eleventh century Islam gained in importance across the eastern part of the Central Asian Silk Road that was under their control.

Other Turkic ruling groups, the Ghaznavids and the Seljuks, also converted to Islam before coming to control large areas from Anatolia to India in the eleventh century. The Ghaznavids became Islamicized in the service of the Iranian Samanids of Bukhara, then challenged and eventually took much of the southern territory of their former employers.

The Oghuz Turkish chieftain Seljuk converted to Islam around 985, apparently for political reasons. His descendants took control of the Ghaznavid lands in 1040. From 1055 the Seljuks established hegemony over Baghdad and, with the somewhat reluctant acquiescence of the caliph, assumed the role of champions of Sunni Islam. Islamization was therefore central to their legitimizing ideology. At the same time, the Seljuks were a major force in the Turkicization of the Muslim world, especially with their conquest of much of Byzantine Anatolia by the late eleventh century and the establishment of the Sultanate of Rum (i.e., eastern "Rome").[35]

Along the northwestern spur of the Silk Road, which included the Volga Basin, the Turkic Bulgars became Islamized during the tenth century. This seems to have been largely an effect of their trade connections with the Muslim world. An eleventh-century Muslim Bulgar historian, Ya'qub b. Nu'man al-Bulgari, writes that the Bulgar king had converted to Islam after a Muslim merchant healed him and his wife from some disease.[36]

Among the eastern Turks, Islam was still very much tied to the merchant class by the eve of the Mongol conquest. Buddhism remained strong in the towns of the Tarim Basin, as did Nestorianism and traditional shamanistic religion among the steppe nomads.

The *pax mongolica* established through the thirteenth-century conquests of Chinggis Khan and his successors was a boon to overland trade. Thus, no doubt at first unintentionally, the Mongols strengthened the position of the Silk Road Muslims by creating conditions under which their business could prosper as never before. Although many of the Mongol elite held onto their native traditions for several more generations, sooner or later those most concerned with trade tended to throw their support behind the Muslims, and many themselves adopted Islam.

The Further Islamization of the Tarim

With the support of a converted ruler, Sufi missionaries could travel and preach more freely among the Turkish and Mongol general populations. Most of the later Turkic tribal groups developed origin legends which attributed their Islamization to a particular charismatic individual from the Muslim West, one of a class which came to be known as *khojas* (from the Persian *khwaja*, or "master").

Many of the earliest Sufi missionaries who came from Transoxiana to the Tarim Basin (or *alti shahr*, "Six Cities," as it is known in Muslim sources) were members of the popular and predominantly Turkish Yasavi order. By the late fourteenth century, however, the more shariʿa-bound and politically involved Naqshbandiyya began to displace them.[37] Hagiographies and histories from the sixteenth and seventeenth centuries portray the subsequent Islamization of the Tarim region as very much the story of these Naqshbandi shaykhs and their inspiring, pious deeds, which often included taking up arms against non-Muslim Turks, Mongols, and Chinese to support candidates for power who were pro-Muslim.

CHINESE MUSLIMS

Today there are about 5 million ethnically Chinese Muslims, known as Hui, living in China. Just exactly who the Hui are and where they came from continues to be a matter of debate.

Persian and Arab Muslim traders traveled to China from the very beginnings of Islamic expansion. Modern legends have the prophet's uncle, Saʿad Waqqas, bringing Islam to China during the Prophet's lifetime, but this story lacks evidence.[38] The earliest written reference to Muslims traveling the Silk Road to China is in the *New Tʿang History*, which states that a delegation sent by the Caliph ʿUthman arrived at Chʿang-an in 651.[39]

In 757 the T'ang emperor requested the aid of various mercenary groups to help him put down the rebellion of An Lu-shan; in addition to the then-pagan Uighurs, Muslims are mentioned as being among those who helped restore T'ang power. In reward for their services the Muslim soldiers were given lands in Central China. A number of them settled and took Chinese wives. In 801 another contingent of Arab and Sogdian Muslims were hired by the Tibetans who were attacking Yunnan in the southwest of China. Although the Tibetans and Muslims were defeated, the T'ang allowed the Muslims to settle there and marry Chinese women.[40] The Hui are presumed to have been originally descended from these mercenary groups.

Like other foreign communities, the Muslims in China lived mainly in self-governing enclaves and resisted sinicization. They had their own educational systems, their own community leaders, and their own economy, which was connected by the Silk Road with that of Muslim communities to the west.

There is little evidence that individual Chinese actually chose to convert to Islam. Once Muslim communities were established in China, however, a significant aspect of their growth was the adoption of unwanted Chinese children, who were raised as Muslims. This influx of Chinese blood, combined with the fact that Muslim soldiers and merchants who settled in China married Chinese women, contributed to the eventual creation of a distinct Chinese Muslim ethnicity. Again, the fact that mixed marriages were the rule suggests significant (if unverifiable) women's input into the early development of Chinese Islam.

During the period of the Yüan (i.e., Mongol) dynasty in the thirteenth and fourteenth centuries, Persian and Arab Muslims were brought to China to serve as administrators. Because of their experience in commerce, Muslims were the favored candidates for positions in finance, tax collection, and so forth. This trend reinforced existing Chinese stereotypes of Persian and Arab Muslims (whom, incidentally, the Chinese did not distinguish from Jews) as conniving, untrustworthy merchants. An exception to this negative image is seen in the case of Sayyid 'Ajall of Bukhara, governor of Yunnan province under the Mongols, whom Chinese sources (such as the later Ming chronicles) treat as a fair and talented administrator and, curiously, as a proponent of Confucian ethics.[41]

A REVERSAL FOR ISLAM

During the first half of the twelfth century, the Islamicized Qara-khanids were displaced in eastern Central Asia by a Mongolian non-Muslim group, the Qara-khitai. (It was from the name of this latter group that Europeans derived the term "Cathay," which they long applied to China). The next two centuries would pose the greatest challenge to Muslim domination of the Silk Road.

The Qara-khitai had been forced out of their original territory farther east by a tribe or confederation called the Jürchens. They moved westward and conquered many Silk Road towns that had been under Muslim control for several centuries. Various religions were represented among the Qara-khitai. The Muslim writer Ibn al-Athir states that their first leader, called the *Gür-khan,* was a Manichaean. Other references suggest he may have been a Nestorian Christian.[42] Most likely, in keeping with steppe tradition, he saw potential value in all religions.

In any event, under the Qara-khitai Muslims lost their preeminent position along the central part of the Silk Road, to the benefit of the followers of other traditions. In some places the Qara-khitai had mosques turned into Buddhist temples or Christian churches. Whether this indicates merely the preferences of the Qara-khitai themselves or their attempt to win the support of non-Muslim populations that had been living under Muslim rule cannot be known from the historical evidence. The fact is we simply do not know what proportion of the population in any given locality adhered to any particular religious tradition. Clearly, however, Central Asian Christianity, Manichaeism, and Buddhism had fallen into a defensive phase of their respective histories. The activities of first the Qara-khitai and then the Mongols reversed that trend and put Muslims on the defensive, at least temporarily.

The most significant conquests in the westward movement of the religiously mixed Qara-khitai were the Silk Road cities of Samarqand and Bukhara, which they wrested from the Muslim Sultan Sanjar in

1141.[43] This reverse in the supremacy of Islam in Central Asia inaugurated two centuries of exacerbated tensions and competitive intrigue among exponents of Christianity, Buddhism, and Islam, which crested under Mongol rule in the thirteenth century. Muslims would emerge dominant once again by the end of the Mongol period, but throughout this time such an outcome was far from being a given.

CHAPTER SIX

Ecumenical Mischief

Echoes and rumors of the Qara-khitai exploits reached the Frankish Crusaders in the Levant, who through a bit of creative phonetics interpreted the ruler's title, *Gür-khan*, as "Prester John" (Syriac: Yuhanan) and developed the myth of a Christian king from the East who would come to join forces with them in the Holy Land and help to crush Islam there.[1] This myth was to persist for nearly two centuries, as the persona of Prester John came optimistically to be associated with a succession of Turkish or Mongolian steppe figures having Christian connections.

It was at least partly in hopes of contacting this nonexistent ally that a series of embassies was sent from Western Europe into the far-off depths of Inner Asia. The ambassadors themselves often joined in the struggle for supremacy that took place at the Mongol courts between representatives of the major world religions of the time.

Prester John stories circulated vigorously during the early thirteenth century. First there were the successes of the mostly Christian Naiman Mongols against the Khwarazm-shah Sultan Muhammad, perhaps the most powerful figure in the Muslim world at that time. Then as details filtered westward regarding the new scourge of the steppes, Temujin (who would become known as Chinggis Khan), information regarding Christian members of his household (particularly women) gave rise to yet further hopes. This, of course, was at a time when the Mongol army under Temujin's grandson Batu had not yet laid waste to Eastern Europe, and the Mongols' westward advances could still be interpreted as directed specifically at Muslim centers of power.

In fact, the Naimans' appearance in western Central Asia was due to the fact that they were fleeing Temujin's attempts to consolidate the various Mongol and Turkic tribes under his solitary command. The Naiman leader, Küchlük, is referred to as a Buddhist, while his wife was a Christian, or possibly the other way around.[2] In any event, he was no friend of Muslims, and when his ally the ruler of Kashgar was killed in a local uprising, he intervened to put down the rebellion and subsequently launched a full-scale persecution of the local Muslim community, forbidding the ritual prayer *(salat)* and commanding Muslims to convert to Christianity or Buddhism.[3]

The Muslim population of Kashgar by that time must have been significant, since when Temujin sent an army against Küchlük and promised to give Kashgar religious freedom, a large number of the inhabitants allied themselves with Temujin's forces. Following Küchlük's expulsion, Temujin's general Jäbä issued a proclamation that "everyone should follow the religion of his ancestors and leave others alone."[4] The Persian historian Juvaini later reported that the Kashgarians told him Chinggis Khan's army had come as an act of "divine mercy."[5]

Sometimes, however, the Muslims were their own worst enemies. According to a later Persian writer, Khwand Amir, when Jäbä and another Mongol general, Sübödei, turned their attentions to the city of Rayy in northern Iran, the local jurists of the Shafite school of law "went out to greet them and encouraged Jäbä and Sübödei to slaughter the half of the city that was Hanafite." The Mongols did so, but then, saying to themselves "What good can be expected of men who plot to have their own countrymen's blood shed?" they killed the Shafites too. Likewise, when they proceeded south to the city of Qom, it was on the urging of some Sunnis that the Mongols put the local population, which was mostly Shi'ite, to death.[6]

RELIGION AMONG THE MONGOLS

The religiosity of the Mongols and related steppe peoples was generally reflected in what goes under the rubric of shamanism and featured a somewhat vague notion of a supreme sky god, Tangri. However, their interest in spiritual matters centered largely on applications to real-life issues, such as the acquisition of food, victory in battle, and personal health. Thus, they were open to any sort of religious practice or ritual which might help them to find success in realizing their immediate aims.

This led to a kind of religious toleration, in which any religion tended to be seen as being potentially effective, at least until proven otherwise. Successive Mongol *khans* repeatedly asked representatives of every religion—Christianity, Islam, Buddhism, Taoism—to pray for them, and the Mongol elite frequently patronized all of these religions through the construction of places of worship and the giving of gifts to religious figures. They drew the line on foreign religious practice only when it infringed on their own, such as the Muslim method of slaughtering animals for meat or bathing in running water.[7] Edicts against these practices were promulgated by Chinggis Khan and enforced sporadically by his successors.[8]

Like previous steppe conquerors, the Mongols aimed to reap the benefits of controlling the trans-Asian trade routes. Among all those groups fitting this historical pattern, they were the most successful in bringing the greater part of Eurasia under their rule. This meant that once Mongol power was firmly established, travel across Asia, although still difficult, was facilitated as never before. This led to a surge in long-distance trade and attendant cultural exchanges. The Polos have left the best-known legacy of these times, but Roman Catholic monks such as William of Rubruck, John of Plano Carpini, and others made the trip before and after them, often combining proselytization with diplomacy. Coming the other direction from the Turkish Nestorian town of Kosheng (Marco Polo's Tenduc) north of China, the monks known as Rabban Sauma and Markos (who later became the Nestorian patriarch

Mar Yaballaha) traveled to the West, with Rabban Sauma going on to Italy and France. They were preceded on the westward road by a Taoist monk named Ch'ang Ch'un, whom Chinggis Khan had summoned while on campaign in what is now Afghanistan.[9]

In more worldly matters Chinggis was aided by information gained from merchants whom he enlisted to accompany him. This meant especially Muslims, since by that time Silk Road commerce was largely dominated by them.[10] As the Mongol victories expanded the territories under their control, they required both advisors and administrators experienced in matters of rule. For this they engaged the services of individuals native to or familiar with the cultures of the conquered regions. Often, especially in Central and western Asia, this meant relying on Muslims, but Christians, Buddhists, and others were not excluded from positions of influence. Muslim merchants, valued for their financial acumen, were appointed as fiscal advisors and tax collectors[11] (although this led to their being stereotyped by the subject populations as greedy and corrupt). Finally, during their bloody campaigns the Mongols made a point of sparing craftsmen and other talented people of whatever race or religion and sending them off to work in Mongolia or wherever their services were needed.

Another aspect of the Mongols' attitude toward religions is that they tended to perceive them as being identified with a particular community.[12] The Mongols recognized the need to earn legitimacy in the eyes of their subjects, and Chinggis Khan "cultivated the religious leaders of the conquered areas, believing that good relations with the clergy would translate into good relations with the people whom they led."[13] In particular, he issued an edict which exempted Christian, Muslim, and Buddhist priests and scholars from taxation.[14] In general, Mongol attitudes were based on practical considerations, which helps to explain the eventual conversion of the western Mongols to Islam and those of the East to Buddhism.

Steppe Christianity

The European Christians cannot be faulted too severely for what appears in hindsight to have been an unrealistic assessment of the Mongols' attachment to Christianity. It is true that overall perhaps only a small percentage of the steppe population professed Christianity, and even their knowledge of the tradition may have been fairly superficial. Still, of the world religions, initially Christianity seems to have been the best represented within steppe society.

Not long after the Christianization of the Kerait and Öngöt tribes in the eleventh century, Christian names appear within the central Mongolian Merkits and even farther east among the Tatars.[15] As a result of such conversions, whatever their depth or meaning in terms of the religious life of the steppe, we have a definite Christian presence in Inner Asia by Chinggis Khan's time, reflected in the loyalties of Küchlük the Naiman and several members of the Chinggisid royal family. Sorgh-aghtani Begi, the mother of two future Great Khans, Möngke and Khubilai, as well as of Hülegü, the founder of the Il-khan dynasty of Iran, was a Nestorian Christian, although she patronized other religions as well.[16] Rumors of this Christian presence at the Mongol court, together with several forged "letters from Prester John" circulating in the Medi-terranean world at the time, fed European hopes of gaining a powerful ally in their struggle against their Muslim neighbors.[17]

Favor to Muslims

Like the Christians, the Muslims writers often tried to portray the early Mongol conquerors as supporters and therefore potential converts to their religion. Unlike the Christian sources, however, the major Muslim accounts of the period were written under Mongol patronage and therefore demonstrate a clear tendency toward revisionism. The Persian historian Rashid al-Din, writing as an official of the later Mongol Il-khan dynasty in Iran, portrays Chinggis' successor Ögödei as a defender of the expatriate Muslim community in China from the bigotry of locals by having him say:

> The poorest Tazik Muslim has several Khitayan slaves standing before
> him, while not one of the great amirs of Khitai has a single Muslim
> captive. And the reason for this can only be the wisdom of God, who

knows the rank and station of all the peoples of the world; it is also in conformity with the auspicious *yasa* of Chinghiz-Khan, for he made the blood-money for a Muslim 40 *balish* and that for a Khitayan a donkey. In view of such clear proofs and testimonies how can you make a laughing stock of the people of Islam?[18]

It may be noted that a defensive tone seems to underlie this passage— apparently the Chinese *were* "making a laughing stock of the people of Islam."

Rashid al-Din likewise has Ögödei rescue a Muslim who, unable to repay a loan from an Uighur, had been told to embrace idolatry (presumably Buddhism) or be publicly humiliated and beaten; the *khan* is said to have given over the Uighur's house and wife to the Muslim and ordered the Uighur to be beaten instead.[19] Juzjani, writing in India in the late thirteenth century, cites another example of Buddhist intrigue against the Muslims: At the instigation of Chaghatai Khan (who was known for his antipathy toward Muslims), one of the Buddhist priests claimed to have heard from Chinggis Khan in a dream that the Muslims would bring about the end of Mongol rule and that to prevent this they should all be killed. Ögödei, according to Juzjani, "perceived that this statement was false . . . and that it appeared to have been hatched by his brother, Chaghatai," and had the priest executed.[20]

Rashid al-Din states that the Mongols credited Muslims with "great sexual powers,"[21] and later claims of Möngke Khan that "of all the peoples and religious communities he showed most honor and respect to the Muslims and bestowed the largest amount of gifts and alms upon them."[22]

Thus, while Christian and Muslim accounts each made certain claims of Mongol sympathy, the reasoning was different. The Christian accounts were wishful thinking and propaganda aimed at a remote Christian audience; Muslim accounts such as those of Juvaini and Rashid al-Din were written to satisfy and flatter their Mongol patrons. On the other hand, the Central Asian Muslim exile Juzjani, writing from India, and post-Mongol writers such as the early-sixteenth-century historian Khwand Amir are more circumspect.

EARLY EUROPEAN
EMBASSIES TO THE MONGOL COURT

By 1238 news of Mongol devastations in the Ukraine and Russia was beginning to reach Europe. The Mongol invasions of Poland in 1240 and Hungary in 1241 made it disappointingly clear to Europeans that the hordes from the East were not aiming exclusively at the conquest of Muslim-held lands. A full-scale Mongol attack on Europe was avoided fortuitously, however, by the Great Khan Ögödei's death, which necessitated the recall of all the royal generals to Mongolia in order to choose a successor.

Encouraged by this reprieve, and no doubt misunderstanding its nature, Pope Innocent IV sent an embassy led by the Franciscan monk John of Plano Carpini to the Mongol court in 1245. This mission, which called upon the Mongols to be baptized and submit to the Pope's authority, was also intended as a means for gathering intelligence regarding possible future Mongol plans to invade Europe. Thus John and subsequent ambassadors represented what Sinologist and explorer Owen Lattimore has wryly termed "the C.I.A., or Christian Intelligence Agency of its time."[23]

John's account of his sojourn at the Mongol court, during which he was privileged to witness the coronation of Güyük as Great Khan in 1246, bears witness to the sectarian intrigues already taking place there. Güyük appears to have looked favorably on Christianity. According to Rashid al-Din, he had had a Christian attendant, Qadaq, since childhood, and

> To this was afterward added the influence of [his secretary] Chinqai. He therefore always went to great lengths in honoring priests and Christians, and when this was noised abroad, priests set their faces toward his court from the lands of Syria and Rum [Byzantium] and the As [Ossetia] and the Oros [Russia]. And because of the attendance of Qadaq and Chinqai he was prone to denounce the faith of Islam, and the cause of the Christians flourished during his reign, and no Muslim dared to raise his voice to them.[24]

At his accession Güyük quickly did away with several Muslims who had become very powerful during the regency of his mother Töregene, including her financial advisor, ʿAbd al-Rahman, and her confidante, a Persian woman by the name of Fatima.[25] Conversely he reinstated Ögödei's former chief secretary, the Nestorian Chinqai mentioned earlier, whom Töregene had forced out.[26]

Chinqai oversaw the rendering into Latin of Güyük's reply to Pope Innocent and probably was responsible for the passage in which the Mongol emperor rebukes the pontiff for his "arrogance" in claiming Catholicism to be the only true form of Christianity.[27] While Güyük's "cabinet reshuffling" may have been more politically than religiously motivated from his own point of view, it must have appeared otherwise to representatives of the competing religious sects.

Juzjani claims that Buddhist priests were constantly inciting Güyük to persecute Muslims. One well-known Buddhist advisor is said to have told the Great Khan, "If thou desirest that the sovereignty and throne of the Mughals should remain unto thee, of two thing do one: either massacre the whole of the Musalmans, or put a stop to their generating and propagating." Güyük then issued an order for all Muslim men under his rule to be castrated; this disaster was averted only by a "miracle" in which one of the Buddhist conspirators had his genitals ripped off by the khan's dog, which was taken as a sign to leave the Muslims alone.[28] Elsewhere, however, Juzjani confirms Güyük's partiality to Christians.[29]

One of the earliest and most cynical examples of the Mongols courting Christian hopes for political ends is seen in a letter sent in 1248 to King Louis, then in Cyprus about to launch the Seventh Crusade, by a Mongol official named Eljigidei in Tabriz. In this letter, Eljigidei "prays God for the success of the Christian forces against the enemies of the Cross." He claims to have been sent by Güyük to protect the Christians and rebuild their churches and affirms that "Latins, Greeks, Armenians, Nestorians, Jacobites and all worshippers of the Cross are one in the eyes of God and the Mongol emperor."[30]

Actually Eljigidei, recently appointed commander of the western Mongol forces, was planning an attack on Baghdad and hoped to entice Louis to carry out a diversionary invasion of Egypt. Furthermore, the

two Persian Nestorians who brought the letter told the French king that
Güyük was Prester John's grandson and that both he and Eljigidei had
embraced Christianity and wished to help the Crusaders recapture
Jerusalem.[31] Louis' response, carried by the Dominican monk Andrew
of Longjumeau, eventually reached the Mongol court in 1250 some time
after Güyük's death, and the Empress Dowager Oghul Qaimish sent a
reply which simply demanded annual tribute, echoing nothing of
Eljigidei's promises.[32]

The report which Andrew brought back included mention of
German slaves languishing in Central Asia. This notice sparked the
imagination of a Franciscan friar named of William of Rubruck, who
was attached to King Louis' court at the time. Word was also circulating
that Chinggis Khan's great-grandson Sartaq, head of the Juchid Golden
Horde which ruled Russia, was a Christian. William resolved to travel
via Sartaq's court to Inner Asia and preach Christianity to the Mongols,
and if possible minister to Christians living there.[33]

William's trip was a mixed success. He never found the German
slaves, and Möngke Khan, Güyük's successor, did not allow him to stay
on permanently in Mongolia to carry out his intended missionary effort.
Furthermore, William's interpreter was an uncooperative drunkard who
frustrated what opportunities the friar might have had to spread his view
of the Gospel. On the other hand, William's account of his journey,
which lasted from 1253 to 1255, is one of the most detailed and
informative travelogues of its time.

Among other things, William is the first medieval European to
encounter and describe Buddhism. His first impression was that Buddhists were simply wayward Christians:

> In the town of Cailac [Qayaliq, in present-day Kazakhstan] they
> possessed three idol temples, two of which I entered in order to see
> their stupid practices. In the first one, I encountered a man who had
> on his hand a little cross in black ink, which led me to believe he was
> a Christian, since he answered like a Christian all the questions I put
> to him. So I asked him: "And why do you not have here a cross and
> an effigy of Jesus Christ?" "It is not our custom," he replied. From this

I concluded that they were Christians, and that the omission was due to faulty doctrine.[34]

William was frustrated in his attempt to learn more about this strange sect from the local Muslims, who refused to talk about them. Subsequently whenever he asked any Muslims about the Buddhists' religion, "they were scandalized."[35]

According to Rubruck, in China the Nestorians and Muslims lived with alien status. His impression of his fellow Christians in the East was not positive:

> The Nestorians there are ignorant. They recite their office and have the Holy Scriptures in Syriac, a language they do not know, so that they chant like the monks among us who know no grammar; and for this reason they are completely corrupt. Above all they are usurers and drunkards, and some of them, furthermore, who live among the Tartars, have several wives just as the Tartars have. On entering the church they wash their lower members, in the Saracen manner [i.e., the Muslim *wudhu,* or "lesser ablution"]; they eat meat on Friday and follow the Saracens in having their feasts on that day. . . . The result is that when any of them rear the sons of aristocratic Mo'als [i.e., Mongols], even though they instruct them in the Gospels and the Faith, nevertheless by their immorality and their greed they rather alienate them from the Christian religion.[36]

William also states that the Nestorians would not allow members of other Christian sects, such as the many Hungarian, Alan, Russian, Georgian, and Armenian slaves, into their churches unless they would be rebaptized as Nestorians.[37] In addition, they practiced divination and even resorted to the services of Muslim diviners.[38] The Nestorians shunned the symbol of the cross, and when the captive French craftsman Guillaume Boucher fashioned one as a gift for the chief of police, Bulghai, Nestorian priests stole it and the object was never found.[39]

During his stay at Möngke's court William was hosted by an Armenian monk named Sargis (Sergius), who was constantly at odds with the Muslims at court. Once during a court ceremony Möngke's younger brother Arigh Böke indicated a pair of Muslims and asked Sargis whether he knew them. "I know that they are dogs," he answered. In response the Muslims said, "Why do you insult us when we do not insult you?" The ensuing argument was broken up by Arigh Böke, but the next day Sargis started a brawl with some Muslims in the street. As a result of this the troublemaker was ordered to move his tent away from the center of the encampment and William, as his guest, had to go with him.[40]

William had earlier been exposed to the anti-Muslim intrigues of Armenians while en route, when he discovered that Armenian translators had taken liberties in transforming his letter of introduction from King Louis into a call for a joint war against the Muslims.[41] Likewise he discovered that Sargis "had told Mangu Chan that if he were prepared to become a Christian the whole world would enter into subjection to him, and that the Franks and the Great Pope would obey him. . . ."[42]

One factor demonstrating Möngke's respect for Christianity was his appointment of Bulghai, a Nestorian Christian, as his chief secretary.[43] However, soon after his accession, his predecessor's Christian minister, Chinqai, was accused of conspiracy and handed over to the Muslim courtier Danishmand Hajib for execution; likewise, a Buddhist plot in the town of Beshbaliq which aimed to massacre the Muslim population during their Friday prayer was discovered by Möngke, who ordered the local Uighur governor publicly executed instead.[44]

It is clear that in typical Mongol fashion, Möngke's policy was to support each religion equally in view of what powers they might provide.[45] William mentions that on feast days, the clergy of each religion in turn come before the *khan* to pray for him and bless his cup. In William's somewhat cynical view, the *khan* "believes in none of them . . . and yet they [the clerics] all follow his court as flies do honey, and he makes them all gifts and all of them believe they are on intimate terms with him. . . ."[46]

Nowhere is the failure of the Christian, Muslim, and Buddhist leaders to understand the Mongol attitude toward religion clearer than in the preceding passage; William alone seems to have assessed the situation with any accuracy. Later he tried to explain to the Mongols that his purpose in coming to Möngke was not for any diplomatic reason but simply "to utter the words of God, if he were willing to hear them." The reaction of the Mongols was that "They seized on this and asked what were the words of God that I wanted to say, thinking that I intended to foretell some success for him as many others do."[47]

Möngke, like Güyük before him, enjoyed setting the competing clerics against each other in formal debates.[48] As a prelude to holding such a debate between William and others at court, Möngke declared, "Here you are, Christians, Saracens, and *tuins* [Buddhist priests], and each of you claims that his religion is superior and that his writings or books contain more truth."[49] The only account we have of the ensuing debate is William's, in which he portrays himself as putting the Buddhists, Muslims, and Nestorians to shame. "But for all that," he admits, "no one said, 'I believe, and wish to become a Christian.'"[50]

In William's final interview with the *khan*, Möngke explains to him that "We Mo'als believe that there is only one God, through whom we have life and through whom we die, and towards him we direct our hearts. . . . But just as God has given the hand several fingers, so he has given mankind several paths. To you God has given the Scriptures and you Christians do not observe them." Möngke then criticizes the Christians for their divisiveness and greed, although tactfully explaining that he is not referring to William.[51]

In 1258 Möngke convened a debate similar to the one in which William had participated, but this time limited to Taoists and Buddhists, whose rivalry in China went back to the T'ang period. The *khan* appointed his younger brother Khubilai to preside, and following the debate Möngke expressed his preference for Buddhism, saying that it was like the palm of the hand and the other religions like fingers.[52]

Meanwhile back in the West, Mongol ambitions were leading to the revived possibility of a Christian-Mongol alliance against the Muslims. The presence of Christians close to the Mongol ruler of Iran, Hülegü, including his wife, Doquz Khatun, and his general Kitbuqa, lent weight to these renewed hopes. In 1254 Hethum, the king of Armenia, agreed to provide troops for the Mongol army in return for protection of Anatolia's Christian communities and, once again, the promise that Jerusalem would revert to the Christians. Following the Mongol conquest of Baghdad in 1258, during which Muslims were slaughtered while Christians were spared, Hülegü gave over the royal palace to the Nestorian Catholicus Mar Makikha and had a new cathedral built for him.[53]

Kitbuqa's conquest of Aleppo and Damascus in early 1260 made it appear that Jerusalem would soon be in Mongol hands. This hope was quashed, however, by the Mongols' unexpected defeat by Mamluk forces from Egypt at 'Ain Jalut later in the year. The Mamluk victory ended Mongol expansion to the southwest and may have caused at least some of the Mongols to begin to doubt the power of Christianity and to wonder if Islam might be the more powerful religion. The stability of Mamluk power was further ensured by an alliance with the Mongol Golden Horde under Juchi's son Berke, who had either converted to Islam or perhaps been raised as a Muslim and was hostile to Hülegü.[54]

Juzjani relates an interesting anecdote to illustrate Berke's defense of Islam. A young Christian of Samarqand had converted to Islam; failing to persuade the youth to renounce Islam and return to Christianity, an unnamed visiting Mongol official, "the inclinations of which accursed one were towards the Christian faith," executed him. On hearing of this, Berke sanctioned the slaughter of Samarqand's Christians while they were assembled in church.[55] Juzjani also claims that Sartaq died as a result of Berke's praying for his death.[56]

Berke's conversion did not lead to the complete Islamization of the Golden Horde at that point, however. Christian missionaries—mainly Latin but also Russian Orthodox—continued to compete for influence there well into the fourteenth century. Their major rivals appear to have been individual Sufi shaykhs. Sometime around 1320 a Dominican missionary by the name of William Adam wrote a treatise calling for increased missionary activity in the Volga region in order to meet the challenge of growing Muslim influence there. William attributes the conversion of the Juchid ruler Özbek Khan, whom Central Asian Muslims credit with Islamizing the Golden Horde, to the activity of Sufi *faqir*s sent by the Mamluk sultan. He also claims that because of the Sufis, the ruler of the Golden Horde "has lately, along with many other

Tartars, become a most evil Saracen, an enemy and persecutor of Christians."[57]

Mongol rule reached its greatest sophistication under Khubilai Khan, who became Great Khan following Möngke's death in 1259. Khubilai's initial attitude toward the great religious traditions was a typical Mongol openness to anything that could be of use. Marco Polo quotes him as saying: "There are four prophets who are worshipped and to whom all the world does reverence. The Christians say their God was Jesus Christ; the Saracens Mahomet; the Jews Moses; and the idolaters Sakyamuni Burkhan, who was the first to be represented as God in the form of an idol; and I do honour and reverence to all four, so that I may be sure of doing it to him who is greatest in heaven and truest, and to him I pray for aid."[58]

Likewise the Muslim historian Khwand Amir states that: "Khubilai Khan used to tend to administrative affairs from sunup until midmorning, and then he used to gather the *ulema* [religious scholars] of Islam, the learned of the Jews, Christian monks, and the wise men of China and hold deliberations, for he enjoyed listening to philosophical and religious debates. During his reign he ordered the Qur'an, the Torah, the Gospel, and Sakyamuni's book translated into Mongolian."[59]

Khubilai took pains to avoid religious rivalries at court. Rashid al-Din states that the Great Divan included four ministers (Pers. *finjan*, Ch. *P'ing-chang*) "from amongst the great amirs of the various peoples, Taziks, Khitayans, Uighurs, and Christians."[60] Further, according to Khwand Amir "It was Khubilai Khan's practice to appoint to the post of vizier four men who were of the same religion in order that disputes and disagreements on religion would not arise and so that the ministry's funds would be safe from embezzlement."[61]

This policy does not seem to have been particularly effective, however, as the following case illustrates. Rashid al-Din records that at one point Khubilai appointed a presumably Buddhist Uighur by the name of Sanga, who was hostile to Muslims, to a ministerial position. After a Muslim at court accused Sanga of lying to the Khan about his wealth, Khubilai had the Uighur executed.[62]

Tibetan Buddhists, meanwhile, maintained their rivalry with native Chinese Taoists, and eventually used their influence (through the monk

'Phags-pa) to persuade Khubilai to suppress the latter and destroy their books in 1281; the only Taoist text to survive this purge was the *Tao Te Ching*.[63] A notable aspect of Khubilai's administrative policy was his distrust of the native Chinese in his service. Although he had shifted his court to China and built a new capital, Khanbaliq (present-day Beijing), several early betrayals by Chinese advisors led him to turn increasingly to foreigners, particularly Muslims.[64] Since the foreigners had no support base in China apart from their Mongol patrons, Khubilai saw them as being more reliable.[65] Likewise, perhaps, Khubilai's suppression of Taoists and Confucians was "intended to deprive of their spiritual support the Chinese who were subject to the Mongol dynasty."[66]

The most well-known Muslim figure at Khubilai's court was his infamous finance minister, Ahmad, whose twenty-year campaign of extortion earned him the hatred of Khubilai's Chinese subjects and foreigners alike. His relations with the Great Khan's Buddhist and Confucian officials were particularly bitter. The Chinese advisors would accuse Ahmad of profiteering, and he would respond by charging them with embezzlement. Eventually Ahmad's Chinese opponents were dismissed or executed at his instigation, died of natural causes, or resigned their posts in disgust, with the result that by 1280 Ahmad's power was almost unchallenged.[67] Two years later, however, he was assassinated by a Chinese general named Ch'ien-hu. Khubilai put to death many Chinese whom he suspected of having a part in this conspiracy, but when Ahmad's house was searched and it was discovered how much treasure he had accumulated, the *khan* had his body exhumed and flung to the dogs, in Marco Polo's account, or wagons driven over it, according to Rashid al-Din.[68]

Following Ahmad's posthumous disgrace Khubilai took a more restrictive attitude toward his subject Muslim population, by, for example, reinstating the ban on *halal* slaughter.[69] Rashid al-Din asserts that the anti-Muslim policies, which also banned circumcision, were implemented at the instigation of a Christian official by the name of 'Isa Tarsah Kelemechi (Ch. Ai-hsüeh), whom Rashid further accuses of inciting slaves of Muslims to denounce their masters. As a result, he claims, "most Muslims left the country of Khitai."[70]

'Isa Kelemechi appears to have nearly sealed the Muslims' fate for good by pointing out to Khubilai the Qur'anic verse which commands, "Kill the polytheists, all of them!"[71] The *khan* then somewhat sarcastically asked the Muslims at his court why they didn't carry out this directive and kill their Mongol overlords. None of the Muslims could reply, until one finally volunteered, "Thou art not a polytheist since thou writest the name of the Great God at the head of thy *yarlighs* [edicts]."[72] This response saved the Muslims for the time being, but the restrictions against them remained in place for several more years. During that time revenues from Muslim trade declined severely, so that in 1287 Khubilai lifted the ban on *halal* slaughter.[73]

This was the same year that, in the West, the Il-khan ruler Arghun sent his second embassy to the Vatican, this time led by the Nestorian Turk Rabban Sauma. In his letter to the Pope, Arghun repeats an earlier request for European assistance in attacking the Levant and Egypt, and states that if he succeeds in capturing Jerusalem, he will become a Christian.[74]

INTRIGUE AND
MAYHEM IN THE IL-KHAN LANDS

Arghun was the son of Abaqa, who is presented in Christian sources as a patron of Christianity.[75] In 1281 Abaqa gave his blessing to the ordination of Yaballaha III, whom the Nestorians had elected as catholicus. An Öngöt Turk from China who had traveled to the West with Rabban Sauma in hopes of making a pilgrimage to Jerusalem, Mar Yaballaha had been chosen by the Nestorians to head their church because of his cultural affinities with the new Mongol rulers. The following year Abaqa is said to have attended Easter mass in Baghdad.[76] Shortly thereafter, however, Abaqa died and was succeeded by his brother Tägüdar, who had converted to Islam and taken the name Sultan Ahmad. One of the new ruler's first acts was to dismiss the Christian and Jewish astrologers and physicians at the Il-khan court. In addition, "Idol temples, churches and synagogues were destroyed, and in their place rose mosques."[77]

A pair of high-ranking Syrian clergy, who were jealous of the foreigner Mar Yaballaha's appointment as catholicus and Rabban Sauma's as visitor general, passed to Sultan Ahmad the accusation that the two Turks favored the succession of another of Abaqa's sons, Arghun. The evidence condemning Mar Yaballaha and Rabban Sauma was found to be inadequate, but their position was clearly precarious until Arghun's victory over Sultan Ahmad in 1284. When Arghun heard of the conspiracy of the two Syrians he ordered their executions; they were saved, however, through the intervention of Mar Yaballaha, who asked only that they be stripped of their ranks.[78]

During Arghun's reign a Jewish physician by the name of Sa'ad al-dawla rose to the position of chief tax collector and later prime minister. According to Muslim sources, "Sa'ad al-dawla gave the governorships of most of Arghun Khan's realm to his relatives." The same sources state that "in all fairness, it must be said that during the time of Sa'ad al-dawla's vizierate all of the realm flourished, and none of Arghun Khan's amirs or retinue was able to transgress the rights of the subjects and peasants in any way."[79]

Sa'ad al-dawla appears to have nominally converted to Islam, although he is said to have urged the *khan* to claim prophethood and found a new religion "that would wipe out all traces of former religions." As a result of this advice, Arghun barred Muslims from the court and at Sa'ad al-dawla's suggestion decided "that the Kaaba should be turned into an idol temple and that the Muslims and all others should be made to worship images instead of God." Finally, while Arghun had fallen ill, a group of courtiers captured Sa'ad al-dawla and executed him, and "the friends of Islam were given a new lease on life."[80]

In 1291 Arghun died and was succeeded by his younger brother Kaikatu, who in typical Mongol fashion "confirmed all the religious sectaries each in his status and honored all the chief dogmas, whether of Christians or Arabs or Jews or Pagans, and showed partiality to none."[81] He did, however, bestow gifts upon the Nestorian Catholicus, to the order of 20,000 dinars. He also commissioned the construction of a new cathedral at the Il-khan capital of Maragha, which he visited twice during the following year. Finally, Kaikhatu commissioned the building of a new monastery north of the capital; in short, "anything that the Mar

Catholicus opened his mouth about and desired he did not refuse."[82] The effects of this apparent favoritism on relations with the Muslims of the realm would soon manifest themselves.

In 1295 Kaikhatu was overthrown and put to death by his nobles. A cousin, Baidu, seized power, but his accession was challenged by Ghazan, Kaikhatu's brother. Ghazan had been baptized and raised a Christian. His chief general, however, a man by the name of Amir Nawruz, was a Muslim,[83] and offered the support of a Muslim army if Ghazan would promise to embrace Islam in the event of his victory over Baidu. This was soon accomplished, and Ghazan accordingly converted.

The Muslim accounts of this event make it clear that part of the religious struggle in the Il-khan territories was between Mongols who had converted to Islam and those that had not: "Also accepting to obey Islamic law, [Ghazan] abandoned polytheism and the despicable nation of the Turks. That very day nearly a hundred thousand obstinate polytheists became believing monotheists and were delivered from the darkness of infidelity and idolatry."[84]

Within a few months, however: "a group of princes and noyans . . . who had been opposed to the adoption of Islam, conspired to do away with Ghazan Khan and Amir Nawroz by any means possible and then turn Muslim mosques into churches and temples."[85]

In the East, meanwhile, Khubilai's successor, Temür Khan, had appointed a cousin, Ananda (who must have been a Buddhist), to govern the Tungut Province. The urban population there had become largely Chinese Muslim, while the countryside remained pagan. Ananda converted to Islam as a result of falling in love with a Muslim woman and coerced most of his 150,000 soldiers into converting as well. This caused some friction with Temür Khan, who tried to force him to renounce Islam, but when Ananda heard of Ghazan's conversion in Iran "and that all the Mongols in Persia had become Muslims, breaking all the idols and destroying idol-temples" (presumably, mainly churches) he took heart and "in imitation of him [Ghazan], strove to strengthen the faith of Islam"[86]—one imagines, by equally forceful means.

It is against this backdrop of tension among the Mongols themselves that we should see the persecutions of Nestorians in the West described in Christian sources. According to Mar Yaballaha's history, it was Nawruz who issued the following edict: "The Churches shall be uprooted, and the altars overturned, and the celebrations of the Eucharist shall cease, and the hymns of praise, and the sounds of calls to prayer shall be abolished; and the heads [chiefs?] of the Christians, and the heads of the congregations [i.e., synagogues] of the Jews, and the great men among them shall be killed."

Immediately the Muslims broke into and looted the Maragha cathedral and took the priests hostage. Some they tied up naked; Mar Yaballaha himself was hung upside down and beaten while his captors urged him to renounce his faith in favor of Islam. In the end he was ransomed by local Christians for 5,000 dinars. King Hethum of Armenia finally intervened with his private armed retinue to stop the looting of Maragha's churches and bought off the Muslim mob.[87] Nawruz continued to harass Mar Yaballaha, however, and sent orders that the Catholicus return the cash gifts Kaikhatu had bestowed upon him.[88] In addition, Nawruz ordered the destruction of the churches of Tabriz and Hamadan. Those of Mosul and Baghdad ransomed themselves, while the caliphal palace given to the Patriarch by Hülegü was taken back by the Muslims, who also converted the Nestorian cathedral into a mosque and had the bones of the Patriarchs Mar Makikha and Mar Denha exhumed and taken away.[89]

When Ghazan heard of the tribulations being inflicted upon the Christians, he issued an edict exempting them from the *jizya,* and stated further that "none of them shall abandon his faith, that the Catholicus shall live in the state to which he hath been accustomed, that he shall be treated with the respect due his rank, that he shall rule over his throne, and shall hold the staff of strength over his dominion." In addition, the new *khan* sent Mar Yaballaha 5,000 dinars by way of reparation.[90] Yet not surprisingly, "in proportion as the king [Ghazan], little [by little], was increasing the honour which he paid to the Catholicus, the hatred which was in the hearts of the enemies [of the Catholicus] increased, and they forged evil plots, and they sent information about everything which took place to . . . Nawruz."[91]

The following year "a certain man, who was called by the name of Shenâkh êl-Tâmûr, came into Maraghah, and he cast about a report that he had with him an Edict ordering that every one who did not abandon Christianity and deny his faith be killed."[92] This news, though false, inspired the Muslims to indulge in a fresh round of looting at the cathedral. Among the items they carried off were a gold seal given the Patriarch by Möngke Khan and a silver one from Arghun.

An attempt by local officials to bring the perpetrators to justice sparked off a general uprising, during which the cathedral was severely damaged and many of the monks killed. Mar Yaballaha himself escaped with some companions and took refuge in the house of one of Ghazan's Christian wives, a woman by the name of Burgesin Argi.[93] When Ghazan, who was traveling at the time, heard of the incident, he ordered the Muslims of Maragha rounded up and tortured until they returned what they had looted, but they returned only "a very small part of what they had stolen, and the rest remained with them."[94]

Some time later in Arbil, local Kurds began circulating a story that some of Ghazan's Christian soldiers had attacked them and killed one of their elders. According to Yaballaha's history, "fighting and hatred followed, and revolt increased, and evil grew, and fury and bitter hatred flourished in both parties, namely, in both Christians and the Arabs [i.e., the Muslims]. And they laid ambushes each party for the other, and they fought pitched battles."[95] During this time Ghazan was occupied in putting down a rebellion which Nawruz had launched in Khurasan. The Christians of Arbil, meanwhile, had fled to the citadel where they were besieged by Muslims, who greatly outnumbered them. Ghazan's Muslim advisors characterized the situation as a Christian revolt. In response to this Mar Yaballaha came to court to present the case of the besieged Christians. The *khan* ordered a reconciliation between the Christians and Muslims of Arbil, which cost the Christians 20,000 dinars in indemnities. They were, however, allowed to keep control of the citadel.[96]

LATER PAPAL MISSIONS

The first genuine successes of the Latin church in the Mongol east were due to the efforts of John of Montecorvino, a Franciscan monk sent to the Mongol court at Khanbaliq in 1290. Over the next four decades, until his death in 1328, John tirelessly propagated Catholicism among the various Christians of the realm, who were by then quite numerous. In addition to the local Turkic and Mongol Nestorian communities, large numbers of Armenians, Slavs, Greeks, and other Christians had been brought forcibly from Europe and the eastern Mediterranean following the Mongol victories earlier in the century.

John's first great coup was to win over the Nestorian Öngöt ruler Körgüz Küregen ("Prince George") for the Pope, and his subjects along with him, although following George's death the local Nestorian priests turned the people back to their original faith. John also had great influence with the Caucasian Alans who followed the Greek Orthodox rite and with the Armenians whose language he had learned during a previous mission in their country. In 1307 news of John's efforts in China reached the Pope, who responded by making him the first archbishop of Khanbaliq and Patriarch of the Orient.

John's efforts were constantly hampered by the Nestorian priests, however, who quite naturally saw him as a competitor trying to muscle in on their turf. Eventually they went so far as to accuse him of being an impostor and nearly succeeded in bringing about his ruin, as he describes in the following passage from the second of three letters he hoped would reach the Pope:

> . . . the Nestorians, who call themselves Christians, but behave in a
> very unchristian manner, have grown so strong in these parts that they
> did not allow any Christian of another rite to have any place of
> worship, however small, nor preach any doctrine but their own. For
> these lands have never been reached by any apostle or disciple of the
> apostles and so the aforesaid Nestorians both directly and by the
> bribery of others have brought most grievous persecutions upon me,
> declaring that I was not sent by the Lord Pope, but that I was a spy, a
> magician and a deceiver of men. And after some time they produced
> more false witnesses, saying that another messenger had been sent with
> a great treasure to the Emperor and that I had murdered him in India
> and made away with his gifts. And this intrigue lasted about five years,
> so that I was often brought to judgement, and in danger of a shameful

death. But at last, by God's ordering, the Emperor came to know my innocence and the nature of my accusers, by the confession of some of them, and he sent them into exile with their wives and children.[97]

John's battle for the Catholic faith in Mongol China was a most lonely one, and he claims in his letter that if he had had only two or three other Catholic priests to buttress his position against the Nestorians, he might have succeeded in converting the *khan* himself.[98] Indeed, it appears that John lacked even the support of his fellow Italian Franciscan and theoretical subordinate, Andrew of Perugia, perhaps due to the rift between the Spirituals and the Community which existed within the order at that time.[99]

It is clear that the Mongol emperor continued to exercise a tolerance unknown among the clerics of various sects that operated within his realm. Andrew unwittingly sums up the difference when he says, "In this vast empire there are verily men of every nation under heaven and of every sect; and each and all are allowed to live according to their sect. For this is their opinion, or I should say their error, that every man is saved in his own sect."[100]

Likewise Peregrine, whom the Pope had sent together with Andrew in order to consecrate John as archbishop, reports that under the Mongols, the Catholic monks were allowed to preach to the Buddhists and even in Muslim mosques,[101] although Andrew admits that "of the Jews and the Saracens none is converted" and that "of the idolators [Buddhists] exceedingly many are baptized, but when they are baptized they do not adhere strictly to Christian ways."[102] Nevertheless, it has been estimated that John may have made as many as 10,000 converts to Catholicism during his years in China, mainly of individuals from various Christian sects.[103]

In 1336 the Alans of Khanbaliq wrote the Pope requesting he send a successor to replace John, who had been dead for eight years. It has been suggested that the Alans needed someone who could stand up to the Nestorian clergy as John had done.[104] Although the Pope's appointee never reached China, a papal embassy led by John of Marignolli did, traveling via the Central Asian Silk Road. Along the way they witnessed the effects Muslim persecutions were having on Central Asia's Christian communities following the Islamization of the western Mongols.

At Almaliq they found that the local Chaghatayid ruler, a convert to Islam named Ali Sultan, had wiped out the Franciscan mission there during the previous year.[105] Marignolli and his entourage proceeded to Khanbaliq, where they stayed for three years. During this time he claims to have held "many glorious disputations with the Jews and other sects."[106] It seems the Jews, like the Nestorians and the Muslims, found the sculptures and paintings of the Catholics' saints to be particularly offensive and verging on idol worship.

Choosing the sea route for his return journey to Europe, Marignolli stopped in the port city of Zaytun long enough to commission the casting of two church bells, which as a parting insult he had placed within the Muslim quarter. Upon his arrival at Avignon in 1353 Marignolli conveyed a letter from the Great Khan which requested that the Pope send more Franciscans to China. This was at a time when the plague had begun to sweep Europe, however, and no further Catholic missions were sent to East Asia until the sixteenth century.

A MISCARRIED POLICY

Although individual Mongol rulers occasionally favored one or another of the religions of their domains, their general policy was to attempt to balance the various traditions so that each might serve them to the extent it could. This policy, by variously allowing representatives of each tradition to believe they were gaining the upper hand vis-à-vis their rivals and could act against them with impunity, led to an enormous amount of destruction and bloodshed. The situation was perhaps analogous to the Qur'anic observation in regard to the fair treatment of multiple wives: "Ye will not be able to deal equally between [your] wives, however much ye wish [to do so]"(Qur'an 4:129). In practice the Mongols could not hope to treat the adherents of diverse faiths equally, since any favor shown to one group tended to inflate their sense of importance while incensing the others.

In fact, the tolerance and favor shown by the Mongols to each of the major religions of their realm had the undesired effect of exacerbating existing tensions and rivalries between them, and the Christians, whose status within steppe society at the outset of Mongol rule exceeded that of Muslims and Buddhists, were the ultimate victims of this intensified rivalry. But while in hindsight it appears inevitable that the Mongols had eventually to embrace the faith of the majority in each sphere of their disintegrating empire—Buddhism in the East and Islam in the West—the sources of the time show how much was due to chance and individual personalities.[107] Khubilai Khan's advisor 'Phags-pa seems to have been singularly instrumental in winning support for the Tibetan form of Buddhism which otherwise might never have made such a mark in the Eastern realm of the empire. At least as late as the early fourteenth century, the direction of events in the West was every bit as uncertain.

CHAPTER SEVEN

A Melting Pot No More

By the time the Portuguese, Dutch, and English began their seaborne encounters with Asian civilization, the Silk Road's two-thousand-year-long role in transmitting cultural traditions was ending. A popular form of Islam, driven by Sufi orders such as the Yasaviyya and the Naqshbandiyya, was the dominant religious force throughout Central Asia, reaching even the last holdouts of steppe paganism among the Turkic nomads. By the sixteenth century the religious melting pot into which the Silk Road had continuously poured its various influences was no more.

THE END OF CHRISTIANITY
IN MEDIEVAL CENTRAL ASIA

Historians have tended to breeze over the question of exactly how and when Christianity was extinguished in Central Asia. Modern accounts, echoing the portrayal in Christopher Marlowe's sixteenth-century poem *Tamburlaine the Great,* often offer no more than a curt comment to the effect that Timur himself was the cause, waging holy war to extirpate all religious rivals. The well-known French historian René Grousset typifies the European stereotype in assessing that Timur "killed from piety. He represents a synthesis, probably unprecedented in history, of Mongol barbarity and Muslim fanaticism, and symbolizes the advanced form of primitive slaughter which is murder committed for the sake of abstract ideology, as a duty and a sacred mission."[1]

But although Timur's biographers do mention his victories over Christian rulers in the Caucasus, such as the "infidels" of Georgia, they make no reference to anti-Christian crusades by Timur in Central Asia.[2] Indeed, the Dominican Archbishop of Sultaniyya in Iran, John II, commented that Timur "does not harm Christians—especially Latins— and receives them well; merchants in particular are allowed to go about their business and worship as if they were in Christiandom."[3]

It is true that Timur's historians dubbed him a *ghazi*, a fighter for the faith, but the context of this title is either struggles with competing Muslim sects or with "heathens" such as uncooperative groups of steppe nomads who posed a serious obstacle to his empire-building activities.[4] Christianity, having lost its last Mongol patrons decades earlier, no longer posed any political threat and is not likely to have concerned Timur. On the other hand, for Timur, a political upstart from the recently converted Barlas tribe, orthodox Sunnism was a propaganda tool to be used against rivals whether Muslim or shamanistic.[5]

It may be that by Timur's time there were no Christians left in Central Asia. Nestorian tombstone inscriptions indicate that the communities of the "Seven Rivers" (southern Kazakhstan) were devastated by plague in 1338 and 1339.[6] At that same time the Chaghatayid ruler Jenkshi, who had allowed Roman Catholic missionaries to come from Europe and proselytize within his realm, was murdered as a result of family intrigues. He was succeeded by the convert 'Ali Sultan, who zealously encouraged Muslim pogroms in which all the Catholic missionaries were killed. Presumably local Nestorians were targeted as well, especially since many had enjoyed government positions under Jenkshi.[7]

One effect that Timur's policies did definitely have was to solidify the status of the Muslim elite classes, such as religious scholars and Sufi masters. Timur did this by granting them lands and tax-exempt financial bases through the administration of pious endowments, known as *waqfs*, which could be in the form of buildings—including not only mosques and religious schools but also bazaars—land, or utilities such as water for irrigation.

The trusteeships for these pious endowments could be stipulated to remain within families, guaranteeing their income and status over generations. Under Timur's successors several such families of religious leaders became the economic masters of numerous Silk Road towns, including Samarqand and Bukhara.

In China, after the end of Mongol rule in 1368, it appears that Christianity suffered from its association with the expelled dynasty. Christians of the Öngöt, Kerait, and other Turkish and Mongol tribes were cut off once and for all from the support of any power sympathetic to their tradition. It appears that, over time, the Christians of the steppes turned increasingly to Buddhist lamas for the fulfillment of their spiritual needs. Early in the twentieth century, European Catholic missionaries felt they detected echoes of a forgotten Christian tradition (baptism, confession, extreme unction) among some Mongol groups, such as the Erküts of the Ordos in Inner Mongolia.[8]

The "Failure" of Christianity Along the Silk Road

Christianity was a part of the religious culture of the Silk Road for over a millennium but in the end left strangely little mark. Apart from the remote and politically insignificant Öngöt kingdom north of China, there were no Nestorian-ruled lands to compare even with the brief effects of state sponsorship which Manichaeism enjoyed in the ninth century. By the late fourteenth century the tradition had vanished, leaving only the scantiest traces. Even in the west Asian and North African heartlands of Islam, substantial Christian communities have survived even to the present day, including Nestorians in northern Iraq and Iran. Why was their fate in Central Asia different?

This is a question which has preoccupied and often vexed Christian historians, by whom the history of Asian Christianity has almost exclusively been written. Their tone is one of tragedy, of promise unfulfilled. Many of their explanations focus on the "quality" of Asian

Christianity, which is seen as either simply heretical (from the viewpoint of Western Christians) or at best superficial. The Nestorians have been accused of accepting "converts without making sure that Christianity was a spiritual reality in their lives."[9] Nestorianism was more successful among the steppe peoples on the fringes of Silk Road civilization than it was in the urban centers, which has led to its characterization as a religion of "low civilization."[10]

These arguments are found already in the medieval accounts of William Rubruck and John of Montecorvino, which in many ways set the tone for Western perceptions of the Nestorians in the East. The Western Christians constantly accused the Nestorians of sectarian bias as well, as if the medieval Roman Catholics were somehow more open to ecumenical cooperation (and as the accounts of Rubruck and Montecorvino show, they weren't).

More recent, circumspect accounts have pointed out the complexity of Christian doctrine, which the steppe peoples do not appear ever to have fully mastered, and the alien nature of many Christian concepts in a Central Asian setting.[11] Buddhism, however, was neither less complex nor more inherently compatible with either the Central Asian or the Chinese mind-sets, at least initially; it had to be transformed. Christianity too was transformed in the East, yet it still failed to take hold.

One aspect which has not been emphasized is the lack of a powerful Nestorian body sponsoring trade. Even where Nestorianism was officially tolerated and protected, as in the Sasanian Empire, Nestorian merchants never enjoyed the kind of preferential advantages accorded by Buddhist or Muslim rulers along the Silk Road to members of their traditions. The only exception to this is under the rule of some of the Mongols, when policies favoring Nestorians backfired by provoking anti-Christian reaction from Muslims.

The major successes of Nestorian missionaries in converting Central Asians were among the steppe peoples, who were after all peripheral participants in the Silk Road commercial system. Given the dramatic change in lifestyle and values which the adoption of a new culturo-religious traditions often entails, perhaps we should marvel at the "success" of Christianity in Asia, which thrived for over a thousand years despite the factors just indicated, rather than bemoan its ultimate "failure."[12]

THE LAST MANICHAEAN COMMUNITY

Manichaeism, known in Chinese as the "Religion of Light" *(Ming chiao)*, survived in China by going underground following the persecutions of 841 to 846. Manichaeans met in secret and outwardly resembled Taoists or Buddhists. At that time a Manichaean teacher by the namer of Hulu (perhaps Turk. *Ulugh*, "great") traveled from the capital at Ch'ang-an to Fu-chou in the southeastern province of Fu-ch'ien, where he developed a following. Marco Polo encountered this Manichaean community during the course of his travels in the thirteenth century, although he mistook them for Christians.[13]

A Chinese tradition developed whereby Lao Tze, the putative founder of Taoism, traveled to the West and was transformed into a pomegranate; centuries later the fruit was eaten by an Iranian queen, who became pregnant by it and gave birth to the prophet Mani. According to this tradition, Mani united the teachings of Lao Tze and the Buddha.[14] This appropriation of Taoism enabled Chinese Manichaeans to represent their temples as Taoist and their religion as a school of Taoism, a strategy which proved useful in enabling Manichaeism to persist under the Sung rulers, who viewed the foreign religion with suspicion and outlawed Manichaean temples.[15] Even so Manichaeans often were vilified during the Sung period, referred to as "vegetarian demon-worshippers"—it was unfortunate that the initial character in the Chinese transcription of Mani's name, *mo*, means "demon."[16]

Like the Christians in pagan Rome, the sect was seen as a threat not because of its beliefs so much as because of its secretive nature.[17] This persecution was eased under the Mongols, who placed the Manichaeans under the jurisdiction of the Nestorian bishop.[18] The Ming dynasty, however, which expelled the Mongols during the fifteenth century, forced the Manichaeans of China underground once again.

Despite this renewed assault the religion survived in Fu-ch'ien as late as the seventeenth century,[19] and traces of it remain there today. A

Manichaean temple survives at Ts'ao-an, about fifteen miles south of the modern city of Ch'üan-chou, the great medieval port known to Westerners as Zaytun. The shrine contains a stone statue which appears at first glance to represent the Buddha; on closer inspection, however, numerous features indicate that it is the prophet Mani. An inscription in the courtyard, moreover, mentions "Mani, the Buddha of Light."[20] Eating vessels with Manichaean inscriptions have recently been unearthed nearby.[21] According to one report, "The Cao'an temple is still in use today. It is inhabited by pious old women who worship and take care of the Mani relief, considering [it] to be a picture of Buddha Sakyamuni."[22]

FURTHER ISLAMIZATION IN THE EAST

The army of Chinggis Khan was a confederation of Turkic and Mongol tribes that he succeeded briefly in bringing under his authority. After Chinggis' death the vast empire he had established slowly began its long process of disintegration. Throughout the subsequent years, decades, and centuries, these tribal groups would band together and disband again to meet the needs of the time and place, whether it be to defend themselves against intertribal raiding or to launch an attack on oasis states.[23]

Often individual aspirants to power would embrace Islam in an effort to consolidate their authority among merchants and other town-dwellers, but this procedure sometimes backfired, as many of the steppe nomads reacted to such conversions with hostility.[24] According the *Tarikh-i Rashidi,* during the mid-fifteenth century one such convert, the Chaghatayid Tughluq Temür, executed any of his entourage who refused to convert with him: "[Tughluq and his spiritual master] then decided that for the propagation of Islam, they should interview the princes one by one, and it should be well for those who accepted the faith, but those who refused should be slain as heathens and idolaters."[25] Later, after a frail sufi missionary miraculously defeated a well-known warrior in single combat, "The people raised loud shouts of applause, and on that day 160,000 persons cut off the hair of their heads and became Musulmans."[26]

In the last decade of the fourteenth century, Tughluq Temür's youngest son and eventual successor Khizr Khwaja "undertook a holy war *(ghazat)* against Khitai" (here, apparently meaning the Tarim region). He conquered the Silk Road towns of Qara Khoja and Turfan, "and forced their inhabitants to become Musulmans, so that at the present time it is called 'Dar al-Islam.'"[27]

Khizr Khwaja's son Muhammad Khan in turn continued the policy of pressuring his subjects to become Muslim. He is said to have pursued this policy so vigorously "that during his blessed reign most of the tribes of the Moghuls became Musulmans." These efforts apparently were met with some resistance, for "It is well known what severe measures he had recourse to, in bringing the Moghuls to be believers in Islam. If, for instance, a Moghul did not wear a turban, a horseshoe nail was driven into his head: and treatment of this kind was common."[28]

The groups known today as Kazakh and Kyrgyz, who have given their names to two present-day republics in Central Asia, were the last of these ever-reshuffling tribal alliances to be Islamicized. Another component group, the Mongol Qalmaqs, never were, but instead embraced Buddhism.

The designation "Kyrgyz" (by which name the modern Kazakhs are known prior to the twentieth century; the modern Kyrgyz were called "Qara-Qyrgyz") first appears in Muslim sources of the tenth century in reference to the conquerors of the town of Aq Su (Whitewater) in the Seven Rivers region of southern Kazakhstan.[29]

Chinese records state that Muslim caravans brought silk from Kucha to this tribe every three years. Most of the Kyrgyz-Kazakhs must have remained apart from this sedentarizing group, however, since Muslim sources refer to them as infidels as late as the mid-sixteenth century.[30] One such source calls the Kyrgyz "the originators of all the revolts in Moghulistan" and explains that "they were still infidels, and hence their hostility to Islam."[31]

Another Muslim, writing in 1582, offers the qualification that "they are neither infidels, nor Muslims."[32] A seventeenth-century writer says that the Kyrgyz worship idols and are not "true" Muslims.[33] By the latter statements we can understand that the people in question had accepted certain Islamic practices, symbols, and vocabularies while retaining or "Islamicizing" much of their traditional religious heritage. This is in fact the very blending of traditions that one finds among these peoples today.

The Islamic content absorbed by these steppe tribes during the centuries immediately before and after the Mongol period can be attributed largely to the work of Sufi missionaries, such as Ahmad Yasavi (1103-1167), Najm al-Din Kubra (d. 1221), and their followers, who were often perceived to have magical powers and, like Christians and others before them, often assumed a role traditionally filled by shamans. Like shamans, they were sometimes believed to be able to fly.[34] To this day among the Kazakhs one can find shamans who perform traditional shamanistic rituals using the Qur'an, Arabic letters, and such.[35]

Miracle-working (karamat) had always been a successful strategy for missionaries among the steppe peoples, and few are the Sufi masters who don't at very least acquire postumous miraculous or healing powers in their hagiographies.[36] According to the fourteenth-century traveler Ibn Battuta, even before becoming Muslims the nomads around Samarqand used to visit the tomb of Qusam ibn Abbas (a cousin of the Prophet who was martyred there in 676), in order "to gain blessing as the result of the miraculous signs which they witnessed on its behalf."[37]

It seems some of the shaykhs were not above verbal deception either as a way of securing influence. Ibn Battuta relates that a preacher by the name of Badr al-din Maydani was once asked by Kebek, ruler of the Chaghatayid White Horde in Transoxiana from 1309 to 1326, whether the Qur'an, which Muslims claimed to contain everything, mentioned his name. "Yes," the preacher replied. "It is in His word (most High is He), 'In whatsoever form He would He hath composed thee (Ar. rakkabak).'" As a result of this flattery Kebek "showed great favor to him and increased respect for Muslims."[38]

Sufi preachers, like Nestorians and Manichaeans before them, usually traveled to the steppes as part of trade missions. In conjunction with the charismatic appeal of these Muslim missionaries, therefore, the more commercially minded nomads must have perceived the advantages that could accrue from adopting at least enough of the religio-cultural tradition of the town-based merchants to foster good business relations.

CONCLUSIONS

European historians, the conceptualizers of the Silk Road, generally agree that the concept loses its meaning by the sixteenth century. Lack of a unifying political authority in Central Asia made long-distance overland trade in expensive goods less and less viable,[39] although regional commerce in essential commodities remained active.[40]

Instead, long-distance trade realigned itself along a new axis connecting India in the southeast with the emerging power of Russia in the northwest.[41] Western Central Asians, at least, were able to maintain their role as middlemen between the tsarist and Mughal empires throughout the seventeenth and eighteenth centuries. Increasingly an even more important role was played by Hindus, who established trading communities throughout Iran and Central Asia and whose networks extended as far as Moscow and Amsterdam.

During the nineteenth century, British and Russian empires converged on Central Asia, turning it into a mere buffer zone and shutting off the flow of trade altogether but for a smugglers' trickle. The Chinese began consolidating their hold on East Turkestan, turning Asia into a colonial pie split three ways. For most of the twentieth century the peoples of Central Asia have lived separated and under the rule of foreign regimes; only in the past two decades have the imperial borders slowly started to open again and the commercial and cultural contacts of the Silk Road begun to resume.

In terms of religious culture, sixteenth-century Central Asia was one of the most thoroughly Islamicized areas of the Muslim world, more so than the Arab and Iranian heartlands of western Asia and Egypt, which retain significant non-Muslim minorities even to the present day. Only North Africa, also relatively peripheral to the heartland of Islamic civilization, matched Central Asia's nearly total degree of Islamization.

It has been suggested that this apparent paradox can be accounted for by the fact that Central Asia was removed from the centers of rival religions such as Christianity, that preexisting religious institutions were weak, and that communication with central religious authority was difficult or nonexistent.[42] This explanation begs certain questions, however. Why, for example, did Christianity survive in southern India, and how did Manichaeism in Fu-ch'ien maintain for so long a distinct identity within the sea of popular Chinese religion?

An alternative explanation, which does not preclude accommodation with the one preceding, is that the peoples of Central Asia were almost entirely dependent, either directly or indirectly, on trade which was dominated by Muslims. This is true even for the Kazakh and Kyrgyz nomads who were the last to be Islamicized. Islamization was likewise most complete in other areas of the world most directly plugged into the Muslim-controlled trade routes, such as the coasts of Africa and Southeast Asia. Conversely in India and Spain, which retained non-Muslim majorities, the dependence of local economies on long-distance trade was nowhere near as generalized.

Direct coercion was at most a minor aspect of the Islamization of the Silk Road. The major factor, from which others derived, was the early and lasting involvement of Muslims in long-distance trade.

The story of the religions of the Silk Road is a part of the broader history of the conversation of cultures, a conversation made possible by the activities of individuals possessing sufficient commercial skills and sense of adventure to overcome profitably the immense difficulties and dangers of travel across the center of the vast Eurasian continent.

NOTES

CHAPTER 1

1. See Morris Rossabi, "The 'Decline' of the Central Asian Caravan Trade," in James Tracy, ed., *The Rise of Merchant Empires: Long-Distance Trade in the Early Modern World 1350-1750*, Cambridge: Cambridge University Press, 1990, pp. 351-370; also Niels Steensgard, *The Asian Trade Revolution of the Seventeenth Century: The East India Company and the Decline of the Caravan Trade*, Chicago: University of Chicago Press, 1974. A number of scholars have recently sought to revise the conventional view of decline in overland trade during this period; see, for example, Muzaffar Alam, "Trade, State Policy and Regional Change: Aspects of Mughal-Uzbek Relations, c.1550-1750," *Journal of the Economic and Social History of the Orient* 37 (1994), pp. 202-227, and Robert McChesney, *Central Asia: Foundations of Change*, Princeton, NJ: Darwin Press, 1996, pp. 53-54, note 3.

2. See Peter Hopkirk, *The Great Game*, Tokyo: Kodansha International, 1992.

3. Laszlo Torday, *Mounted Archers: The Beginnings of Central Asian History*, Durham: Durham Academic Press, 1997, p. 91.

4. John Noble Wilford, "New Finds Suggest Even Earlier Trade on Fabled Silk Road," *New York Times*, March 16, 1993, pp. C1, C8.

5. Francesco de Balducci Pegolotti, *La Pratica della Mercatura*, in Henry Yule and H. Cordier, eds. and trs., *Cathay and the Way Thither*, 4 vols., London: Hakluyt Society, 1937 [1913-16].

6. By the fifth century even silk was not making the complete trip from China, as it was being produced in Iran, India, and eventually the Byzantine Empire (Xinru Liu, *Silk and Religion*, Delhi: Oxford University Press, 1996, p. 9).

7. See Peter Hopkirk, *Foreign Devils on the Silk Road*, Amherst, MA: University of Massachusetts Press, 1984 [1980].

8. Sir Aurel Stein, *The Ruins of Desert Cathay*, 2 vols., New York: Dover, 1987 [1912], v. 2, p. 194.

9. Albert von le Coq, *Die buddhistische Spätantike in Mittelasien: v.2, Die manichäischen Miniaturen*, Berlin: D. Reimer, 1913.

10. D. S. Margoliouth, "An Early Judeo-Persian Document from Khotan in the Stein Collection, with Other Early Persian Documents," *Journal of the Royal Asiatic Society*, (1903), pp. 735-761; B. Utas, "The Jewish-Persian Fragment from Dandan-Uiliq," *Orientalia Suecana* 17 (1968), pp. 123-126.

11. A. V. W. Jackson, H. W. Bailey, W. B. Henning, I. Gershevitch, and Mary Boyce in England, and W. Bang, A. von Gebain, W. Sundermann, P. Zieme, and H.-J. Klimkeit in Germany, have been some of the major contributors to this effort.

12. See, for example, Jerry Bentley, *Old World Encounters*, New York: Oxford University Press, 1993 and Philip Curtin, *Cross-Cultural Trade in World History*, Cambridge: Cambridge University Press, 1984.

13. See Xinru Liu, *Ancient India and Ancient China: Trade and Religious Exchanges, AD 1-600*, Delhi: Oxford University Press, 1988, especially pp. 68-69.
14. Gavin Hambly, *Central Asia*, London: Weidenfeld and Nicolson, 1967, p. 7.
15. The travels of the Japanese pilgrim Ennin (793-864) have been translated by Edwin O. Reischauer as *Ennin's Diary: The Record of a Pilgrimage to China in Search of the Law*, New York: Ronald Press, 1955.
16. Bentley, *Old World Encounters*.
17. On Africa see Mervyn Hiskett, *The Course of Islam in Africa*, Edinburgh: Edinburgh University Press, 1994, pp. 100, 108; and J. S. Trimingham, *The Influence of Islam Upon Africa*, New York: Praeger, 1968, pp. 38-40. On Indian Ocean trade see André Wink, *Al-Hind: The Making of the Indo-Islamic World*, vol. 1, Leiden: Brill, 1990, especially pp. 25-85, and K. N. Chaudhuri, *Asia Before Europe: Economy and Civilisation of the Indian Ocean from the Rise of Islam to 1750*, Cambridge: Cambridge University Press, 1990.
18. For a fictionalized portrait of a Sogdian merchant's world in the eighth century, see Susan Whitfield, *Life Along the Silk Road*, London: John Murray, 1999, pp. 27-54.
19. See the studies in G. L. Semenow, *Studien zur sogdischen Kultur an der Seidenstraße*, Wiesbaden: Harrassowitz, 1996.
20. Stein, *Ruins;* v. 2, pp. 114-115; Frantz Grenet and N. Sims-Williams, "The Historical Context of the Sogdian Ancient Letters," *Transition Periods in Iranian History* (*Studia Iranica*, cahier 5), Paris, 1987, pp. 101-122.
21. Stein, *Ruins*, v. 2, p. 186.
22. See Richard Frye, *The Golden Age of Persia*, London: Weidenfeld and Nicolson, 1975, pp. 150-174.
23. See Richard Frye, *Bukhara: the Medieval Achievement*, Costa Mesa, CA: Mazda Publishers, 1997 [1965].
24. See Donald Leslie, *The Survival of the Chinese Jews*, Leiden: Brill, 1972, pp. 18 ff.
25. Abu Nasr Ahmad Qubawi, preface to Abu Bakr Muhammad Narshakhi, *Tarikh-i Bukhara*, tr. R. N. Frye, *History of Bukhara*, Cambridge, MA: Mediaeval Academy of America, 1954, p. 1.
26. Sergei P. Poliakov, *Everyday Islam: Religion and Tradition in Rural Central Asia*, Armonk, NY: M. E. Sharpe, 1992, especially pp. 59-75. For many Poliakov, a lifelong member of the communist party, is a suspect source. However, while one is well-advised to be mindful of his ideological biases, no other scholar has had access to or amassed comparable data for the people and period he studies.
27. Richard Eaton, *The Sufis of Bijapur, 1300-1700*, Princeton, NJ: Princeton University Press, 1978, pp. 155-174.
28. Peter Bryder, ". . . Where the Faint Traces of Manichaeism Disappear," *Altorientalische Forschungen* 15/1 (1988), pp. 201-208; Bryder, "Cao'an Revisited," *Research Into China Overseas Communication History* 16/2 (1989), pp. 35-42.

CHAPTER 2

1. René Grousset, *The Empire of the Steppes*, tr. Naomi Walford, New Brunswick, NJ: Rutgers University Press, 1970, p. ix.
2. See, for example, Georges Dumézil, *Mythe et Epopée*, 3 vols., Paris: Gallimard, 1968-1973; also J. P. Mallory, *In Search of the Indo-Europeans: Language, Archaeology, and Myth*, London: Thames and Hudson, 1989.
3. Joseph Fletcher, "The Mongols: Ecological and Social Perspectives," *Harvard Journal of Asiatic Studies* 46/1 (1986), p. 31.

4. B. A. Litvinskii, "Prehistoric Religions: The Eurasian Steppes and Inner Asia," in Mircea Eliade, ed., *Encyclopedia of Religion*, New York: Macmillan, 1987, v. 11, p. 517.

5. Litvinskii, "Prehistoric Religions," pp. 517-18.

6. See David W. Anthony and Nokolai B. Vinogradov, "Birth of the Chariot," *Archaeology* 48/2 (1995), pp. 36-41; and David W. Anthony and Dorcas R. Brown, "The Origins of Horseback Riding," *Antiquity* 65 (1991), pp. 22-38.

7. Old Iranian *Saka*, Greek *Scythai* (Scythian), and Sogdian *Sughde*, as well as the biblical Hebrew *Ashkenaz* (via Assyrian *Askuzai*) appear all to derive from **skuza*, an ancient Indo-European word for archer; cf. English "shoot" (Torday, *Mounted Archers*, pp. 248-280).

8. Herodotus, *The Histories*, tr. Aubrey de Sélincourt, rev., A. R. Burn, New York: Penguin, 1972, pp. 291-295 (Book 4: 71-72, 75, 65); Peter Golden, *An Introduction to the History of the Turkic Peoples*, Wiesbaden: Otto Harrassowitz, 1992, p. 49.

9. Herodotus, *Histories*, pp. 127-128 (2: 215-216).

10. Herodotus, *Histories*, p. 289 (4: 59). Herodotus treats the Massagatae and the Scythians as separate peoples, but they were both Saka groups.

11. Ruth Meserve, "Inner Asian Religions," in Mircea Eliade, ed., *Encyclopedia of Religion*, New York: Macmillan, 1987, v. 7, p. 241.

12. Herodotus, *Histories*, pp. 278-279 (4: 24). See also E. D. Phillips, "The Argippaei of Herodotus," *Artibus Asiae* 23 (1960), pp. 124-128.

13. A large number of Indo-European mummies have recently been discovered in western China, some as much as three thousand years old. See Elizabeth Wayland Barber, *The Mummies of Urumchi*, New York: Norton, 1999; Victor Mair, "Prehistoric Caucasoid Corpses of the Tarim Basin," *Journal of Indo-European Studies* 23/3-4 (1995), pp. 281-307.

14. Meserve, "Inner Asian Religions," p. 241.

15. On the persistence of horse sacrifice see J. A. Boyle, "A Form of Horse Sacrifice Amongst the 13th- and 14th-century Mongols," *Central Asiatic Journal* 10 (1965), pp. 145-150.

16. See the overview of these ongoing disagreements in Mary Boyce, *Zoroastrianism: Its Antiquity and Constant Vigour*, Costa Mesa, CA: Mazda Publishers, 1992, pp. 1-26.

17. After decades of scholarly speculation, the hallucinogenic component in *haoma/soma* has been identified as harmaline. See David Flattery and Martin Schwartz, *Haoma and Harmaline: The Botanical Identity of the Indo-Iranian Sacred Hallucinogen "Soma" and Its Legacy in Religion, Language, and Middle Eastern Folklore*, Berkeley: University of California Press, 1989.

18. Although in modern Persian *div* means "demon," the original positive character of the *daevas* survives in later Iranian names, such as the Sogdian Devashtic and the Persian Divdad.

19. Shahin Bekhradnia, "The Tajik Case for a Zoroastrian Identity," *Religion, State and Society* 22/1 (1994), p. 109.

20. For example, Jamsheed Choksy, *Conflict and Cooperation: Muslim Elites and Zoroastrian Subalterns in Medieval Iranian Society*, New York: Columbia University Press, 1997, p. 4.

21. On Achaemenid religion, see M. Schwartz, "The Religion of Achaemenian Iran," in Ilya Gershevitch, ed., *Cambridge History of Iran*, v. 2, *The Median and Achaemenian Periods*, Cambridge: Cambridge University Press, 1985, pp. 664-697.

22. Janos Harmatta, "Religions in the Kushan Empire," in *History of the Civilizations of Central Asia*, v. 2, Paris: UNESCO, 1994, p. 315.

23. K. Maurer Trinkhaus, "Mortuary Ritual and Mortuary Remains," *Current Anthropology* 25/5 (1984), p. 677.

24. A. Christensen, "Die Moschee Makh in Buhara," *Orientalische Litteraturzeitung* 7 (1904), pp. 49-51.
25. Behistun inscription, column 5; cf. Richard Frye, *The Heritage of Central Asia,* Princeton: Markus Wiener, 1996, p. 83.
26. W. B. Henning, "A Sogdian God," *Bulletin of the School of Oriental and African Studies* 28/2 (1965), p. 251.
27. Henning, "A Sogdian God," p. 247.
28. Henning, "A Sogdian God," p. 251; Grenet and Sims-Williams, "The Historical Context of the Sogdian Ancient Letters."
29. Schwartz, "Religion of Achaemenian Iran," p. 681.
30. Allen H. Godbey, "From Persia to China," in William C. White, ed., *Chinese Jews,* 2nd edition, New York: Paragon, 1966, pp. 136-137.
31. Irene Franck and David M. Brownstone, *The Silk Road,* New York: Facts on File, 1986, p. 63.
32. Itzhak Ben-Zvi, *The Exiled and the Redeemed,* Philadelphia: Jewish Publication Society of America, 1957, p. 67; Julius Brutzkus, "Bukhara," *Encyclopaedia Judaica,* Berlin, 1929, vol. 4, p. 1126.
33. L. Rabinowitz, *Jewish Merchant Adventurers: A Study of the Radanites,* London: Goldston, 1948, p. 51.
34. David Law, *From Samaria to Samarkand,* Lanham, MD: University Press of America, 1992.
35. V. A. Livshits and Z. I. Usmanova, "New Parthian Inscriptions from Old Merv," in Shaul Shaked and Amnon Metzer, eds., *Irano-Judaica III,* Jerusalem: Ben Zvi Institute, 1994, pp. 99-105.
36. Jacob Neusner, "Jews in Iran," in Ehsan Yarshater, ed., *Cambridge History of Iran,* v. 3, *The Seleucid, Parthian, and Sasanian Periods,* Cambridge: Cambridge University Press, 1983, p. 912.
37. See Shaul Shaked, "Iranian Influence on Judaism: First Century B.C.E. to Second Century C.E.," in W. D. Davies and Louis Finkelstein, eds., *Cambridge History of Judaism,* v. 1, Cambridge: Cambridge University Press, 1984, pp. 308-325; David Winston, "The Iranian Component in the Bible, Apocrypha, and Qumran: A Review of the Evidence," *History of Religions* 6 (1966), pp. 183-216.
38. See, for example, Gedaliahu G. Stroumsa, "A Zoroastrian Origin to the *Sefirot?*" in Shaked and Metzer, eds., *Irano Judaica III,* pp. 17-33.
39. Shaul Shaked, "Iranian Functions in Esther," *Irano-Judaica,* Jerusalem: Ben-Zvi, 1982, pp. 292-303.
40. James Russell, "Zoroastrian Elements in the Book of Esther," in Shaked and Metzer, eds., *Irano-Judaica II,* Jerusalem: Ben-Zvi, 1990, pp. 33-40.
41. Almut Hintze, "The Greek and Hebrew Versions of the Book of Esther and its Iranian Background," in Shaked and Metzer, eds., *Irano Judaica III,* pp. 34-39.
42. David Flusser, "Hystaspes and John of Patmos," in Shaul Shaked, ed., *Irano-Judaica,* Jerusalem: Ben Zvi Institute, 1982, pp. 12-75.
43. Carsten Colpe, "Development of Religious Thought," in Ehsan Yarshater, ed., *Cambridge History of Iran,* v. 3, *The Seleucid, Parthian, and Sasanian Periods,* Cambridge: Cambridge University Press, 1983, pp. 831-833.
44. Shaked, "Iranian Influence," p. 324.
45. Quoted in Leslie, *Survival of the Chinese Jews,* p. 3.
46. Michael Pollock, *Mandarins, Jews and Missionaries,* Philadelphia: Jewish Publication Society, 1980, pp. 255-256.
47. Pollock, *Mandarins,* p. 257.
48. Wilford, "New Finds."

49. Leslie, *Survival*, p. 4.

50. Rudolf Loewenthal, *The Jews of Bukhara*, (Central Asian Collectanea, no. 8), Washington, D.C., 1961, p. 6.

51. Victor Mair, "Old Sinitic *M^{y}ag, Old Persian Magus, and English 'Magician,'" *Early China* 15 (1990), pp. 27-47.

52. Homer H. Dubs, "Taoism," in H. F. MacNair, ed., *Philosophy and Religion*, Berkeley: University of California Press, 1946, pp. 286-287.

53. Iwamoto Yutaka, *Bukkyo setsuwa kenkyu, v. 4: Jigoku meguri no bungaku*, Tokyo: Kaimei shoten, 1979, pp. 184-199; cited in Stephen F. Teiser, *The Ghost Festival in Medieval China*, Princeton: Princeton University Press, 1988, p. 24.

54. See, for example, Ts'un-yan Liu, "Traces of Zoroastrian and Manichaean Activities in pre-T'ang China," in *Selected Papers from the Hall of Harmonious Winds*, Leiden: Brill, 1976, pp. 2-55.

CHAPTER 3

1. His dates have been posited variously as 624-544, 563-483, or 448-368 BCE; current consensus is that at least part of his life was in the fifth century BCE.

2. Peter Harvey, *An Introduction to Buddhism: Teachings, History and Practices*, Cambridge: Cambridge University Press, 1990, p. 74.

3. The Theravada tradition has been questioned on this point; see Richard Gombrich, *Theravada Buddhism*, London: Routledge, 1988, p. 133.

4. On various traditional accounts of the schism, see Etienne Lamotte, *History of Indian Buddhism*, Louvain: Peters Press, 1988, pp. 274-292.

5. Harvey, *Introduction to Buddhism*, pp. 74-75.

6. Ge Ling Shang, personal communication, 1998.

7. Paul Harrison, "Searching for the Origins of the Mahayana: What Are We Looking For?" *The Eastern Buddhist* 28/1 (1995), pp. 56, 67.

8. Sasaki Shizuka, "A Study on the Origin of Mahayana Buddhism," *The Eastern Buddhist* 30/1 (1997), pp. 79-113.

9. Paul Williams, *Mahayana Buddhism: The Doctrinal Foundations*, London: Routledge, 1989, pp. 277-278, note 7.

10. Williams, *Mahayana Buddhism*, p. 49.

11. Paul Harrison, "Who Gets to Ride in the Great Vehicle? Self-Image and Identity Among the Followers of the Early Mahayana," *Journal of the International Association of Buddhist Studies* 10/1 (1987), p. 80.

12. Williams, *Mahayana Buddhism*, p. 5.

13. Hsüan-tsang, *Records of the Western Countries (Ta T'ang Si Yu Ki)*, in Samuel Beal, tr., *Buddhist Records of the Western World*, New Delhi: Oriental Reprints, 1969 [1884], vol. 1, pp. 47-48.

14. See J. Harmatta, "Sino-Indica," *Acta Antiqua* 12/1-2 (1964), p. 4. The inscriptions speak of spreading the *dharma*, however, not Buddhism per se.

15. Janos Harmatta, "Religions in the Kushan Empire," in *History of the Civilizations of Central Asia*, v. 2, Paris: UNESCO, 1994, p. 314.

16. On the interaction between Iranian and Greek religious ideas, see Colpe, "Development of Religious Thought."

17. Hsüan-tsang, *Records*, v. 1, p. 139.

18. Sally Hovey Wriggins, *Xuanzang: A Buddhist Pilgrim on the Silk Road*, Boulder CO: Westview, 1996, p. 68.

19. B. A. Litvinskii and I. R. Pichikian, "The Hellenistic Architecture and Art of the Temple of the Oxus," *Bulletin of the Asia Institute*, new series, 8 (1994), pp. 47-66; Harmatta, "Religions in the Kushan Empire," p. 314.

20. I. B. Horner, tr., *Milinda's Questions*, 2 vols., London: Luzac & Co., 1969; Lamotte, *History of Indian Buddhism*, pp. 419-426. See also A. K. Narain, *The Indo-Greeks*, London: Oxford University Press, 1957.

21. Guitty Azarpay, "A Jataka Tale on a Sasanian Silver Plate," *Bulletin of the Asia Institute*, new series, 9 (1995), pp. 99-125.

22. Ronald E. Emmerick, "Buddhism in Central Asia," in Mircea Eliade, ed., *Encyclopedia of Religion*, New York: Macmillan, 1987, v. 2, p. 401.

23. A. D. H. Bivar, in Gavin Hambly, *Central Asia*, London: Weidenfeld and Nicolson, 1969, p. 47; cf. Stein, *Ruins*, v. 2, p. 414.

24. Harmatta, "Religions in the Kushan Empire," pp. 317-318.

25. Oskar von Hinüber, "Expansion to the North: Afghanistan and Central Asia," in Heinz Bechent and Richard Gombrich, *The World of Buddhism*, London: Thames and Hudson, 1984, p. 104.

26. Jan Nattier, "The Meanings of the Maitreya Myth: A Typological Analysis," in Alan Sponberg and Helen Hardacre, eds., *Maitreya, the Future Buddha*, Princeton, NJ: Princeton University Press, 1988, p. 46, note 60, citing Przyluski.

27. Ronald E. Emmerick, "Buddhism Among Iranian Peoples," in Yarshater, ed., *Cambridge History of Iran*, v. 3, pp. 955-956; Lamotte, *History of Indian Buddhism*, pp. 498-499.

28. Lamotte, *History of Indian Buddhism*, pp. 668-75.

29. Lamotte, *History of Indian Buddhism*, pp. 677-8.

30. Litvinsky, "Buddhism in Central Asia," p. 25.

31. Litvinsky, "Buddhism in Central Asia," p. 25. It has been suggested that the name "Bukhara" is originally derived from "vihara," which could indicate that a Buddhist temple once stood there.

32. Emmerick, "Buddhism Among Iranian Peoples," p. 960.

33. See G. Koshelenko, "The Beginnings of Buddhism in Margiana," *Acta Antiqua Academiae Scientarum Hungaricae* 14/1-2 (1966), p. 182.

34. David Utz, "Arshak, Parthian Buddhists, and 'Iranian' Buddhism," paper presented at the conference "Buddhism Across Boundaries: The Sources of Chinese Buddhism," Hsi Lai University, 3-6 January 1993; and Takayasu Higuchi, "Buddhist Ruins of West Turkestan," *Bukkyoshigaku Kenkyu* 27/1 (1984), pp. 119-141 (in Japanese).

35. Mariko Namba Walter, "Buddhism in Western Central Asia," paper presented at the American Historical Association annual conference, Seattle, WA, January 1998, pp. 1, 3.

36. Litvinsky, "Buddhism in Central Asia," p. 25.

37. Walter, "Buddhism in Western Central Asia," p. 7.

38. Walter, "Buddhism in Western Central Asia," p. 8.

39. Mariko Namba Walter, "Mahayana and Hinayana in Central Asian Buddhist History: The Nature of Buddhism in Chinese Turkestan," paper presented at the Association for Asian Studies annual conference, January 1997, pp. 5-6.

40. Erik Zürcher, *The Buddhist Conquest of China*, Leiden: Brill, 1959, p. 26.

41. Zürcher, *Buddhist Conquest*, p. 27.

42. Harrison, "Who Gets to Ride in the Great Vehicle?" p. 68; Harrison, "The Earliest Chinese Translations of Mahayana Sutras: Some Notes on the Works of Lokaksema," *Buddhist Studies Review* 10/2 (1993), pp. 135-177; and Harrison, "Searching for the Origins of the Mahayana," p. 55.

43. Zürcher, *Buddhist Conquest*, p. 35.

44. Walter, "Buddhism in Western Central Asia," p. 4.
45. Mariko Namba Walter, "Tokharian Buddhism in Kucha: Buddhism of Indo-European Speakers in Chinese Turkestan before the 10th century C.E.," unpublished paper.
46. Higuchi, "Buddhist Ruins of West Turkestan." I thank Mariko Walter for this reference.
47. Walter, "Buddhism in Western Central Asia," p. 6.
48. Emmerick, "Buddhism Among Iranians," pp. 960-961.
49. Jan Nattier, "Church Language and Vernacular Language in Central Asian Buddhism," *Numen* 37/2 (1990), pp. 195-219.
50. He may have been the one responsible for introducing into India the popular Heart Sutra as well. Jan Nattier, "The Heart Sutra: A Chinese Apocryphal Text?" *International Journal of Buddhist Studies* 15/2 (1992), p. 180.
51. Antonino Forte, "An Ancient Chinese Monastery Excavated in Kirgiziya," *Central Asiatic Journal* 38/1 (1994), pp. 41-57.
52. Chou Yi-liang, "Tantrism in China," *Harvard Journal of Asiatic Studies*, 8 (1945), pp. 241-332.
53. Bentley, *Old World Encounters*, p. 97.
54. Fa-hsien, *Buddhist Country Records (Fo Kwo Ki)*, in Beal, tr., *Buddhist Records*, v. 1, pp. xxiii-lxxxiii.
55. Sung-yün, *Buddhist Books in the Western Countries*, in Beal, tr., *Buddhist Records*, v. 1, p. xciii.
56. Chang-yüeh, "Preface," in Beal, tr., *Buddhist Records*, v. 1, p. 6. Chang claims Hsüan-tsang translated all of these texts, but this is unlikely.
57. For reasons that are not clear, local Muslim governors occasionally did permit Buddhist missions to transit their territories in Central Asia. Often, however, the missionaries were robbed or detained. Jan Yün-hua, "Buddhist Relations Between India and Sung China," *History of Religions* 6 (1966), pp. 142-143.
58. Hui-li, *Life of Hsuan-tsang*, tr. Yung-hsi Li, Peking: The Chinese Buddhist Association, 1959, p. 46.
59. Hui-li, *Life of Hsuan-tsang*, p. 47.
60. No incontrovertibly Buddhist remains have been unearthed in Sogdiana proper, in contrast to areas to the south of the Hissar Mountains, where they abound.
61. B. A. Litvinsky, "Buddhism in Central Asia," p. 50.
62. Narshakhi, *History of Bukhara*, p. 23.
63. G. Uray, "Tibet's Connections with Nestorianism and Manicheism in the 8th-10th Centuries," *Wiener Studien zur Tibetologie und Buddhismuskunde* 10 (1983), pp. 407, 421. On the Ladakh paintings, see Hans-Joachim Klimkeit, *Manichaean Art and Calligraphy*, Leiden: Brill, 1982; on the inscriptions, see Nicholas Sims-Williams, *Sogdian and Other Iranian Inscriptions of the Upper Indus*, 2 vols., London: School of Oriental and African Studies, 1989-92.
64. See Christopher I. Beckwith, *The Tibetan Empire in Central Asia*, Princeton, NJ: Princeton University Press, 1987.

CHAPTER 4

1. Quoted in S. N. C. Lieu, *Manichaeism in the Later Roman Empire and Medieval China*, 2nd ed., Tübingen: Mohr, 1992, p. 98.
2. Chabot, *Synodicon Orientale*, p. 302, quoted in Samuel H. Moffett, *A History of Christianity in Asia*, vol. 1, San Francisco: Harper, 1992, p. 197.

3. See Moffett, *Christianity in Asia,* pp. 51-53.

4. Alphonse Mingana, *The Early Spread of Christianity in Central Asia and the Far East: A New Document,* Manchester: Manchester University Press, 1925, pp. 7-8.

5. Mingana, *Early Spread of Christianity,* p. 4.

6. Neusner, "Jews in Iran," in Ehsan Yarshater, ed., *Cambridge History of Iran,* v. 3, *The Seleucid, Parthian, and Sasanian Periods,* Cambridge: Cambridge University Press, 1983, p. 914.

7. Bedjan, *Acta Martyrum* 2: 351; quoted in Moffett, *Christianity in Asia,* p. 142.

8. Abu Rayhan Biruni, *Chronology of Ancient Nations,* tr. E. Sachau, Lahore: Hijra International, 1983 [1879], p. 282.

9. Mingana, *Early Spread of Christianity,* p. 74.

10. Emile Benveniste, "Le Vocabulaire Chrétien dans les Langues d'Asie Central," *L'Oriente Cristiano nella Storia della Civiltà,* Rome: Accademia Nazionale dei Lincei, 1964, pp. 85-91.

11. Nicholas Sims-Williams, "Syro-Sogdica I: An Anonymous Homily on the Three Periods of Solitary Life," *Orientalia Christiana Periodica* 47 (1981), p. 441.

12. Sims-Williams, "Syro-Sogdica," p. 443.

13. Mingana, *Early Spread of Christianity,* p. 9.

14. Lieu, *Manichaeism in the Later Roman Empire,* p. 228.

15. See Mircea Eliade, *Shamanism: Archaic Techniques of Ecstasy,* Princeton, NJ: Princeton University Press, 1964. The term "shaman" comes from the Tungus language; the Turkish word is *qam,* and the Mongolian *bö'e.* Medieval Muslim sources use the Arabic term *kahin* (as in Hebrew).

16. Mingana, *Early Spread of Christianity,* pp. 11-12; Erica C. D. Hunter, "The Conversion of the Kerait to Christianity in A.D. 1007," *Zentralasiatische Studien* 22 (1989-91), p. 160.

17. J. A. Boyle, "Turkish and Mongol Shamanism in the Middle Ages," *Folklore* 83 (1972), pp. 184-93.

18. Mingana, *Early Spread of Christianity,* p. 12.

19. Mingana, *Early Spread of Christianity,* p. 13.

20. Hunter, "The Conversion of the Kerait."

21. Mingana, *Early Spread of Christianity,* p. 15.

22. See Edward H. Schafer, *The Golden Peaches of Samarkand: A Study of T'ang Exotics,* Berkeley: University of California Press, 1962.

23. Kazuo Enoki, "Nestorian Christianism in Medieval Times," *L'Oriente Cristiano nella Storia della Civiltà,* Rome: Academia Nazionale dei Lincei, 1964, pp. 72-73.

24. Paul Pelliot, "Les influences iraniennes en Asie Central et en Extrême-Orient," *Revue d'Histoire et de Littérature Réligieuses* 3/2 (1912), p. 108.

25. Schafer, *Golden Peaches,* p. 50.

26. Schafer, *Golden Peaches,* pp. 53-4.

27. Ibn Nadim, *Fihrist of al-Nadim: A Tenth Century Survey of Muslim Culture (Fihrist al-'ulum),* tr. B. Dodge, 2 vols., New York: Columbia University Press, 1970, pp. 836-837.

28. The Mandaeans survive to this day in small communities throughout southern Iraq and Iran.

29. W. B. Henning, "Mani's Last Journey," *Bulletin of the School of Oriental and African Studies* 10 (1939-42), pp. 941-953.

30. Jacob Neusner, "Rabbi and Magus in Third-century Sasanian Babylonia," *History of Religions* 6 (1966), p. 173.

31. Geo Widengren and Gherardo Gnoli have argued that Manichaeism is in essence Iranian, while more recently Samuel Lieu has argued eloquently in favor of its more Semitic character.

32. Jason BeDuhn has suggested that rather than being gnostic in essence, Manichaeism used gnostic ideas to win converts in regions where gnosticism was popular, but turned to other vocabularies (e.g., Buddhist) farther east. Jason David BeDuhn, review of Hans-Joachim Klimkeit, *Gnosis on the Silk Road, Journal of the American Oriental Society* 115/2 (1995), pp. 344-346.

33. Hans-Joachim Klimkeit, *Gnosis on the Silk Road,* San Francisco: Harper, 1993, p. 314. This story is similar to one in the apocryphal Acts of John and reappears in Islamic guise in a tenth-century work by Ibn Babai. The conception of the physical body as "a bag of blood and pus," used as a mental means to overcome lust, comes from Buddhist teaching.

34. See, for example, the sixteenth-century treatise by Qazi Ahmad Qumi, *Gulistan-i hunar,* tr. V. Minorsky, *Calligraphers and Painters,* Washington: Smithsonian, 1959, pp. 177-180.

35. S. N. C. Lieu, *Manichaeism in Central Asia and China,* Leiden: Brill, 1998, p. 138.

36. Lieu, *Manichaeism in the Later Roman Empire,* pp. 112-113, 220.

37. Some evidence has been derived from Taoist sources, however, of even earlier Manichaean activity in China; see Liu, "'Traces of Zoroastrian and Manichaean Activities in pre-T'ang China."

38. Lieu, *Manichaeism in the Later Roman Empire,* p. 230.

39. Lieu, *Manichaeism in the Later Roman Empire,* p. 236.

40. E. Chavannes and P. Pelliot, *Un traité Manichéen retrouvé en Chine,* Paris: Imprimérie Nationale, 1913, p. 154.

41. This model of Chinese-nomadic relations is explained in Thomas Barfield, *The Perilous Frontier,* Oxford: Blackwell, 1989. The Uighur case is addressed on pp. 150-157.

42. Colin Mackerras, "The Uighurs," in Denis Sinor, ed., *Cambridge History of Early Inner Asia,* Cambridge: Cambridge University Press, 1990, p. 331.

43. Xijuan Zhou, "Buddhists or Manichaeans? Some Characteristics of the Manichaean Missionaries Along the Silk Road," paper presented at the American Historical Association annual conference, 1998, pp. 9-10.

44. Mackerras, "The Uighurs," p. 335; Chavannes and Pelliot, *Un Traité Manichéen,* pp. 193-4, 198.

45. Ibn Nadim, *Fihrist,* p. 803.

46. Reischauer, tr., *Ennin's Diary,* p. 232.

47. Lieu, *Manichaeism in the Later Roman Empire,* p. 238.

48. Zhou, "Buddhists or Manichaeans?" pp. 6-7.

49. Klimkeit, *Gnosis,* p. 273.

50. Pelliot, "Influences iraniennes," p. 114. This law remained on the books in China and also Vietnam into the twentieth century, leading Pelliot to remark that the French colonial government of Indochina in his time was continuing to proscribe a religion which had long ceased to be practiced.

51. Lieu, *Manichaeism in the Later Roman Empire,* p. 107.

52. Klimkeit, *Gnosis,* p. 52.

53. Mary Boyce, *A Reader in Manichaean Middle Persian and Parthian,* Leiden: Brill, 1975, p. 139; Lotus Sutra, chapter 24.

54. Boyce, *Reader,* p. 51.

55. Hans-Joachim Klimkeit, "Christians, Buddhists and Manichaeans in Medieval Central Asia," *Buddhist-Christian Studies* 1 (1981), p. 49.

56. Klimkeit, *Gnosis,* p. 151.

57. Hans-Joachim Klimkeit, "Jesus' Entry into Parinirvana: Manichaean Identity in Buddhist Central Asia," *Numen* 33 (1986), p. 225.
58. Klimkeit, *Gnosis,* p. 69.
59. Larry Clark, "The Manichaean Turkic *Pothi-Book,*" *Altorientalische Forschungen* 9 (1982), pp. 189-90; cf. Lieu, *Manichaeism in Central Asia and China,* pp. 46-47.
60. D. M. Lang, "St. Euthymius the Georgian and the Barlaam and Ioasaph Romance," *Bulletin of the School of Oriental and African Studies* 17/2 (1955), pp. 306-325.
61. P. Y. Saeki, *The Nestorian Documents and Relics in China,* 2nd ed., Tokyo: Academy of Oriental Culture, 1951, p. 26.
62. Saeki, *Nestorian Documents and Relics,* p. 55.
63. Saeki, *Nestorian Documents and Relics,* p. 6.
64. Saeki, *Nestorian Documents and Relics,* p. 125.
65. Moffett, *Christianity in Asia,* p. 310.
66. Lieu, *Manichaeism in Central Asia and China,* pp. 67-68.
67. Huang Yung-wu, *Tunhuang Pao Tsang,* Taipei: Hsin wen feng, vol. 48, pp. 361-362, cited in Zhou, "Buddhists or Manichaeans?" p. 14.

CHAPTER 5

1. Abu Ja'far Muhammad b. Jarir al-Tabari, *Ta'rikh al-rusul w'al-muluk,* 3 vols., ed. M. J. DeGoeje, Leiden: Brill, 1879-1901, v. 3, p. 272.
2. Narshakhi, *History of Bukhara,* p. 66.
3. Narshakhi, *History of Bukhara,* p. 66.
4. Narshakhi, *History of Bukhara,* p. 67-68.
5. Narshakhi, *History of Bukhara,* pp. 74-75.
6. Ehsan Yarshater, "Mazdakism," in *Cambridge History of Iran,* v. 3, pp. 1005-1006.
7. Jiger Janabel, "The Islamization of Southern Qazaqstan in the Ninth and Tenth Centuries," paper presented at the American Historical Association annual conference, Seattle, WA, 9 January 1998.
8. A detailed case study of one such figure, Baba Tükles, is given by Devin DeWeese in *Islamization and Native Religion in the Golden Horde,* State College, PA: Penn State University Press, 1994.
9. See Richard Bulliet, "Conversion to Islam and the Emergence of a Muslim Society in Iran," in Nehemia Levtzion, ed., *Conversion to Islam,* New York: Holmes and Meier, 1979, pp. 30-51.
10. Bulliet, "Conversion to Islam," p. 62.
11. Trinkhaus, "Mortuary Ritual," p. 676.
12. W. Barthold, *Four Studies on the History of Central Asia,* 3 vols., Leiden: Brill, 1959-61, v. 1, p. 16.
13. Edward H. Schafer, "Iranian Merchants in T'ang Dynasty Tales," *Semitic and Oriental Studies Presented to William Popper,* Berkeley: University of California Press, 1951, pp. 403-422.
14. Richard Bulliet, "Naw Bahar and the Survival of Iranian Buddhism," *Iran* 14 (1976), pp. 140-145.
15. Bulliet, "Naw Bahar," p. 144.
16. Bulliet, "Naw Bahar," p. 145.
17. al-Tabari, *Ta'rikh,* v. 3, p. 1841.
18. Narshakhi, *History of Bukhara,* pp. 20-21.
19. Ibn Hawkal, in M. J. DeGoeje, ed., *Bibliotheca Geographorum Arabicorum,* Leiden: Brill, 1889, v. 2, p. 365.

20. Stein, *Ruins*, v. 2, pp. 440-441.
21. Julian Baldick, *Imaginary Muslims: the Uwaysi Sufis of Central Asia*, New York: I. B. Tauris, 1993, pp. 163-165.
22. See Ibn Khurdadbih, *Kitab al-masalik wa'l-mamalik*, in M. J. DeGoeje, ed., *Bibliotheca Geographorum Arabicorum*, v. 6, p. 114.
23. Rabinowitz, *Jewish Merchant Adventurers*, p. 15.
24. Omeljan Pritsak, *The Origin of Rus*, v. 1, Cambridge, MA: Harvard University Press, 1981, p. 25.
25. See Golden, *Introduction*, pp. 241-242.
26. Quoted in Rabinowitz, *Jewish Merchant Adventurers*, p. 9.
27. Rabinowitz, *Jewish Merchant Adventurers*, p. 10.
28. Rabinowitz, *Jewish Merchant Adventurers*, pp. 41-42, 86.
29. Wheeler M. Thackston, Jr., tr., *Naser-e Khosraw's Book of Travels*, Albany: State University of New York Press, 1986, p. xi.
30. See Bernard Lewis, *The Assassins: A Radical Sect in Islam*, New York: Oxford University Press, 1967.
31. Stories of a childhood friendship between Hasan, Nizam al-Mulk, and the astronomer-poet Omar Khayyam most likely belong to legend. See Lewis, *The Assassins*, p. 40.
32. Nasr appears in some accounts as Abu'l Nasr Samani. For a legendary account of Satoq Bughra in the sixteenth-century hagiographical *History of the Uwaysis*, see Baldick, *Imaginary Muslims*, pp. 77-81.
33. On the Qara-khanids, see Peter Golden, "The Karakhanids and Early Islam," in Denis Sinor, ed., *Cambridge History of Early Inner Asia*, Cambridge: Cambridge University Press, 1990, pp. 343-370, and Golden, *Introduction*, pp. 214-19.
34. Ibn al-Athir, *Al-Kamil fi'l-ta'rikh*, in DeGoeje, *Bibliotheca Geographorum Arabicorum*, v. 8, p. 396; Ibn Miskawayh, *Tajarub al-Umam*, tr. D. S. Margoliouth, Oxford: Oxford University Press, 1920-21, p. 181.
35. See Golden, *Introduction*, pp. 217-18.
36. See Golden, *Introduction*, p. 258. The modern Bulgarians are descended from a western branch of the Bulgars who became slavicized.
37. See Joseph Fletcher, "The Naqshbandiyya in Northwest China," in B. F. Manz and Jonathan Lipman, eds., *Studies on Chinese and Islamic Inner Asia*, London: Variorum, 1995, p. 5.
38. Donald D. Leslie, *Islam in Traditional China: A Short History*, Canberra: Canberra College of Advanced Education, 1986, pp. 72-74.
39. Ou-yang Hsiu, *New T'ang History*, Shanghai: Commercial Press, 1936, 221b/11b-12; cited in Hajji Yusuf Chang, "The Hui (Muslim) Minority in China: An Historical Overview," *Journal of the Institute of Muslim Minority Affairs* 8/1 (1987), p. 63. On apocryphal stories of the introduction of Islam into China, see Isaac Mason, "The Mohammadans of China: When, and How, They First Came," *Journal of the North China Branch of the Royal Asiatic Society*, 60 (1929), pp. 42-78.
40. Chang, "The Hui Minority in China," p. 63.
41. See Jacqueline Armijo-Hussein, "Sayyid 'Ajall Shams al-Din: A Muslim from Bukhara, Serving the Mongols in China, and Bringing 'Civilization' to Yunnan," Ph.D. dissertation, Harvard University, 1997.
42. Barthold, *Four Studies*, v. 1, p. 103.
43. The anti-Muslim character of Qara-khita'i rule is glossed over by the thirteenth century Muslim writer Juzjani, who suggests that the Gür-khan "had secretly become a Muslim" and states that the Qara-khita'i "were just sovereigns, and were adorned with equity, and ability, and used to treat Muhammadans with great reverence . . ."

(Minhaj al-Din Juzjani, *Tabaqat-i Nasiri*, tr. H. G. Raverty, 2 vols., New Delhi: Oriental Reprints, 1970 [1881], v. 2, p. 912.

CHAPTER 6

1. See Igor de Rachewiltz, *Papal Envoys to the Great Khans*, London: Faber and Faber, 1971, pp. 29-40.
2. Ghiyas al-din Muhammad Khwand Amir, *Habib al-siyar*, tr. W. M. Thackston, Jr., Cambridge, MA: Dept. of Near Eastern Languages and Civilizations, 1994, v. 1, p. 14. According to de Rachewiltz, Küchlük was born a Christian but converted to Buddhism at the instigation of his wife. De Rachewiltz, *Papal Envoys*, pp. 49-50.
3. Barthold, *Four Studies*, v. 1, p. 35.
4. Khwand Amir, *Habib al-siyar*, v. 1, p. 15.
5. Barthold, *Four Studies*, v. 1, 37.
6. Khwand Amir, *Habib al-siyar*, v. 1, 18.
7. See, for example, the anecdotes in Juzjani (v. 2, pp. 1107-1115) and Rashid al-Din Fazlullah, *Jami' al-tawarikh*, tr. J. A. Boyle, *The Successors of Genghis Khan*, New York: Columbia University Press, 1971, pp. 77-8.
8. Morris Rossabi, "The Muslims in the Early Yüan Dynasty," in John Langlois, ed., *China Under Mongol Rule*, Princeton, NJ: Princeton University Press, 1981, p. 261.
9. Accounts of the journeys of Ch'ang Ch'un and other Chinese are found in Emilii Bretschneider, *Medieval Researches from Asiatic Sources*, Osnabruck: Biblio Verlag, 1987 [1875-76].
10. Barthold, *Four Studies*, v. 1, p. 39.
11. See, for example, Rashid al-Din, *Successors*, p. 94.
12. Devin DeWeese suggests that "what is at work in Mongol attitudes towards religions such as Christianity and Islam is hardly 'tolerance' or ecumenism, and certainly not religious indifference, but an assumption that religion is above all a matter of practice and communal affiliation, not of 'belief.'" DeWeese, *Islamization and Native Religion*, pp. 100-101, note 73. DeWeese somewhat overstates the case, since his argument overlooks the Mongols' interest in "using" religions as described above.
13. Morris Rossabi, *Khubilai Khan: His Life and Times*, Berkeley: University of California Press, 1988, p. 7.
14. Rashid al-Din, *Successors*, pp. 219-20. Jews, however, were not granted this exemption.
15. de Rachewiltz, *Papal Envoys*, p. 46.
16. Rashid al-Din, who calls her "the most intelligent woman in the world," states that "though she was a follower and devotee of the religion of Jesus she made great efforts to declare the rites of the law of Mustafa and would bestow alms and presents upon imams and sheikhs." Rashid al-Din, *Successors*, pp. 199-200.
17. See de Rachewiltz, *Papal Envoys*, pp. 34-35, 39.
18. Rashid al-Din, *Successors*, p. 78.
19. Rashid al-Din, *Successors*, p. 87. Juzjani likewise asserts that "By nature, Ögödei was exceedingly beneficent and of excellent disposition, and a great friend to Musalmans. During his reign the Muhammadans in his dominons were tranquil and prosperous in condition, and treated with respect." Juzjani, *Tabaqat-i Nasiri*, v. 2, p. 1106. The Muslim sources are equally unanimous, however, in describing Chinggis' son Chaghatai as an enemy of Muslims. Juzjani, *Tabaqat-i Nasiri*, v. 2, pp. 1107, 1144-48; Khwand Amir, *Habib al-siyar*, v. 1, p. 44.
20. Juzjani, *Tabaqat-i Nasiri*, v. 2, pp. 1110-1115.
21. Rashid al-Din, *Successors*, p. 90.

22. Rashid al-Din, *Successors,* p. 220.
23. Owen and Eleanor Lattimore, *Silks, Spices and Empire,* New York: Dell, 1968, p. 68.
24. Rashid al-Din, *Successors,* pp. 184, 188.
25. Ata Malik Juvaini, *Tarikh-i Jahan-gusha,* tr. J. A. Boyle, *History of the World Conqueror,* Seattle: University of Washington Press, 1997 [1958], p. 246; Rashid al-Din, *Successors,* pp. 176-177.
26. Rashid al-Din, *Successors,* p. 177; de Rachewiltz, *Papal Envoys,* pp. 100-101.
27. de Rachewiltz, *Papal Envoys,* p. 103.
28. Juzjani, *Tabaqat-i Nasiri,* v. 2, pp. 1157-1158.
29. Juzjani, *Tabaqat-i Nasiri,* v. 2, pp. 1160-1164.
30. de Rachewiltz, *Papal Envoys,* p. 120.
31. de Rachewiltz, *Papal Envoys,* p. 121.
32. She was executed in 1252 following Möngke's accession. Rashid al-Din, *Successors,* p. 215.
33. William of Rubruck, ed. and tr. Peter Jackson and David Morgan, *The Mission of Friar William of Rubruck,* London: Hakluyt Society, 1990, p. 42.
34. Rubruck, *Mission,* p. 150.
35. Rubruck, *Mission,* p. 151.
36. Rubruck, *Mission,* pp. 163-164.
37. Rubruck, *Mission,* p. 213.
38. Rubruck, *Mission,* pp. 217, 220.
39. Leonardo Olschki, *Guillaume Boucher: A French Artist at the Court of the Khans,* Baltimore: Johns Hopkins Press, 1946, pp. 33-37.
40. Rubruck, *Mission,* p. 225.
41. Rubruck, *Mission,* p. 171.
42. Rubruck, *Mission,* p. 174.
43. Rashid al-Din, *Successors,* p. 207; Rubruck, *Mission,* pp. 173, 192. Möngke also kept on two Muslim scribes, 'Imad al-Mulk and Fakhr al-Mulk. Rashid al-Din, *Successors,* p. 222.
44. Rashid al-Din, *Successors,* p. 215.
45. Juzjani claims, implausibly, that Berke Khan converted Möngke to Islam at the event of the latter's succession. Juzjani, *Tabaqat-i Nasiri,* v. 2, pp. 1181-1182.
46. Rubruck, *Mission,* p. 187.
47. Rubruck, *Mission,* p. 228.
48. Juzjani claims these debates were instigated by the Christians and Buddhists in order to discredit the Muslims. Juzjani, *Tabaqat-i Nasiri,* v. 2, pp. 1160-1163.
49. Rubruck, *Mission,* p. 229.
50. Rubruck, *Mission,* p. 235.
51. Rubruck, *Mission,* pp. 236-237.
52. Rubruck, *Mission,* pp. 236-237.
53. E. A. Wallis Budge, tr., *The Monks of Kublai Khan: The History of the Life and Travels of Rabban Sawma,* London: Religious Tract Society, 1928, p. 223. Juzjani states that Baghdad was betrayed by Shi'is in the service of the Caliph. *Tabaqat-i Nasiri,* v. 2, pp. 1228-1252.
54. Jean Richard, "La conversion de Berke et les débuts de l'islamisation de la Horde d'Or," *Revue des études islamiques* 35 (1967), pp. 173-184.
55. Juzjani, *Tabaqat-i Nasiri,* v. 2, pp. 1288-1290.
56. Juzjani, *Tabaqat-i Nasiri,* v. 2, p. 1291.
57. William Adam, "De modo sararcenos extirpandi," ed. Ch. Kohler, in *Recueil des historiens des Croisades, Documents Arméniens,* Paris: Imprimerie Nationale, 1902, v. 2, p. 530; cited in DeWeese, *Islamization,* p. 141.

58. Marco Polo, *The Travels*, tr. Ronald Latham, New York: Penguin, 1959, p. 119.
59. Khwand Amir, *Habib al-siyar*, v. 1, p. 38.
60. Rashid al-Din, *Successors*, p. 278.
61. Khwand Amir, *Habib al-siyar*, v. 1, p. 39.
62. Khwand Amir, *Habib al-siyar*, v. 1, p. 39.
63. Leonardo Olschki, *Marco Polo's Asia*, Berkeley: University of California Press, 1960, pp. 195, 198.
64. Rossabi, "Muslims," pp. 272-273. Rashid al-Din mentions Khubilai's vizier Sayyid 'Ajall Sham al-Din 'Umar of Bukhara, his son Nasir al-Din who was appointed governor of Qara-Jang, and grandson Abu Bakr who was made governor of Zaytun. Rashid al-Din, *Successors*, pp. 287-288.
65. Rossabi, *Khubilai Khan*, p. 142.
66. Olschki, *Marco Polo's Asia*, pp. 198-199.
67. Rossabi, "Muslims," pp. 280-281.
68. Polo, *Travels*, pp. 133-135; Rashid al-Din, *Successors*, p. 293.
69. Polo, *Travels*, p. 135; Rashid al-Din, *Successors*, p. 294. Boyle notes that according to the *Yüan Shih*, however, Khubilai's restrictive edict occurred in 1280, prior to Ahmad's death.
70. Rashid al-Din, *Successors*, p. 294. See also A. C. Moule, *Christians in China Before the Year 1550*, London: Society for Promoting Christian Knowledge, 1930, pp. 228-229.
71. Qur'an 9:5. The verse in question refers to Muhammad's Meccan opponents; whether it condones the killing of polytheists in general is a matter of debate.
72. Rashid al-Din, *Successors*, p. 295. Khwand Amir states that the verse had earlier been brought to the attention of the Il-Khan Abaqa by "a vile Jew, intent upon doing the Muslims in." *Habib al-siyar*, v. 1, p. 37.
73. Rashid al-Din, *Successors*, p. 294.
74. J. A. Montgomery, tr., *The History of Yaballaha III, Nestorian Patriarch and of His Vicar Bar Sawma*, New York: Columbia University Press, 1927, pp. 8-9.
75. Montgomery, tr., *History of Yaballaha III*, pp. 45-46.
76. Montgomery, tr., *History of Yaballaha III*, p. 46, note 21.
77. Khwand Amir, *Habib al-siyar*, v. 1, p. 67.
78. Montgomery, tr., *History of Yaballaha III*, p. 50.
79. Khwand Amir, *Habib al-siyar*, v. 1, p. 74.
80. Khwand Amir, *Habib al-siyar*, v. 1, pp. 74-5.
81. Montgomery, tr., *History of Yaballaha III*, p. 75.
82. Montgomery, tr., *History of Yaballaha III*, p. 79.
83. On him see J. A. Boyle, ed., *Cambridge History of Iran*, v. 6, *The Saljuk and Mongol Periods*, Cambridge: Cambridge University Press, 1968, pp. 376-379, 380, 382-384. Rashid al-Din says of Nawruz's earlier rebellion that "because of Nauruz, much damage was done [in Khurasan] and many Muslims were killed." *Successors*, p. 141.
84. Khwand Amir, *Habib al-siyar*, v. 1, p. 81.
85. Khwand Amir, *Habib al siyar*, v. 1, p. 82.
86. Rashid al-Din, *Successors*, p. 325. The conversions of Ghazan and Ananda seem to have persuaded Temür Khan that Islam was an acceptable religion, and to have encouraged further conversions at the Mongol court.
87. Budge, tr., *Monks of Kublai Khan*, pp. 210-214.
88. Budge, tr., *Monks of Kublai Khan*, pp. 216-219.
89. Budge, tr., *Monks of Kublai Khan*, pp. 223-224.
90. Budge, tr., *Monks of Kublai Khan*, pp. 221-222.
91. Budge, tr., *Monks of Kublai Khan*, p. 225.

92. Budge, tr., *Monks of Kublai Khan*, p. 226.
93. Budge, tr., *Monks of Kublai Khan*, p. 229.
94. Budge, tr., *Monks of Kublai Khan*, p. 230.
95. Budge, tr., *Monks of Kublai Khan*, p. 231.
96. Budge, tr., *Monks of Kublai Khan*, pp. 234-238.
97. John of Montecorvino, in Christopher Dawson, ed., *The Mongol Mission*, London: Sheed and Ward, 1955, pp. 224-225.
98. Dawson, ed., *The Mongol Mission*, p. 226.
99. de Rachewiltz, *Papal Envoys*, p. 184.
100. Dawson, ed., *The Mongol Mission*, p. 237.
101. Dawson, ed., *The Mongol Mission*, p. 233.
102. Dawson, ed., *The Mongol Mission*, p. 237.
103. de Rachewiltz, *Papal Envoys*, p. 169.
104. de Rachewiltz, *Papal Envoys*, p. 189.
105. de Rachewiltz, *Papal Envoys*, p. 192.
106. de Rachewiltz, *Papal Envoys*, p. 195.
107. Fletcher suggests that since Islam arose among largely nomadic Arabs and Tibetan nomads had "adapted Tibetan Buddhism for nomadic consumption," these two traditions were the most appealing to the peoples of the steppes. "The Mongols," p. 44. This argument, however, disregards the immense popularity of Nestorian Christianity in Inner Asia, which lasted many centuries.

CHAPTER 7

1. Grousset, *Empire of the Steppes*, p. 434. See also Moffett, *Christianity in Asia*, pp. 480, 483-6, 504; G. W. Houston, "An Overview of Nestorians in Inner Asia," *Central Asiatic Journal* 24 (1980), p. 67; Bertold Spuler, "The Disintegration of the Caliphate in the West," in P. M. Holt et al., *Cambridge History of Islam*, 4 vols., Cambridge: Cambridge University Press, 1970, v. 1, p. 170; G. W. Thacker, "A Nestorian Gravestone from Central Asia in the Gulbenkian Museum," *Durham University Journal* (March 1967), p. 100.
2. Khwand Amir, *Habib al-siyar*, v. 1, pp. 229, 250, 260, 271-272; likewise over Hindu rulers in India (pp. 264, 266, 268-269) as well as plans to do the same to the Chinese (p. 292).
3. H. Moranville, *Mémoire sur Tamerlan et Sa Cour par un Dominicain en 1403*, Bibliothèque de l'école de Chartres, v. 55, Paris, 1894; quoted in Moffett, *Christianity in Asia*, p. 486.
4. Khwand Amir, *Habib al-siyar*, v. 1, pp. 234, 249.
5. It is not impossible, given the long presence of Nestorianism among the steppe peoples, that some of Timur's nomadic rivals had Christian affinities, but nowhere do the sources mention this explicitly as a factor.
6. These come from two graveyards containing a total of some 610 tombstones dating from 858 to 1342. See Saeki, *Nestorian Documents and Relics*, 408-419, and Thacker, "A Nestorian Gravestone."
7. Barthold, *Four Studies*, v. 1, p. 136.
8. Antoine Mostaert, *Ordosica* (*Bulletin of the Catholic University of Peking* 9), Peking: Catholic University, 1934; cf. Henri Bernard, *La Découverte de nestoriens mongols aux Ordos*, Tientsin: Hautes Études, 1935. The tribal name Erküt appears to be derived from the Persian *Arkhun*, or high priest (Saeki, *Nestorian Documents and Relics*, p. 426).

9.   L. E. Browne, *The Eclipse of Christianity in Asia from the Time of Muhammad till the Fourteenth Century,* Cambridge: Cambridge University Press, 1933, p. 108.
10.   Franck and Brownestone, *The Silk Road,* p. 259.
11.   Bentley, *Old World Encounters,* p. 107.
12.   I am grateful to Jerry Bentley for this observation.
13.   Polo, *Travels,* pp. 235-237.
14.   Lieu, *Manichaeism in Central Asia and China,* p. 194.
15.   Lieu, *Manichaeism in Central Asia and China,* p. 106.
16.   Lieu, *Manichaeism in Central Asia and China,* p. 133.
17.   Lieu, *Manichaeism in Central Asia and China,* p. 168.
18.   Lieu, *Manichaeism in Central Asia and China,* p. 180.
19.   The history of the sect is given by a seventeenth-century source translated into French by Paul Pelliot, "Les traditions manichéennes au Fou-kien," *T'oung Pao* 22 (1923).
20.   This relief and the temple which houses it are described in detail by Peter Bryder, ". . . Where the Faint Traces," p. 203; see also Lieu, *Manichaeism in the Later Roman Empire,* pp. 256-257, and Lieu, *Manichaeism in Central Asia and China,* pp. 56-58, 188-195.
21.   Lieu, *Manichaeism in Central Asia and China,* p. 58.
22.   Bryder, "...Where the Faint Traces," p. 207.
23.   See Jiger Janabel, "From Mongol Empire to Qazaq Juzder: Studies on the Steppe Political Cycle (13-18 cc.)," Ph.D. dissertation, Harvard University, 1997.
24.   The continual tension between steppe peoples who had converted to Islam and those that hadn't is a recurring theme in the *Habib al-Siyar;* for example, v. 1, pp. 97, 163, 234, 249, and elsewhere.
25.   Muhammad Haydar Dughlat, *Tarikh-i Rashidi,* tr. D. Ross, ed. N. Elias, New York: Praeger, 1970 [1895], p. 14.
26.   Dughlat, *Tarikh-i Rashidi,* pp. 14-15.
27.   Dughlat, *Tarikh-i Rashidi,* p. 52.
28.   Dughlat, *Tarikh-i Rashidi,* pp. 57-58.
29.   For more on this ethnonym see Golden, *Introduction,* pp. 176-177.
30.   Barthold, *Four Studies,* v. 1, pp. 91-92; Joseph Fletcher, "Confrontations Between Muslim Missionaries and Nomad Unbelievers in the Late Sixteenth Century: Notes on Four Passages from the Diya al-Qulub," in Walther Heissig, ed., *Tractata Altaica,* Wiesbaden: Otto Harrassowitz, 1976, pp. 170-171.
31.   Dughlat, *Tarikh-i Rashidi,* pp. 125, 148.
32.   Barthold, *Four Studies,* v. 1, p. 159.
33.   Mahmud b. Amir Wali, *Bahr al-Asrar fi manaqib al-akhyar,* tr. Buri Ahmedov, *More tain otnositel'no doblestei blagorodnyx,* Tashkent, 1977, p. 41, cited in Golden, *Introduction,* p. 344.
34.   Baldick, *Imaginary Muslims,* p. 174.
35.   Thomas Oller interviewed and photographed several of these Kazakh shamans, including a fourteen-year-old girl, during the course of visits to northwestern Mongolia in 1994 and 1995 (personal communication).
36.   Some examples are mentioned in DeWeese, *Islamization,* p. 209; Fletcher, "Confrontations," p. 171; and Baldick, *Imaginary Muslims.*
37.   Ibn Battuta, *The Travels of Ibn Battuta,* tr. H. A. R. Gibb, 4 vols., Cambridge: Hakluyt Society, 1958-94, v. 3, p. 568.
38.   Ibn Battuta, *Travels,* p. 556.
39.   The English merchant Anthony Jenkinson reports in 1558 that the Kazakhs and the Kyrgyz between them had completely cut off Silk Route trade with the East (*The Voyage of Master Anthony Jenkinson,* London: Hakluyt Society, 1886, p. 86).
40.   See Alam, "Trade, State Policy and Regional Change," pp. 202-227.

41. On this see Stephen Dale, *Indian Merchants and Eurasian Trade,* Cambridge: Cambridge University Press, 1994.

42. Frye, *Bukhara,* pp. 100-101; Bentley, *Old World Encounters,* p. 14.

BIBLIOGRAPHY

Alam, Muzaffar, "Trade, State Policy and Regional Change: Aspects of Mughal-Uzbek Commercial Relations ca. 1550-1750," *Journal of the Economic and Social History of the Orient* 37 (1994), pp. 202-227.

Anthony, David W., and Dorcas R. Brown, "The Origins of Horseback Riding," *Antiquity* 65 (1991), pp. 22-38.

Anthony, David W., and Nokolai B. Vinogradov, "Birth of the Chariot," *Archaeology* 48/2 (1995), pp. 36-41.

Armijo-Hussein, Jacqueline, "Sayyid 'Ajall Shams al-Din: A Muslim from Bukhara, Serving the Mongols in China, and Bringing 'Civilization' to Yunnan," Ph.D. dissertation, Harvard University, 1997.

Asmussen, Jes P., *Manichaean Literature*, Delmar, NY: Scholars' Facsimiles and Reprints, 1975.

———, "The Sogdian and Uigur-Turkish Christian Literature in Central Asia Before the Real Rise of Islam: A Survey," in L. A. Nercus, ed., *Indological and Buddhist Studies. Volume in Honour of Professor J.W. Jong on his Sixtieth Birthday*, Canberra: Australian National University, 1982, pp. 11-29.

Asmussen, Jes P., ed., *Xᵘastvanift: Studies in Manichaeism*, Copenhagen: Munksgaard, 1965.

Azarpay, Guitty, "A Jataka Tale on a Sasanian Silver Plate," *Bulletin of the Asia Institute*, new series, 9 (1995), pp. 99-125.

Bailey, H.W., "Iranica," *Bulletin of the School of Oriental and African Studies* 11 (1943).

Baldick, Julian, *Imaginary Muslims: The Uwaysi Sufis of Central Asia*, London and New York: I. B. Tauris, 1993.

Barber, Elizabeth Wayland, *The Mummies of Urumchi*, New York: Norton, 1999.

Bareau, André, *Les Sectes bouddhiques du petit véhicule*, Saigon: École Française d'Extrême-Orient, 1955.

Barfield, Thomas J., *The Perilous Frontier*, Oxford: Blackwell, 1989.

Bartol'd, V. V., "Mesta do-Musulmanskogo kulta v Bukhare," *Vostochnye Zapiski* 1 (1927), pp. 11-25.

Barthold, W., "The Burial Rites of the Turks and Mongols," *Central Asiatic Journal* 14/1-3 (1970), pp. 195-227.

————, *Turkestan Down to the Mongol Invasion*, 3rd. ed., London: Luzac, 1987 [1928].

————, *Four Studies on the History of Central Asia*, tr. V. and T. Minorsky, 3 vols., Leiden: Brill, 1962 [1958].

Beal, Samuel, tr., *Buddhist Records of the Western World*, New Delhi: Oriental Reprints, 1969 [1888].

Beckwith, Christopher I., *The Tibetan Empire in Central Asia*, Princeton, NJ: Princeton University Press, 1987.

BeDuhn, Jason David, review of Hans-Joachim Klimkeit, *Gnosis on the Silk Road*, *Journal of the American Oriental Society* 115/2 (1995), pp. 344-346.

Bekhradnia, Shahin, "The Tajik Case for a Zoroastrian Identity," *Religion, State and Society* 22/1 (1994), pp. 109-120.

Bennigsen, Alexandre, and Fanny E. Bryan, "Islam in Central Asia," in Mircea Eliade, ed., *Encyclopedia of Religion*, New York: Macmillan, 1987, v. 7, pp. 367-377.

Bentley, Jerry, *Old World Encounters: Cross-Cultural Contacts and Exchanges in Premodern Times*, New York: Oxford University Press, 1993.

————, "Cross-Cultural Interaction and Periodization in World History," *American Historical Review* 101/3 (1996), pp. 749-770.

Benveniste, Emile, "Le Vocabulaire Chrétien dans les Langues d'Asie Central," *L'Oriente Cristiano nella Storia della Civiltà*, Rome: Accademia Nazionale dei Lincei, 1964, pp. 85-91.

Ben-Zvi, Itzhak, *The Exiled and the Redeemed*, 3rd ed., Philadelphia: Jewish Publication Society, 1957.

Bernard, Henri, *La Découverte de nestoriens mongols aux Ordos*, Tientsin: Hautes Études, 1935.

Biruni, Abu Rayhan, *Chronology of Ancient Nations*, tr. E. Sachau, Lahore: Hijra International, 1983 [1879].

Boyce, Mary, *A Reader in Manichaean Middle Persian and Parthian*, Leiden: Brill, 1975.

————, *A History of Zoroastrianism*, 3 vols. to date, Leiden: Brill, 1975-.

————, *Zoroastrianism: Its Antiquity and Constant Vigour*, Costa Mesa, CA: Mazda, 1992.

Boyle, J. A., "A Form of Horse Sacrifice Amongst the 13th and 14th-century Mongols," *Central Asiatic Journal* 10 (1965), pp. 145-150.

————, "Turkish and Mongol Shamanism in the Middle Ages," *Folklore* 83 (1972), pp. 184-193.

————, "The Thirteenth Century Mongols' Conception of the Afterlife," *Mongolian Studies* 1 (1974), pp. 5-14.

Boyle, J. A., ed., *Cambridge History of Iran*, v. 6, *The Saljuk and Mongol Periods*, Cambridge: Cambridge University Press, 1968.

Bretschneider, Emilii, *Medieval Researches from Asiatic Sources*, Osnabruck: Biblio Verlag, 1987 [1875-76].

Browne, L. E., *The Eclipse of Christianity in Asia from the Time of Muhammad till the Fourteenth Century*, Cambridge: Cambridge University Press, 1933.

Brutzkus, Julius, "Bukhara," *Encyclopedia Judaica*, Berlin, 1929, v. 4, p. 1126.

Bryder, Peter, ". . . Where the Faint Traces of Manichaeism Disappear," *Altorientalische Forschungen* 15/1 (1988), pp. 201-208.

———, "Cao'an Revisited," *Research Into China Overseas Communication History* 16/2 (1989), pp. 35-42.

Budge, E. A. T. Wallis, tr., *The Monks of Kublai Khan: The History of the Life and Travels of Rabban Sawma*, London: Religious Tract Society, 1928.

———, *The Chronography of Gregory Abu'l Faraj*, 2 vols., London: Oxford University Press, 1932.

Bulliet, Richard, "Naw Bahar and the Survival of Iranian Buddhism," *Iran* 14 (1976), pp. 140-145.

———, "Conversion to Islam and the Emergence of a Muslim Society in Iran," in Nehemia Levtzion, ed., *Conversion to Islam*, New York. Holmes and Meier, 1979, pp. 30-51.

———, *Conversion to Islam in the Medieval Period: A Study in Quantitative History*, Cambridge, MA: Harvard University Press, 1980.

Chang, Hajji Yusuf, "The Hui (Muslim) Minority in China: An Historical Overview," *Journal of the Institute of Muslim Minority Affairs* 8/1 (1987), pp. 62-78.

Chaudhuri, K. N., *Asia Before Europe: Economy and Civilisation of the Indian Ocean from the Rise of Islam to 1750*, Cambridge: Cambridge University Press, 1990.

Chavannes, E., "Le nestorianisme et l'inscription de Karabalassoun," *Journal Asiatique* (January-February 1897), pp. 43-85.

Chavannes, E., and P. Pelliot, *Un traité Manichéen retrouvé en Chine*, Paris: Imprimérie Nationale, 1913.

Choksy, Jamsheed, *Conflict and Cooperation: Muslim Elites and Zoroastrian Subalterns in Medieval Iranian Society*, New York: Columbia University Press, 1997.

Chou Yi-liang, "Tantrism in China," *Harvard Journal of Asiatic Studies*, 8 (1945), pp. 241-332.

Christensen, A., "Die Moschee Makh in Buhara," *Orientalische Litteraturzeitung* 7 (1904), pp. 49-51.

Clark, Larry, "The Manichaean Turkic *Pothi-Book*," *Altorientalische Forschungen* 9 (1982), pp. 145-218.

Collins, J., "Persian Apocalypses," *Semeia* 14 (1979), pp. 207-217.

Colpe, Carsten, "Development of Religious Thought," in Ehsan Yarshater, ed., *Cambridge History of Iran*, v. 3, *The Seleucid, Parthian, and Sasanian Periods*, Cambridge: Cambridge University Press, 1983, pp. 819-865.

Curtin, Philip, *Cross-Cultural Trade in World History*, Cambridge: Cambridge University Press, 1984.

Dale, Stephen, *Indian Merchants and Eurasian Trade*, Cambridge: Cambridge University Press, 1994.

Dani, A. H., and V. Masson, eds., *History of the Civilizations of Central Asia*, v. 1, Paris: UNESCO, 1992.

Dawson, Christopher, ed., *The Mongol Mission*, London: Sheed and Ward, 1955.

DeGoeje, M. J., ed., *Bibliotheca Geograforum Arabicorum*, 8 vols., Leiden: Brill, 1870-1894.

DeWeese, Devin, *Islamicization and Native Religion in the Golden Horde*, State College, PA: Penn State University Press, 1995.

Dubs, Homer H., "Taoism," in H. F. MacNair, ed., *Philosophy and Religion*, Berkeley and Los Angeles: University of California Press, 1946, pp. 286-287.

Dughlat, Muhammad Haydar, *Tarikh-i Rashidi*, tr. D. Ross, ed. N. Elias, New York: Praeger, 1970 [1895].

Dumézil, Georges, *Mythe et Epopée*, 3 vols., Paris: Gallimard, 1968-1973.

Dunlop, Douglas S., *History of the Jewish Khazars*, Princeton, NJ: Princeton University Press, 1954.

Eaton, Richard, *The Sufis of Bijapur, 1300-1700*, Princeton, NJ: Princeton University Press, 1978.

Eliade, Mircea, *Shamanism: Archaic Techniques of Ecstasy*, Princeton, NJ: Princeton University Press, 1964.

Eliade, Mircea, ed., *Encyclopedia of Religion*, 16 vols., New York: Macmillan, 1987.

Emmerick, Ronald E., "Buddhism Among Iranian Peoples," in Yarshater, ed., *Cambridge History of Iran*, v. 3, *The Seleucid, Parthian, and Sasanian Periods*, Cambridge: Cambridge University Press, 1983, pp. 955-956.

————, "Buddhism in Central Asia," in Mircea Eliade, ed., *Encyclopedia of Religion*, New York: Macmillan, 1987, v. 2, pp. 400-404.

Enoki, Kazuo, "Nestorian Christianity in Medieval Times," *L'Oriente Cristiano nella Storia della Civiltà*, Rome: Accademia Nazionale dei Lincei, 1964, pp. 45-77.

Erdy, Miklos, "Manichaeans, Nestorians, or Bird Costumed Humans in Their Relation to Hunnic Type Cauldrons in Rock Carvings of the Yenisei Valley," *Eurasian Studies Yearbook* 68 (1996), pp. 45-95.

Fa-hsien, *Buddhist Country Records (Fo Kwo Ki)*, in Beal, tr., *Buddhist Records*, v. 1, pp. xxiii-lxxxiii.

Flattery, David, and Martin Schwartz, *Haoma and Harmaline: The Botanical Identity of the Indo-Iranian Sacred Hallucinogen "Soma" and Its Legacy in Religion, Language, and Middle Eastern Folklore*, Berkeley: University of California Press, 1989.

Fletcher, Joseph, "Confrontations Between Muslim Missionaries and Nomad Unbelievers in the Late Sixteenth Century: Notes on Four Passages from the Diya al-Qulub," in Walther Heissig, ed., *Tractata Altaica*, Wiesbaden: Otto Harrassowitz, 1976, pp. 167-174.

———, "The Mongols: Ecological and Social Perspectives," *Harvard Journal of Asiatic Studies* 46/1 (1986), pp. 11-49.

———, " The Naqshbandiyya in Northwest China," in B. F. Manz and Jonathan Lipman, eds., *Studies on Chinese and Islamic Inner Asia*, London: Variorum, 1995.

Flusser, David, "Hystaspes and John of Patmos," in Shaul Shaked, ed., *Irano-Judaica*, Jerusalem: Ben-Zvi Institute, 1982, pp. 12-75.

Foltz, Richard, "When Was Central Asia Zoroastrian?" *Mankind Quarterly* 38/3 (1998), pp. 189-200.

———, "Judaism and the Silk Route," *The History Teacher* 32/1 (1998), pp. 9-16.

———, "Ecumenical Mischief Under the Mongols," *Central Asiatic Journal* 43/1 (1999).

Forte, Antonino, "An Ancient Chinese Monastery Excavated in Kirgiziya," *Central Asiatic Journal* 38/1 (1994), pp. 41-57.

Franck, Irene M., and David M. Brownstone, *The Silk Road*, New York: Facts on File, 1986.

Frye, Richard, *The Golden Age of Persia*, London: Weidenfeld and Nicolson, 1975.

———, "Comparative Observations on Conversion to Islam in Iran and Central Asia," *Jerusalem Studies in Arabic and Islam* 4 (1984), pp. 81-88.

———, "The Fate of Zoroastrians in Eastern Iran," in Rika Gyselen, ed., *Au Carrefour des Réligions: Mélanges offerts à Philippe Gignoux*, Bures-sur-Yvette: Groupe pour l'Étude de la Civilisation du Moyen-Orient, 1995.

———, *The Heritage of Central Asia*, Princeton, NJ: Markus Weiner, 1996.

———, *Bukhara: The Medieval Achievement*, Costa Mesa, CA: Mazda, 1997 [1971].

Gaulier, Simone, et al., *Buddhism in Afghanistan and Central Asia*, 2 vols., Leiden: Brill, 1976.

Gibb, H. A. R., *The Arab Conquests in Central Asia*, London: Royal Asiatic Society, 1923.

Gignoux, Philippe, "Zoroastrianism," in B. A. Litvinsky, ed., *History of Civilizations of Central Asia*, v. 3, *The Crossroads of Civilizations: A.D. 250 to 750*, Paris: UNESCO, 1996, pp. 403-412.

Godbey, Allen H., "From Persia to China," in William C. White, *Chinese Jews*, 2nd ed., New York: Paragon, 1966, pp. 136-149.

Golden, Peter, "The Karakhanids and Early Islam," in Denis Sinor, ed., *Cambridge History of Early Inner Asia*, Cambridge: Cambridge University Press, 1990, pp. 343-370.

————, *An Introduction to the History of the Turkic Peoples*, Wiesbaden: Otto Harrassowitz, 1992.

Gombrich, Richard, *Theravada Buddhism*, London: Routledge, 1988.

Grenet, Frantz, and N. Sims-Williams, "The Historical Context of the Sogdian Ancient Letters," *Transition Periods in Iranian History*, (*Studia Iranica*, cahier 5), Paris: Association pour l'avancement des études iraniennes, 1987, pp. 101-22.

Grenet, Frantz, and Zhang Guangda, "The Last Refuge of the Sogdian Religion: Dunhuang in the Ninth and Tenth Centuries," *Bulletin of the Asia Institute* 10 (1996), pp. 175-186.

Grousset, René, *The Empire of the Steppes*, tr. Naomi Walford, New Brunswick, NJ: Rutgers University Press, 1970.

Guidi, M., *La lotta tra l'Islam e il manicheismo*, Rome, 1927.

Haloun, G., and W. Henning, trs., "The Compendium of the Doctrines, and Styles, of the Teachings of Mani, the Buddha of Light," *Asia Major* 3/2 (1952), pp. 184-221.

Hambly, Gavin, *Central Asia*, London: Weidenfeld and Nicolson, 1969.

Haneda, Akira, "Introduction: Problems of the Turkicization, Problems of Islamization," *Acta Asiatica* 34 (1978), pp. 1-21.

Harmatta, Janos, "Sino-Indica," *Acta Antiqua Academiae Scientarum Hungaricae* 12/1-2 (1964), pp. 3-21.

————, "Religions in the Kushan Empire," in *History of the Civilizations of Central Asia*, v. 2, Paris: UNESCO, 1994, pp. 313-329.

Harmatta, Janos, ed., *History of the Civilizations of Central Asia*, v. 2, Paris: UNESCO, 1994.

Harrison, Paul, "Who Gets to Ride in the Great Vehicle? Self-Image and Identity Among the Followers of the Early Mahayana," *Journal of the International Association of Buddhist Studies* 10/1 (1987), pp. 67-90.

————, "The Earliest Chinese Translations of Mahayan Sutras: Some Notes on the Works of Lokaksema," *Buddhist Studies Review* 10/2 (1993), pp. 135-177.

————, "Searching for the Origins of the Mahayana: What Are We Looking For?" *The Eastern Buddhist* 28/1 (1995), pp. 48-59.

Harvey, Peter, *An Introduction to Buddhism: Teachings, History and Practices*, Cambridge: Cambridge University Press, 1990.

Heissig, Walther, *The Religions of Mongolia*, Berkeley: University of California Press, 1980.

Henning, W. B., "Mani's Last Journey," *Bulletin of the School of Oriental and African Studies* 10 (1939-42), pp. 941-953.

———, "The Book of Giants," *Bulletin of the School of Oriental and African Studies* 11 (1943-46), pp. 52-74.

———, "A Sogdian God," *Bulletin of the School of Oriental and African Studies* 28/2 (1965), pp. 242-254.

Herodotus, *The Histories*, tr. Aubrey de Sélincourt, rev. A. R. Burn, New York: Penguin, 1972.

Herzfeld, Ernst, *Zoroaster and His World*, 2 vols., New York: Octagon Press, 1974 [1947].

Higuchi, Takayasu, "Buddhist Ruins of West Turkestan," *Bukkyoshigaku Kenkyu* 27/1 (1984), pp. 119-141 (in Japanese).

Hintze, Almut, "The Greek and Hebrew Versions of the Book of Esther and Its Iranian Background," in Shaul Shaked, and Amnon Metzer, eds., *Irano-Judaica III*, Jerusalem: Ben-Zvi Institute, 1994, pp. 34-39.

Hinüber, Oskar von, "Expansion to the North: Afghanistan and Central Asia," in Heinz Bechert and Richard Gombrich, eds., *The World of Buddhism*, London: Thames and Hudson, 1984, pp. 99-107.

Hiskett, Mervyn, *The Course of Islam in Africa*, Edinburgh: Edinburgh University Press, 1994.

Hodgson, Marshall, *The Venture of Islam*, 3 vols., Chicago: University of Chicago Press, 1974.

Hoffman, H., "Kalacakra Studies: I," *Central Asiatic Journal* 13 (1969), pp. 52-73.

Hopkirk, Peter, *Foreign Devils on the Silk Road*, Amherst: University of Massachusetts Press, 1984 [1980].

———, *The Great Game*, Tokyo: Kodansha International, 1992.

Horner, I. B., tr., *Milinda's Questions*, 2 vols., London: Luzac & Co., 1969 [1963].

Houston, G. W., "An Overview of Nestorians in Inner Asia," *Central Asiatic Journal* 24 (1980), pp. 60-68.

Hsüan-tsang, *Records of the Western Countries* (*Ta T'ang Si Yu Ki*), in Samuel Beal, tr., *Buddhist Records of the Western World*, New Delhi: Oriental Reprints, 1969 [1884].

Hui-li, *The Life of Hsuan-Tsang*, tr. Li Yung-hsi, Peking: Chinese Buddhist Association, 1959.

Hunter, Erica C. D., "The Conversion of the Kerait to Christianity in A.D. 1007," *Zentralasiatische Studien* 22 (1989-91), pp. 143-163.

Ibn al-Athir, *Al-Kamil fi'l-ta'rikh*, in M. J. DeGoeje, ed., *Bibliotheca Geographorum Arabicorum*, v. 8.

Ibn Battuta, *The Travels of Ibn Battuta*, tr. H. A. R. Gibb, 4 vols., Cambridge: Hakluyt Society, 1958-94.

Ibn Khurdadbih, *Kitab al-masalik wa'l mamalik*, ed. M. J. DeGoeje, *Biblotheca Geographorum Arabicorum*, v. 6; tr. C. Barbier de Meynard, "Le Livre des Routes et des Provinces par Ibn Khordadbeh," *Journal Asiatique* 6/5 (1865), pp. 5-127, 227-280, 446-527.

Ibn Miskawayh, *Tajarub al-Umam*, tr. D. S. Margoliouth, Oxford: Oxford University Press, 1920-21.

Ibn Nadim [Abu'l-Faraj Muhammad ibn Ishaq al-Warraq], *Fihrist al-'ulum*, tr. B. Dodge, *The Fihrist of al-Nadim: A Tenth Century Survey of Muslim Culture*, 2 vols., New York: Columbia University Press, 1970.

Jan, Yün-hua, "Buddhist Relations Between India and Sung China," *History of Religions* 6 (1966), pp. 24-42, 135-168.

Janabel, Jiger, "From Mongol Empire to Qazaq Juzder: Studies on the Steppe Political Cycle (13-18 cc.)," Ph.D. dissertation, Harvard University, 1997.

————, "The Islamization of Southern Qazaqstan in the Ninth Century," paper presented at the American Historical Association annual conference, Seattle, WA, 1998.

Jenkinson, Anthony, *The Voyage of Master Anthony Jenkinson*, London: Hakluyt Society, 1886.

Juvaini, Ata Malik, *Tarikh-i Jahan-gusha*, tr. J. A. Boyle, *History of the World Conqueror*, Seattle: University of Washington Press, 1997 [1958].

Juzjani, Minhaj al-Din, *Tabaqat-i Nasiri*, 2 vols., tr. H. G. Raverty, New Delhi: Oriental Reprints, 1970 [1881].

Kashgari, Mahmud, *Divan Lughat al-Turk*, tr. R. Dankoff and J. Kelly, 3 vols., Cambridge, MA: Dept. of Near Eastern Languages and Civilizations, 1982-85.

Khwand Amir, *Habib al-siyar*, v. 3, tr. W. M. Thackston, Jr., 2 vols., Cambridge, MA: Dept. of Near Eastern Languages and Civilizations, 1994.

Klimkeit, Hans-Joachim, "Christians, Buddhists and Manichaeans in Medieval Central Asia," *Buddhist-Christian Studies* 1 (1981), pp. 46-50.

————, *Manichaean Art and Calligraphy*, Leiden: Brill, 1982.

————, "Christian-Buddhist Encounter in Medieval Central Asia," in G. W. Houston, *The Cross and the Lotus*, Delhi: Motilal Banarsidass, 1985, pp. 9-24.

————, "Jesus' Entry into Parinirvana: Manichaean Identity in Buddhist Central Asia," *Numen* 33 (1986), pp. 225-240.

————, "Christian Art on the Silk Road," in Thomas W. Gaehtgens, ed., *Kunstlerischer Austaush: Akten des XXVIII Internationalen Kongresses für Kunstgeschichte, Berlin, 15-20 Juli 1992*, Berlin: Akademie Verlag, 1993, pp. 477-488.

————, *Gnosis on the Silk Road*, San Francisco: Harper, 1993.

Koshelenko, G., "The Beginnings of Buddhism in Margiana," *Acta Antiqua Academiae Scientarum Hungaricae* 14 (1966), pp. 175-183.

Kyuzo, Kato, "Cultural Exchange on the Ancient Silk Road," *Senri Ethnological Studies* 32 (1992), pp. 5-20.

Lamotte, Etienne, *History of Indian Buddhism*, Louvain: Peters Press, 1988.

Lang, D. M., "St. Euthymius the Georgian and the Barlaam and Ioasaph Romance," *Bulletin of the School of Oriental and African Studies* 17/2 (1955), pp. 306-325.

Lattimore, Owen and Eleanor, *Silks, Spices and Empire*, New York: Dell, 1968.

Law, David, *From Samaria to Samarkand*, Lanham, MD: University Press of America, 1992.

le Coq, Alexander von, *Die buddhistische Spätantike in Mittelasien*, v. 2, *Die manichäischen Miniaturen*, Berlin: D. Reimer, 1913.

———, *Buried Treasures of Chinese Turkestan*, London: Allen & Unwin, 1928.

Leslie, Donald D., *The Survival of the Chinese Jews*, Leiden: Brill, 1972.

———, *Islam in Traditional China: A Short History*, Canberra: Canberra College of Advanced Education, 1986.

LeStrange, Guy, *The Lands of the Eastern Caliphate*, New York: Barnes and Noble, 1966 [1905].

Lewis, Bernard, *The Assassins: A Radical Sect in Islam*, New York: Oxford University Press, 1967.

Lieu, S. N. C., *Manichaeism in the Later Roman Empire and Medieval China*, Tübingen: Mohr, 1992 [1985].

———, *Manichaeism in Central Asia and China*, Leiden: Brill, 1998.

Litvinsky [Litvinskii], B. A., "Central Asia," in G. P. Malalasekera, ed., *Encyclopaedia of Buddhism*, v. 4, fasc. 1, Columbo: Government Press, 1979, pp. 21-52.

———, "Prehistoric Religions: The Eurasian Steppes and Inner Asia," in Mircea Eliade, ed., *Encyclopedia of Religion*, New York: Macmillan, 1987, v. 11, pp. 516-522.

Litvinsky [Litvinskii], B. A., ed., *History of the Civilizations of Central Asia*, v. 3, Paris: UNESCO, 1996.

Litvinskii, B. A., and I. R. Pichikian, "The Hellenistic Architecture and Art of the Temple of the Oxus," *Bulletin of the Asia Institute*, new series, 8 (1994), pp. 47-66.

Liu, Ts'un-yan, "Traces of Zoroastrian and Manichaean Activities in pre-T'ang China," in *Selected Papers from the Hall of Harmonious Winds*, Leiden: Brill, 1976, pp. 2-55.

Liu, Xinru, *Ancient India and Ancient China, Trade and Religious Exchanges AD 1-600*, New Delhi: Oxford University Press, 1988.

———, "Silks and Religions in Eurasia, c. A.D. 600-1200," *Journal of World History* 6 (1995), pp. 25-48.

————, *Silk and Religion,* Delhi: Oxford University Press, 1996.

Livshits, V. A., "The Sogdian Letters from Mt. Mugh," *XXV International Congress of Orientalists,* Moscow: Nauka, 1960.

Livshits, V. A., and Z. I. Usmanova, "New Parthian Inscriptions from Old Merv," in Shaul Shaked, and Amnon Metzer, eds., *Irano-Judaica III,* Jerusalem: Ben-Zvi Institute, 1994, pp. 99-105.

Loewenthal, Rudolf, "The Jews of Bukhara," *Central Asian Collectanea,* no. 8, Washington, DC, 1961.

MacKenzie, D. N., "Mani's *Šabuhragan,*" *Bulletin of the School of Oriental and African Studies* 42 (1979), pp. 500-534, and 43 (1980), pp. 288-310.

Mackerras, Colin, "The Uighurs," in Denis Sinor, ed., *Cambridge History of Early Inner Asia,* Cambridge: Cambridge University Press, 1990, pp. 329-335.

Maenchen-Helfen, O., "Manichaeans in Siberia," *Semitic and Oriental Studies Presented to William Popper,* Berkeley: University of California Press, 1951, pp. 311-326.

Mair, Victor, "Old Sinitic *Mʸag, Old Persian Magus, and English 'Magician,'" *Early China* 15 (1990), pp. 27-47.

————, "Prehistoric Caucasoid Corpses of the Tarim Basin," *Journal of Indo-European Studies* 23/3-4 (1995), pp. 281-307.

Mallory, J. P., *In Search of the Indo-Europeans: Language, Archaeology, and Myth,* London: Thames and Hudson, 1989.

Margoliouth, D. S., "An Early Judeo-Persian Document from Khotan in the Stein Collection, With Other Early Persian Documents," *Journal of the Royal Asiatic Society* (1903), pp. 735-761.

Mason, Isaac, "The Mohammadans of China: When, and How, They First Came," *Journal of the North China Branch of the Royal Asiatic Society* 60 (1929), pp. 42-78.

McChesney, Robert, *Central Asia: Foundations of Change,* Princeton, NJ: Darwin Press, 1996.

Meserve, Ruth I., "Inner Asian Religions," in Mircea Eliade, ed., *Encyclopedia of Religion,* New York: Macmillan, 1987, v. 7, pp. 238-247.

Messina, Giuseppe, *Cristianismo, buddhismo manicheismo nell'Asia antica,* Rome: Pontificio Instituto Biblico, 1947.

Mingana, Alphonse, *The Early Spread of Christianity in Central Asia and the Far East: A New Document,* Manchester: Manchester University Press, 1925.

Minorsky, V., "Tamim ibn Bahr's Journey to the Uighurs," *Bulletin of the School of Oriental and African Studies* 12 (1948), pp. 275-305.

Moffett, Samuel H., *A History of Christianity in Asia,* vol. 1, San Francisco: Harper, 1992.

Montgomery, J. A., tr., *The History of Yaballaha III, Nestorian Patriarch and of His Vicar Bar Sawma,* New York: Columbia University Press, 1927.

Mostaert, Antoine, *Ordosica* (*Bulletin of the Catholic University of Peking*) 9, Peking: Catholic University, 1934.

Moule, A.C., *Christians in China Before the Year 1550*, London: Society for Promoting Christian Knowledge, 1930.

Narain, A. K., *The Indo-Greeks*, Oxford: Oxford University Press, 1957.

Narshakhi, Abu Bakr Muhammad, *Tarikh-i Bukhara*, tr. R. N. Frye, Cambridge, MA: Mediaeval Academy of America, 1954.

Nattier, Jan, "The Meanings of the Maitreya Myth: A Typological Analysis," in Alan Sponberg and Helen Hardacre, eds., *Maitreya, the Future Buddha*, Princeton, NJ: Princeton University Press, 1988, pp. 23-47.

———, "Church Language and Vernacular Language in Central Asian Buddhism," *Numen* 37/2 (1990), pp. 195-219.

———, "The Heart Sutra: A Chinese Apocryphal Text?" *International Journal of Buddhist Studies* 15/2 (1992), pp. 153-223.

Neusner, Jacob, "Rabbi and Magus in Third-century Sasanian Babylonia," *History of Religions* 6 (1966), pp. 169-178.

———, "Jews in Iran," in Ehsan Yarshater, ed., *Cambridge History of Iran*, v. 3, *The Seleucid, Parthian, and Sasanian Periods*, Cambridge: Cambridge University Press, 1983, pp. 909-923.

Olschki, Leonardo, *Guillaume Boucher: A French Artist at the Court of the Khans*, Baltimore: Johns Hopkins Press, 1946.

———, "Manichaeism, Buddhism and Christianity in Marco Polo's China," *Zeitschrift der schweizerischen Gesellschaft für Asienkunde* 5/1-2 (1951), pp. 1-21.

———, *Marco Polo's Asia*, Berkeley: University of California Press, 1960.

Pelliot, Paul, "Les influences iraniennes en Asie Central et en Extrême-Orient," *Revue d'Histoire et de Littérature Réligieuses* 3/2 (1912), pp. 97-119.

———, "Chrétiens de l'Asie centrale et d'Extrême-Orient," *T'oung Pao* 15 (1914), pp. 623-644.

———, "Les traditions manichéennes au Fou-kien," *T'oung Pao* 22 (1923), pp. 193-208.

———, "Neuf notes sur des questions d'Asie Centrale," *T'oung Pao* 26 (1929), pp. 201-265.

———, *Recherches sur les Chrétiens de l'Asie centrale et d'Extrême-Orient*, Paris: Imprimérie nationale, 1973.

Pestalozza, Uberto, "Il manicheismo presso i Turchi occidentali ed orientali," *Rendiconti del Reale Instituto Lombardo di Scienze e Lettere*, 2nd series, 67 (1934), pp. 417-497.

Phillips, E. D., "The Argippaei of Herodotus," *Artibus Asiae* 23 (1960), pp. 124-128.

Piacentini, Valeria Fiorani, *Turchizzazione ed islamizzazione dell'Asia Centrale (VI-XVI secolo d. Cr.)*, Milan: Società Editrice Dante Alighieri, 1974.

Plano Carpini, John of, *The Journey of Friar John of Pian de Carpini*, ed. Manuel Komroff, *Contemporaries of Marco Polo*, New York: Dorset, 1989 [1928].

Poliakov, Sergei P., *Everyday Islam: Religion and Tradition in Rural Central Asia*, Armonk, NY: M. E. Sharpe, 1992.

Pollock, Michael, *Mandarins, Jews and Missionaries*, Philadelphia: Jewish Publication Society, 1980.

Polo, Marco, *The Travels*, tr. Ronald Latham, New York: Penguin, 1959.

Pritsak, Omeljan, "The Khazar Kingdom's Conversion to Judaism," *Harvard Ukrainian Studies* 2 (1978), pp. 261-281.

―――, *The Origin of Rus*, v. 1, Cambridge, MA: Harvard University Press, 1981.

Pulleyblank, E. G., "A Sogdian Colony in Inner Mongolia," *T'oung Pao* 46 (1952), pp. 317-356.

―――, "Han China in Central Asia," *International Historical Review* 3 (1981), pp. 278-286.

Puri, B. N., *Buddhism in Central Asia*, Delhi: Motilal Banarsidass, 1987.

Qumi, Qazi Ahmad, *Gulistan-i hunar*, tr. V. Minorsky, *Calligraphers and Painters*, Washington: Smithsonian, 1959.

Rabinowitz, L., *Jewish Merchant Adventurers: A Study of the Radanites*, London: Goldston, 1948.

Rachewiltz, Igor de, *Papal Envoys to the Great Khans*, London: Faber and Faber, 1971.

Rashid al-Din, *Jami' al-tawarikh*, tr. J. A. Boyle, *The Successors of Genghis Khan*, New York: Columbia University Press, 1971.

Reischauer, Edwin O., *Ennin's Diary: The Record of a Pilgrimage to China in Search of the Law*, New York: Ronald Press, 1955.

Richard, Jean, "La conversion de Berke et les débuts de l'islamisation de la Horde d'Or," *Revue des études islamiques* 35 (1967), pp. 173-184.

―――, "Le Christianisme dans l'Asie Centrale," *Journal of Asian History* 16 (1982), pp. 101-124.

Risso, Patricia, *Merchants and Faith: Muslim Commerce and Culture in the Indian Ocean*, Boulder, CO: Westview, 1995.

Rondelez, V., "Un évêché en Asie Centrale au XIVe siècle," *Neue Zeitschrift für Missionswissenschaft* 7 (1951), pp. 1-17.

Rossabi, Morris, "The Muslims of the Early Yüan Dynasty," in *China Under Mongol Rule*, ed. John D. Langlois, Princeton, NJ: Princeton University Press, 1981, pp. 258-299.

―――, *Khubilai Khan: His Life and Times*, Berkeley: University of California Press, 1988.

―――, "The 'Decline' of Central Asian Caravan Trade," in James Tracy, ed., *The Rise of Merchant Empires: Long-Distance Trade in the Early Modern World, 1350-1750*, Cambridge: Cambridge University Press, 1990.

————, *Voyager from Xanadu: Rabban Sauma, First Eastern Emissary to the West*, New York: Kodansha, 1992.

Rubruck, William, *The Mission of Friar William of Rubruck*, Peter Jackson and David Morgan, eds. and trs., London: Hakluyt Society, 1990.

Russell, James R., "Zoroastrianism as the State Religion of Ancient Iran," *Journal of the K. R. Cama Oriental Institute* 53 (1986), pp. 74-142.

————, "Zoroastrian Elements in the Book of Esther," in Shaked and Metzer, eds., *Irano-Judaica II*, Jerusalem: Ben-Zvi, 1990, pp. 33-40.

Saeki, P. Y., *The Nestorian Documents and Relics in China*, 2nd ed., Tokyo: Academy of Oriental Culture, 1951.

Saunders, J., "The Decline and Fall of Christianity in Medieval Asia," *Journal of Religious History* 5 (1968-69), pp. 93-104.

Schafer, Edward H., "Iranian Merchants in T'ang Dynasty Tales," *Semitic and Oriental Studies Presented to William Popper*, Berkeley: University of California Press, 1951, pp. 403-422.

————, *The Golden Peaches of Samarkand: A Study of T'ang Exotics*, Berkeley: University of California Press, 1962.

Schwartz, Martin, "Studies in the Texts of Sogdian Christians," Ph.D. dissertation, University of California, Berkeley, 1967.

————, "The Religion of Achæmenian Iran," in Ilya Gershevitch, ed., *Cambridge History of Iran*, v. 2, *The Median and Achaemenian Periods*, Cambridge: Cambridge University Press, 1985, pp. 664-697.

Scott, David, "Manichaean Views of Buddhism," *History of Religions* 25/2 (1985), pp. 99-115.

————, "Manichaean Responses to Zoroastrianism," *Religious Studies* 25 (1989), pp. 435-458.

————, "The Iranian Face of Buddhism," *East and West* 40 (1990), pp. 43-77.

————, "Buddhist Responses to Manichaeism," *History of Religions* 35 (1995), pp. 148-162.

Semenow, G. L. *Studia zur sogdischen kultur an der Seidenstrasse*, Wiesbaden: Otto Harrassowitz, 1996.

Shaked, Shaul, "Iranian Functions in Esther," in *Irano-Judaica*, Jerusalem: Ben-Zvi, 1982, pp. 292-303.

————, "Iranian Influence on Judaism: First Century B.C.E. to Second Century B.C.E.," in W. D. Davies and Louis Finkelstein, eds., *Cambridge History of Judaism*, v. 1, Cambridge: Cambridge University Press, 1984, pp. 308-325.

————, "First Man, First King: Notes on Semitic Iranian Sycretism and Iranian Mythological Transformations," in Shaked, ed., *Gilgul: Essays on Transformation, Revolution and Permanence*, Leiden: Brill, 1987, pp. 238-256.

Shaked, Shaul, ed., *Irano-Judaica*, Jerusalem: Ben-Zvi Institute, 1982.

Shaked, Shaul and Amnon Metzer, eds., *Irano-Judaica II*, Jerusalem: Ben-Zvi, 1990.

———, *Irano-Judaica III*, Jerusalem: Ben-Zvi Institute, 1994.

Shizuka, Sasaki, "A Study on the Origin of Mahayana Buddhism," *The Eastern Buddhist* 30/1 (1997), pp. 79-113.

Shkoda, V. G., "The Sogdian Temple: Structure and Rituals," *Bulletin of the Asia Institute* 10 (1996), pp. 195-206.

Sims-Williams, Nicholas, "Syro-Sogdica I: An Anonymous Homily on the Three Periods of Solitary Life," *Orientalia Christiana Periodica* 47 (1981), pp. 441-446.

———, "Indian Elements in Parthian and Sogdian," in K. Röhrborn and W. Veenker, eds., *Sprachen des Buddhismus in Zentralasian*, Weisbaden: Harrassowitz, 1983, pp. 132-141.

———, *Sogdian and Other Iranian Inscriptions of the Upper Indus*, 2 vols., London: School of Oriental and African Studies, 1989-92.

Sinor, Denis, ed., *Cambridge History of Early Inner Asia*, Cambridge: Cambridge University Press, 1990.

Spuler, Bertold, "The Disintegration of the Caliphate in the West," in P. M. Holt, ed., *Cambridge History of Islam*, 4 vols., Cambridge: Cambridge University Press, 1970, pp. 143-174.

Stavisky, B. Ya., "Kara Tepe in Old Termez: A Buddhist Religious Centre of the Kushan Period on the Bank of the Oxus," in J. Harmatta, ed., *From Hecataeus to Al-Huwarizmi: Bactrian, Pahlavi, Sogdian, Persian, Sanskrit, Syriac, Arabic, Chinese, Greek and Latin Sources for the History of Pre-Islamic Central Asia*, Budapest: Academiai Kiado, 1984, pp. 95-135.

Steensgard, Niels, *The Asian Trade Revolution of the Seventeenth Century: The East India Company and the Decline of the Caravan Trade*, Chicago: University of Chicago Press, 1974.

Stein, M. Aurel, *Ruins of Desert Cathay*, 2 vols., New York: Dover, 1987 [1912].

Stroumsa, Gedaliahu G., "A Zoroastrian Origin to the *Sefirot*?" in Shaked and Metzer, eds., *Irano Judaica III*, pp. 17-33.

Sundermann, W., "Lo studio dei testi iranici di Turfan," in Gherardo Gnoli, ed., *Iranian Studies*, Rome, 1983, pp. 199-134.

Sung-yün, *Buddhist Books in the Western Countries*, in Beal, tr., *Buddhist Records*, v. 1, pp. lxxxiv-cviii.

al-Tabari, Abu Ja'far Muhammad b. Jarir, *Ta'rikh al-rusul w'al-muluk*, 13 vols., ed. M. J. DeGoeje, Leiden: Brill, 1879-1901.

Tajadod, Nahal, "A Linguistic Voyage through Manichaeism and Chinese Zoroastrianism," *Diogenes* 171 (1995), pp. 63-73.

Teiser, Stephen F., *The Ghost Festival in Medieval China*, Princeton, NJ: Princeton University Press, 1988.

Thacker, T. W., "A Nestorian Gravestone from Central Asia in the Gulbenkian Museum," *Durham University Journal* (March 1967), pp. 94-107.

Thackston, Wheeler M., Jr., tr., *Naser-e Khosraw's Book of Travels*, Albany: State University of New York Press, 1986.

Torday, Laszlo, *Mounted Archers: The Beginnings of Central Asian History*, Durham (UK): Durham Academic Press, 1997.

Trimingham, J. S., *The Influence of Islam Upon Africa*, New York: Praeger, 1968.

Trinkhaus, K. Maurer, "Mortuary Ritual and Mortuary Remains," *Current Anthropology* 25/5 (1984), pp. 674-678.

Upasak, C. S., *History of Buddhism in Afghanistan*, Varanasi, India: Central Institute of Higher Tibetan Studies, 1990.

Uray, G., "Tibet's Connections with Nestorianism and Manicheism in the 8th-10th Centuries," *Wiener Studien zur Tibetologie und Buddhismuskunde* 10 (1983), pp. 399-429.

Utas, B., "The Jewish-Persian Fragment from Dandan-Uiliq," *Orientalia Suecana* 17 (1968), pp. 123-126.

Utz, David A., *A Survey of Buddhist Soghdian Studies*, Tokyo: Reiyukai Library, 1980.

———, "Arshak, Parthian Buddhists, and 'Iranian' Buddhism," paper presented at the conference "Buddhism Across Boundaries: The Sources of Chinese Buddhism," Hsi Lai University, 3-6 January 1993.

Vasary, Istvan, "'History and Legend' in Berke Khan's Conversion to Islam," in Denis Sinor, ed., *Aspects of Altaic Civilization III*, Bloomington, IN: Research Institute for Inner Asian Studies, 1990, pp. 230-252.

Walter, Mariko Namba, "Tokharian Buddhism in Kucha: Buddhism of Indo-European Speakers in Chinese Turkestan before the 10th century C.E.," unpublished paper.

———, "Mahayana and Hinayana in Central Asian Buddhist History: The Nature of Buddhism in Chinese Turkestan," paper presented at the Association for Asian Studies annual conference, January 1997.

———, "Kingship and Buddhism in Central Asia," Ph.D. dissertation, Harvard University, 1997.

———, "Buddhism in Western Central Asia," paper presented at the 111th American Historical Association annual conference, Seattle, WA, January 1998.

Whitfield, Susan, *Life Along the Silk Road*, London: John Murray, 1999.

Widengren, Geo, *Mani and Manichaeism*, London: Weidenfeld and Nicolson, 1965.

Wilford, John Noble, "New Finds Suggest Even Earlier Trade on Fabled Silk Road," *New York Times*, March 16, 1993, pp. C1, C8.

Williams, Paul, *Mahayana Buddhism: The Doctrinal Foundations*, London: Routledge, 1989.

Wink, André, *Al-Hind: The Making of the Indo-Islamic World*, vol. 1, Leiden: Brill, 1990.

Winston, David, "The Iranian Component in the Bible, Apocrypha, and Qumran: A Review of the Evidence," *History of Religions* 5 (1966), pp. 183-216.

Wriggins, Sally Hovey, *Xuanzang: A Buddhist Pilgrim on the Silk Road*, Boulder, CO: Westview, 1996.

Yarshater, Ehsan, "Mazdakism," in *Cambridge History of Iran*, v. 3, *The Seleucid, Parthian, and Sasanian Periods*, Cambridge: Cambridge University Press, 1983, pp. 991-1024.

Yarshater, Ehsan, ed., *Cambridge History of Iran*, v. 3, *The Seleucid, Parthian, and Sasanian Periods*, Cambridge: Cambridge University Press, 1983.

————, *Encyclopaedia Iranica*, London: Routledge & Kegan Paul, 1985-.

Yüan, Ch'en, *Western and Central Asians in China Under the Mongols*, tr. Ch'ien Hsing-hai and L. Carrington Goodrich, Nettetal: Steyler Verlag, 1989.

Yule, Henry, and H. Cordier, *Cathay and the Way Thither*, 4 vols., London: Hakluyt Society, 1937 [1913-16].

Zaehner, R. C., *The Dawn and Twilight of Zoroastrianism*, New York: Putnam, 1961.

Zhou, Xijuan, "Buddhists or Manichaeans? Some Characteristics of the Manichaean Missionaries Along the Silk Road," paper presented at the American Historical Association annual conference, 1998.

Zürcher, Erik, *The Buddhist Conquest of China*, Leiden: Brill, 1959.

INDEX